The Modern Satiric Grotesque

And Its Traditions

The Modern Satiric Grotesque

And Its Traditions

JOHN R. CLARK

THE UNIVERSITY PRESS OF KENTUCKY

Copyright © 1991 by The University Press of Kentucky

Scholarly publisher for the Commonwealth,
serving Bellarmine College, Berea College, Centre
College of Kentucky, Eastern Kentucky University,
The Filson Club, Georgetown College, Kentucky
Historical Society, Kentucky State University,
Morehead State University, Murray State University,
Northern Kentucky University, Transylvania University,
University of Kentucky, University of Louisville,
and Western Kentucky University.

Editorial and Sales Offices: Lexington, Kentucky 40508-4008

Library of Congress Cataloging-in-Publication Data
Clark, John R., 1930–
  The modern satiric grotesque and its traditions / John R. Clark.
      p.   cm.
  Includes bibliographical references and index.
  ISBN: 978-0-8131-5619-4
  1. Grotesque in literature.   2. Satire—History and criticism.
  I. Title.
  PN56.G7C57   1991
  809.7—dc20   90-27474

This book is printed on acid-free paper meeting
the requirements of the American National Standard
for Permanence of Paper for Printed Library Materials.∞

Contents

Preface vii
Introduction 1
Part I. Dark Comedy 7
  1. Deadly Laughter 9
  2. Satiric Gothic, Satiric Grotesque 17
Part II. Stratagems 27
  3. Degrading the Hero 29
  4. Debunking the Author 36
  5. Dislocating the Language 51
  6. Gaming with the Plot 67
  7. Further Intrusion and Obstruction 77
  8. Discordant Endings 83
  9. Infernal Repetition 90
Part III. Themes 103
  10. Ennui 105
  11. Scatology 116
  12. Cannibals 131
  13. Dystopias and Machines 139
  14. Entropy and Armageddon 148
Part IV. Conclusion 157
  15. The Death of the Humanities 159
Notes 165
Index 203

Preface

The intention of this study is to define and illustrate the major tactics and topics deployed by much modern literary "dark" humor. There can be no doubt that, in our era, the themes and modes of our comic literature (and our other literature as well) are usually no laughing matter. The subjects are frightful and ugly, the methods of presentation disruptive; such creations patently seek to foster dis-ease. Nevertheless, this study will argue that critics complaining about our fierce satiric literature because it is dank, cheerless, or unpleasant, naysaying or negative, are too simplistic and prescriptive. Great literature must flower as best it can, choosing whatever myths and means it can best nurture and develop. All such writing, if vigorous, controlled, and imaginative, is definitely creative and thereby affirmative.

Furthermore, as this study attempts to show, all of the strategies, tones, and materials of this extremist literature have been assimilated from a long and spirited usage. Such creations are firmly established in a lasting tradition. Hence it would only be sensible to comprehend and appreciate our comedic literature—whether it be dark or light—in this larger context.

I wish to thank the editors of several journals for granting me permission to reprint material here that previously appeared in somewhat different form in the pages of their periodicals: "The Human Use of Inhuman Beings," *Humanities in the South* 45 (1977): 7-9; "Funny Bones: The Deadly Laughter of the Grotesque," *Thalia* 9 (1987): 24-31; "Modern Gothic: The Satiric Grotesque," *Studies in Contemporary Satire* 13 (1986): 5-15; "Cynical Hercules and the Contemporary Hero," *Classical Bulletin* 57 (1981): 65-69; "Neglected Authors: The Martyrs and Relics of Satire," *Studies in Contemporary Satire* 12 (1985): 6-21; "Chafing Dish: Satire's Adulteration of Language and Style," *Thalia* 5 (1982): 14-26; "Gaming in Modern Literature: Some Causes and Effects," *Modernist Studies* 4 (1982): 146-59; "Intrusion, Obstruction, and the Self-Reflexive Narrator in So-Called Post-Modern Literature," *Classical and Modern*

Literature 7 (1986): 31-37 (reprinted by permission of CML, Inc.); "The Senselessness of an Ending: Comic Intrusions upon the 'Higher Seriousness,' " *West Virginia University Philological Papers* 29 (1983): 1-7; " 'Pangs without Birth, and Fruitless Industry': Redundancy in Satire," *Centennial Review* 26 (1982): 239-55; " 'Bored Out of My Gourd': The Progress of Modern Exhaustion," *West Virginia University Philological Papers* 28 (1982): 1-15; "Bowl Games: Satire in the Toilet," *Modern Language Studies* 4 (1974): 43-53; "The Progress of Cannibalism in Satire," *Midwest Quarterly* 25 (1984): 174-86; "The Machine Prevails: A Modern Technological Theme," *Journal of Popular Culture* 12 (1978): 118-26; "Running Down and Dropping Out: Entropy in Modern Literature," *Studies in Contemporary Satire* 10 (1983): 9-22; "The Death of the Humanities and Other Recent Atrocities," *Humanities in the South* 52 (1980): 1-4.

I also wish to acknowledge Professor Priscilla VanZandt of the University of North Florida, who worked with me on chapter 4. My deepest gratitude goes to Dr. Anna Lydia Motto, my wife, who assisted me in the research, the writing, and the revision of some of these chapters.

The Modern
Satiric Grotesque

And Its Traditions

Introduction

The literature of the modern era immerses us again and again in disillusionment, anomie, alienation, and wretchedness. Matthew Arnold saw man in 1853 facing what the early Greeks had faced—loss of calm, cheerfulness, and disinterested objectivity. In their stead, "the dialogue of the mind with itself has commenced; modern problems have presented themselves; we hear already the doubts, we witness the discouragement, of Hamlet and of Faust."[1] Oswald Spengler anticipated something worse, predicting the decline of the west, and since Spengler's day, man has been haunted by a nagging sense of absurdity and despair. Max Weber similarly predicted such a disenchantment in the West, and recently a typical commentator affirmed that "the writing of Tonnies, Marx, Whyte, Riesman, Kahler, Perkins, and others attest to the prevalence of that belief—that man has become materialized, automated, despiritualized, 'disenchanted'—in the twentieth century."[2]

And, to be truthful, the motifs of the satiric artistry early in this century—in the work of Strindberg, Mayakovsky, Proust, Mann, Joyce, Čapek, Sinclair Lewis, Orwell, Huxley, Waugh, Céline, and Nathanael West—have been dark indeed. The typical reified, denatured, dispirited inhabitant of our period is precisely characterized by Robert Musil's designation: *Der Mann ohne Eigenschaften*. Modern man, stripped of any distinguishing qualities, has arrived in the subbasement of life. Later writings merely continue to record this downward journey. In such a light, we should perceive the oeuvre of the angry young men, the absurdists of the theater, the novelists of black humor, the celebrants of pop art, and the theorists of deconstruction. Critics too tend to define the entire period in gloomy and tenebrous terms, speaking of the "revolt of the masses" and the "betrayal of the intellectuals," noting the proliferation of the "anti-hero" and generating a host of the bleakest terms: "the power of blackness," "the loss of self," the "waiting for the end," "nil," "nightmare," and "silence."[3] Even many of our lighter comedians have grown increasingly bleak and depressed toward the close of their careers; this has certainly been true of Dickens, Twain, Chaplin, Thurber, Waugh, and Lenny Bruce.

Furthermore, one will find precious little among recurrent literary subjects that one can designate beneficent or ameliorative. For instance, traditional utopian literature has turned "sour," fostering the rise of a predominant genre, that of the antiutopia.[4] In addition, literature's concern with the scatological increases significantly in this century, plunging the reader into the urinal and the toilet; many artists of the lavatory—Joyce, Eliot, Golding, Grass, Marcel Duchamp, Southern, Barth, Updike, Claes Oldenburg, Beckett—appear eager to rush in where angels fear to tread. Similarly, modern writings startle readers by confronting them with the unsavory subject of cannibalism, as in works by Twain, Bierce, Waugh, Mailer, Burgess, Bellow, Hawkes, and Donleavy; such writers hint knowingly that man, for all his "humane" posturings and asseverations, secretly is prone (perhaps enthusiastically) to indulge quite savagely in consuming delectable human flesh.

In like manner, as if they utterly endorsed C.P. Snow's concept of the isolated "two cultures" and indeed endorsed the triumph of science alone, numerous modern authors have discerned a grim species of humor in dramatizing the triumph of the machine over mankind. Such writers as E.M. Forster, Zamyatin, Elmer Rice, Čapek, Kafka, Barthelme, Pinter, Vonnegut, Lem, and Mailer generate fictions that portray automation taking over society, triumphing over feeble humanity. The mechanic embodies machismo, and the robot provides the reasonable solution, according to this revolutionary literature of the "revised new syllabus." All these and other similar strategies in our literature diminish the human race, reducing it to manure, monkeydom, savagery, or mechanism. What could be "darker" than this heart of darkness? Can anything be more despoiled after defoliation and depletion? Here is wretchedness par excellence!

Or so, at any rate, would many of our moralists and rhetoricians have it. They extol the "power of positive thinking"; they favor literatue that overtly accentuates the positive. Hence, the trends I have been tracing—consisting of literary explorations of tedium, disenchantment, scatology, machination, and blackness—strike them as monumental negations of hope, kindliness, and mirth. At the least, such interpreters of our century assess this body of literature as unfaithful to humanism. A typical example of such a dismayed observation is Jesse Bier's study *The Rise and Fall of American Humor* (New York, 1968). After surveying the history of American laughter, Bier concludes that a monstrous falling-off has occurred; in the present century he detects a vast and terrible decline of native humor. The contemporary scene, he opines, is wretched, gloomy, decadent, almost barren. Yet who told Jesse Bier that the modern humorist's imitation of a "dark" action in a creative work confirms its author's "immoralism," nihilism, or pathological illness? Bier's premises would allow one in any era to consign half the writers of comedy (and all writers of satire) to Bedlam—or the flames.

Much is wrongheaded in this view. And most wrongheaded of all is Bier's devotion to a prescriptive criticism: American humorists must not practice romantic comedy; American humorists must not be apostates or pessimists; American humorists must discover (and affirm) the power of positive funny-think. Long ago Henry James restated several traditional and seminal tenets for the critic of fiction: the artist must be permitted the "freedom to feel and say." "We must grant the artist his subject, his idea, his *donnée:* our criticism is applied only to what he makes of it."[5] The point seems obvious, yet every generation finds its defense necessary. Ihab Hassan ventures even further, wishing to encourage the artist: "Praise, as we conceive it, is an inherent function of criticism. In an age of mendacity, *kitsch* art, and counterfeit leisure, the pursuit of genuine excellence is a dangerous and noble pursuit. We must raise the standards on ourselves, and raise the price. We should tolerate arrogance in our novelists and encourage the kind of artistic courage and ruthlessness society calls subversive. We must always demand more. And still we must praise, for without praise criticism manages, somehow, to deny the values it sets out to preserve."[6] One might have hoped that such concepts needed no repetition. But as long as pious and somber sermons pronouncing the death of comedy and tragedy, of satire, of poetry, and of Western culture continue to abound, then the tedious but necessary defense of art and artistry must again be made.

Yet I suspect that such vindications will always be necessary. Particularly in our present century, so long as a great body of comic and satiric literature continues to bask in so-called heresies of nightmare, negativism, and despair, moralizers will proceed to decry and denounce. For literature, according to their view, is a question of acquisition: debits and credits are assembled, representing the century's balance sheet. This is the C.P.A.s' assessment of art; their idea of "accountability" merely entails tabulating pluses and minuses, labeling and formulating "affirmatives," dogmatic positives, that they insist be tangibly present in the world's works of art. Yet art is a complex creative amalgam that can never be narrowly quantified, reduced to some lowest arithmetical common denominator.

For all such reasons, art associated with negation, art that shocks its readership or that gives us a regulated glimpse of Avernus or of

4　The Modern Satiric Grotesque

chaos is not "negative art" at all. "I think it can be argued that there is in fact a literature of negative energy which is yet affirmative of life."[7] Indeed, every well-managed work of art is an inventive and fruitful construct; hence it renders an overt and positive contribution to society and to culture. Satirists, too, must be included in this circle of creators; they happen to be the creators of devastation. They dramatize (and explore) weakness, decadence, and denigration. "As no one writer is adequate to all the needs of literature or life, it may be equally appropriate to recommend the satirists as a complement and correction to the literature of philanthropy."[8] In any event, recent satiric literature has virtually supplied an overdose in this kind, providing us with daily examples of *die Ausrottung der Besten*. Perhaps we even secretly require this dosage of bad news. "There is no psychic fact more available to our modern comprehension than that there are human impulses which, in one degree or another, and sometimes in the very highest degree, repudiate pleasure and seek gratification in—to use Freud's word—unpleasure."[9] Indeed, modern art has proved vigorous precisely where it has been unpleasant.

Nonetheless, such negative explorations do render the reader uncomfortable. But it cannot be helped, for our era follows a period of excessive optimism, and the reaction has set in with a vengeance. Our artists now overtly wish to explore and bring to light human paradoxes, the dark/darker/darkest side of mankind. As Dostoevsky's Underground Man perceives, "Man loves to create. . . . But why . . . does he also passionately love destruction and chaos?" Indeed, as we are made to confront man's tormented psyche and to unravel his poor defenses, if we grin at all, we do it crookedly. "He is fond of striving toward achievement, but not so very fond of the achievement itself, and this is, naturally, terribly funny. In short, man is constructed comically; there is evidently some joke in all of this."[10] It is a particularly painful joke, surely, and our century has sought with tragic monomania to seek it out. The resulting literature is almost certain to cause titter and terror, yet it has been a brilliantly rich literature—possibly because of its grotesque intensity and seriousness.

In this century, therefore, positive creation extols the dark thought, the humiliating eventuality, the culpable man. Irving and Harriet Deer rightly assess contemporary artistry as generating the "power of negative thinking." They analyze our art's devotion to "this quality of protest without apparent solution." Again and again, the artist posits "the game of evil," "fondles" obscurity, and "pollutes" our thought.[11] The artist invests positive energy in manifest impiety, violence, madness, and death.

Paradoxically enough, such an art still stands at the center of humanistic concerns. In no way has this art abandoned the Terentian mandate, "Homo sum: humani nil a me alienum puto."[12] For the proper study of mankind in any century, including the twentieth, remains the study of man. Whatever humankind is worth—including its buffoonery, absurdity, ambivalence, and vice—the human being in all forms and disguises must not become alien to us. We must direct our attention implacably at him.

And, contrary to what many presume, twentieth-century art is as concerned for and involved with mankind as any that can be found. This study will consider the *how* and the *why* of such involvement and concern. To facilitate clarity, the present volume is arranged in four parts. Part I explores the dark mood of so much of our literature, tracing the reasons for its fascination with gloom and snicker (chapter 1). Then, traditions of the gothic and the grotesque are analyzed; I argue that horror and grotesquerie are especially suited to the modern era, in which the self has been recognized as being irrational and unstable and a traumatic parade of dreadful current events has helped topple conventional idols of Renaissance *humanitas* and idealism. Very deliberately, much modern literature probes and portrays the swart and seamy side of the human condition (chapter 2).

Part II investigates authors' methods for shocking readers and capturing their attention by utilizing disjunctive tactics that confound normative expectations and defy everyday artistic usage: debasing or destroying the conventional protagonist or hero (chapter 3); undercutting the stature of artistes or even the author (chapter 4); deploying unusually inept language and low diction (chapter 5); treating life and fictions about life as mere games (chapter 6); intruding *in propria persona* upon fictions and otherwise shattering the ordonnance of coherent works of art (chapter 7); jarring the reader with abrupt, ineffectual, or puzzling endings to stories (chapter 8); and often indeed devising tales in which scenes, sections, and experiences repeat themselves and characters, rather than advancing to some new stage of knowledge or fortune, plod aimlessly upon a treadmill, like Sisyphus, getting nowhere at all (chapter 9).

Whereas Part II explores grotesque satire's abuse of normative artistic conventions and forms, Part III surveys a number of such satire's unsavory subjects. It is to be expected that this literature gambols in subject areas normally considered off-limits to decorous works of art. Hence, we encounter displeasing, taboo, and even dreadful topics here: suicide, incest, coprophilia, insanity, child abuse, and so on. Specifically distasteful topics are canvassed, including

6   The Modern Satiric Grotesque

boredom (chapter 10); excrement (chapter 11); cannibalism (chapter 12); machine-tooled totalitarian antiutopias (chapter 13); and even the entropic death of the universe (chapter 14).

Despite the appalling disagreeableness of our art and the ugliness of our belles lettres, Part IV (the conclusion) stresses that we need not respond with groans, with pious censure, or with total revulsion to our era's satiric art. For this disquieting literature has proven vigorous, investigative, oftentimes profound, and astonishingly imaginative and fecund. We should hardly be thinking of giving up, when our literary team is so evidently bent on winning.

Part I. Dark Comedy

Chapter 1 notes that contemporary man as presented in modern literature is caught in a dilemma, facing the paralytic horror that some dread cataclysm awaits him together with the equally shattering fear that nothing whatsover will happen. Thus, he is captured, helpless and suspended, between inertia and catastrophe. The chapter examines the chief reasons for this impasse: decadent romanticism and excessive expectations about a grand individualist self, ideals of progress gone awry, and ruinous revolutions and world wars. The climate is particularly ripe for a satiric literature that laughs ruthlessly at the modern farce of man's angst and tremblings, his lost hopes, posturings, and antiheroic ineptitudes.

Chapter 2 traces the origins of words like gothic and grotesque, illustrating their presence in much of previous world literature. Modern interest in the psyche, in man's troublous inner life, renders the gloomy strategies of gothicism and grotesquerie more pertinent and apt. The tactics and themes of the grotesque are well suited to exaggerate the dark side of human nature, to shock the audience with scenes of the startling, the disturbing, the unnatural, and the absurd. Key exemplers of such modern artistry can be found in the work of Franz Kafka, William Faulkner, Günter Grass, Gabriel García Márquez, and Samuel Beckett. Such darkling artistry cannot help but alienate its audience and upset the bourgeoisie; indeed, it is thus that the traditional satiric artist, treating serious subjects, gains serious attention. Surely he wants it that way.

1

Deadly Laughter

A pathetic image of "suspense" dramatizes the great trauma of modern literature: paranoid and "dangling man," robbed of optimism, awaits some incalculable and ghastly catastrophe, yet he is equally fearful of failure even here, paralyzed by the dread that nothing will happen—alike benumbed by the anticipation that the world—or his own life—will end in a bang, or a whimper.[1] This, of course, is the condition of any number of characters in the early poetry of Eliot and Auden, in Proust, Mansfield, Kafka, Mann's *Buddenbrooks*, Céline, O'Neill, Golding, Burgess, Beckett, and Pinter, and in Karl Kraus's monolithic epic drama, *The Last Days of Mankind* (1918–19). Events appalling enough regularly beset modern man in his fictions, the pages filling in plenty with corpses, slaughter, and bones. But even in less appalling fictions the characters are bemused and atremble about the imminence and the potential of disaster. How did twentieth-century man wind up in such a cul-de-sac, in such traumatic impasse and dither?

For one thing, the last four centuries have witnessed the rise of the bourgeoisie, the triumph of quotidian man, what Ortega y Gasset described as the horde of the masses—man freed of class, caste, roots, and standards—Mencken's Boobocracy. In addition, man in the Age of Reason facilitated the "death of God"—and these two phenomena together conspired to rob modern man of sanctity and heroes, even of heroism itself. The subsequent media explosion fostered what Marshall McLuhan has called the "global village," depriving modern man of new voyages and new frontiers.

The Renaissance and particularly the Enlightenment promised Western man an era of rationalism, the irrevocable march of science and technology. In short, it bequeathed to succeeding generations the myth of indelible growth, the idea of progress.[2] Surely, a flock of optimists promised, we would soon attain nirvana, wherein everything would be found out. Swift's modern in *A Tale of a Tub*, a half-baked apologist for projects and science, boasted that "every Branch of

Knowledge has received such wonderful Acquirements since [Homer's] Age, especially within these last three Years"; hence, it may be "reckoned, that there is not at this present, a sufficient Quantity of new Matter left in Nature, to furnish and adorn any one particular Subject to the Extent of a Volume."[3] Paradoxically, Swift's fool simultaneously prophesies that all will be discovered—or else used up! But the appropriate stance was scientific, hopeful, idealizing: in an imminent earthly paradise, man trusted that he would no longer "see through a glass, darkly; but then face to face" (1 Cor. 13:12). Two hundred years later, Chekhov's battered and pathetic trio of sisters and their friends still melodramatically cling to a wistful yearning for the advent of such a brave new world: "Oh, my God! Time will pass, and we shall be gone forever, we'll be forgotten, our faces will be forgotten, our voices, and how many there were of us, but our sufferings will turn into joy for those who live after us, happiness and peace will come to this earth."[4]

Romanticism in its turn, of course, initiated a great tide (and even the habit) of rebellion and revolution. The romantics boldly disparaged classicism, tradition, and even Enlightenment rationalism, but they still retained an ardent faith in progress. Romanticism's idealization of a "performing self," of a Cartesian solipsistic investigator, of a tormented but swashbuckling Byronic actor, has led us to worship the "cult of the ego"—to seek to cultivate a magnificent and dynamic self that will fulfill all our hopes for a heroism that was lost in the communal and mythic past.[5] We have turned almost desperately to Emersonian "self-reliance," though we harbor increasing misgivings that that self can triumph or even survive.

It is significant to note that the imagery of self-expression and self-fulfillment early in the nineteenth century turned extremist and, in a century of political wars and upheavals, militant. The term *avant-garde*, which became the watchword for bohemian leadership, fashion, and innovation in the arts, is borrowed from army lingo and retains implications of aggression, advance, dangerous missions of reconnaissance.[6] Such imagery continues into the present century. Note D.H. Lawrence's aspiration:

I wish we were all like kindled bonfires on the edge of space, marking out the advance-posts. What is the aim of self-preservation, but to carry us right out to the firing-line; there, what *is* is in contact with what is not. If many lives be lost by the way, it cannot be helped, nor if much suffering be entailed. I do not go out to war in the intention of avoiding all danger or discomfort: I go to fight for myself. Every step I move forward into being brings a newer, juster proportion into the world, gives me less need of storehouse and barn, allows me to leave all, and to take what I want by the way, sure that it will always be there; allows me in the end to fly the flag of myself, at the extreme tip of life.[7]

In some sense, this romantic assertion is ludicrous: the imagery of warfare and slaughter is unusual in this passage; why should Lawrence's "advancing" self-seeking entail the death of many others? Nor is Lawrence's figure even sensible, for he is a reconnaissance man who longs to outrun his own army and even its supplies. He may be "sure" that without supplies he can yet magically "take what [he] want[s] by the way"—but we must infer from the figure that it is far more plausible that he will outrun the war entirely and certainly cease to serve as part of any societal or military team. And worse, if in his isolation he is not captured by the enemy, we can at least anticipate that, without camp food and stores, he can well expect starvation.

Yet the metaphor is retained in the tradition. Guillaume Apollinaire similarly urges, "Pity us who battle ever at the frontiers of infinity and the future," although, as we have noted, frontiers have been increasingly straitened and shut down.[8] But the martial spirit of such egoism could become still more turbulent and severe. In boasting about the contemporary poet's rejection of the past and concern for himself, his own nation, and the immediate future, Filippo Marinetti in the First Futurist Manifesto (February 20, 1909) goes far indeed:

We shall sing the love of danger, the habit . . . of boldness.

The essential elements of our poetry shall be courage, daring and rebellion. . . . we . . . extol aggressive movement, feverish insomnia, the double quick-step, the sommersault, the box on the ear, the fisticuff. . . .

strife. No masterpiece without aggressiveness. . . . We stand upon the extreme promontory of the centuries! . . . We wish to glorify War—the only health giver of the world—militarism, patriotism, the destructive arm of the Anarchist, the beautiful ideas that kill, the contempt for women.

We wish to destroy the museums, the libraries, to fight against moralism, feminism, and all opportunist and utilitarian meannesses.[9]

The fanatic hysteria in the tone, so soon to be perfected by Stalinists and Nazis alike, boded ill for the future such extremists vaunted. Such a romantic self is, in its solipsism, its almost inchoate irrationality, and its rash celebration of power and immediacy, close to self-destruction, a self-destruction archetypally expressed by Jean Anouilh's Antigone: "You [she exclaims to Creon] with your promise of a humdrum happiness—provided a person doesn't ask too much of life. I want everything of life, I do; and I want it now! I want it total, complete: otherwise I reject it! If life must be a thing of fear and lying and compromise; if life cannot be free, gallant, incorruptible— then . . . I choose death!"[10] Indeed this quest for an ideal self has led to self-destruction, to so-called identity crises, and to what Wylie Sypher has called "the Loss of self"—the discovery that no singular fulsome identity exists beneath the surface, merely schizophrenic doubles, multiples, and fragments.[11] With an access of hubris and with the demolition of deities, contemporary man confronts an upsurge of guilt and anxiety. The Freudian hypothesis concerning the dominance of unconscious desires and a repressive id has been too awfully realized in events; our century has been forced to confront undercurrents and even open outbursts of irrationality. Modern physics overthrew laws, only to stress the inaccessibility of knowledge, celebrating instead indeterminacy, probability, randomness, and chance. The great spurt of leaping hearts and elevated hopes initiated by romanticism had by the middle of the nineteenth century turned to dejection and disillusionment. The literary prognosis thereafter increasingly heralded decline, degeneracy, entropy, and decay.[12]

Finally, the experience of the brutish and unprecedented savagery of world wars and further revolutions in this century climaxed in the demise of the idea of progress itself.[13] Instead of hopefulness and anticipation, we now sluggishly observe, in George Santayana's sarcastic words, "the power of idealization steadily [in] decline"; we woodenly scrutinize "the long comedy of modern social revolutions, so illusory in their aims and so productive in their aimlessness."[14]

When wars and rebellions and new manifestos and "movements" incessantly recur—without significant results—the effect is numbing. As Marx once observed: "The first time . . . tragedy, the second . . . farce."[15] Hence, our response to this "long comedy" of recent history has been the hoarse cacophonous laughter of despair, expressed in the recurrent tides of our recent literary movements: decadent symbolism, expressionism, dada, surrealism, the theater of the absurd, the novels of black humor, and the flourishing genre of the dystopia. Knowing recent history and the aspirations of a few brief preceding generations, modern man tends merely to grin with spectral grimness and succumb to disappointment, trivialization, and ennui. He senses, exhaustedly, impotently, in Prufrock's words, that

> I have known them all already, known them all:—
> Have known the evenings, mornings, afternoons,
> I have measured out my life with coffee spoons;
> I know the voices dying with a dying fall.[16]

Needless to say, therefore, in the twentieth century man's avant-garde response to this "long comedy" is a laughter that is militant, extremist, pitiable, and terrible.

In the 1920s Thomas Mann remarked this tendency toward the rash, the unnatural, and the extreme: "I feel that, broadly and essentially, the striking feature of modern art is that it has ceased to recognize the categories of tragic and comic, or the dramatic classifications, tragedy and comedy. It sees life as tragicomedy, with the result that the grotesque is its most genuine style."[17] And consider Eugène Ionesco's program for the theater: "magnifying . . . effects. . . . No drawing room comedies, but farce, the extreme exaggeration of parody. . . . No dramatic comedies either. But back to the unendurable. Everything raised to paroxysm. . . . A theatre of violence: violently comic, violently dramatic."[18] The masterworks of this century have responded nicely, utilizing just such hyena-forms of extremity; the most powerful works develop increasingly bizarre and "forbidden" topics of exorbitancy, violence, and grotesquerie: decadence and homosexuality, child abuse, insanity, suicide, lobotomy, bestiality, incest, cannibalism, and ultimately the apocalyptic, featuring scenarios of the end of the world.[19] These are the immoderate subjects treated by Proust, Mann, Pirandello, Gide, Zamyatin, Čapek, Kafka, Faulkner, Céline, Nabokov, Heller, Ellison, Beckett, Vonnegut, Pinter, García Márquez, Grass, and Pynchon.

Like the romantics, we still call for revolution, imagination, extremity, but unlike them our manner is no longer exalted, earnest, serious, holy; instead, we provoke the paroxysm of hopeless laughter and desperate, unnatural comedy. Our moderns ask, as George Steiner remarks, "inherently destructive questions": "It may be, in fact, that the aspect of demolition, the apocalyptic strain, gently tempt us. We are fascinated by 'last things,' by the end of cultures, of ideologies, of art forms, of modes of sensibility. We are, certainly since Nietzsche and Spengler, 'terminalists.' Our view of history, says Levi-Strauss in a deep pun, is not an anthropology but an 'entropology.' "[20] It is indeed impressive when we consider the vast number of modern masterpieces that employ features of the surrealistic-grotesque and travel upon a journey that runs downhill.

It will prove useful here to mention four seminal works that usher in the century and exemplify modern themes: Dostoevsky's "Notes from Underground" (1864), Conrad's "Heart of Darkness" (1899), James's "The Beast in the Jungle" (1903), and Mann's "Death in Venice" (1912). All these short masterpieces are built upon the premise of "great expectations" that are foiled, disappointed, demolished. All supply to some extent an unnatural setting and an atmosphere of anticipation and waiting, and all of them are "dark comedies."[21] Each introduces a distorted protagonist—Dostoevsky's narrator, Mr. Kurtz, John Marcher, and Gustave von Aschenbach—who is in essence a "humour character," crippled and incapacitated by personality and locale. James's John Marcher is particularly prototypical and unsoldierly, for he literally "marches" to no place at all. All these works deploy key words that suggest extremities—the underworld, darkness, beastliness, and death—symbolizing the debilitating nature of external environment as well as of man's inner life. They handsomely set the stage, the pattern, and the mood for the ensuing century's violent and dread-ridden comedies of manners.

In a sense, such themes of antiheroism and destruction can be seen from two different perspectives. On the one hand, betraying comedy's traditional tendency to sustain social standards and to foster the reintegration of characters into society, modern grotesqueries dramatize the corruption of entire communities. Archetypal works of this kind include Mark Twain's "The Man That Corrupted Hadleyburg" (1900) and Friedrich Dürrenmatt's *The Visit* (1956): in both, dollar bills and rampant greed insidiously "tempt" an entire society until if "falls." The populace is induced to renounce amity and *humanitas*, degenerating as individuals into isolated particles; all become petty, lying, cheating, and even committing ritual murder. Writers in our century frequently explore such a theme of inane and corrupt society. It flourishes in most science fiction, in the great quantity of writings categorized as dystopias. Perhaps Gabriel García Márquez's *One Hundred Years of Solitude* (1967) represents the apex of such explorations.

On the other hand, individualism and the noble protagonist are equally perverted and destroyed. As extreme versions of the *Don Quixote* and *Candide* motif, we should consider John Crowe Ransom's poem "Captain Carpenter" (1924) and Nathanael West's novel *A Cool Million* (1934). In both, the naive central character sets out upon a romantic quest to attain fortune and maturation but is instead savagely and systematically "dismantled," losing limb after limb until the antihero's very "heart" is penetrated or torn from his torso and he is blatantly extirpated. These modern versions of satiric decline and fall offer no opportunity for growth, recantation, or the "cultivation of one's garden"; rather, characters are reduced to mutilated corpses. Again, the motif of the dismembered antihero can be traced through a great many instances of wounded heroes, castrati, and lobotomized vegetables who appear in our literature throughout the century and who are perhaps most luridly depicted in the fictions and dramas of Samuel Beckett.

Both extremes—society's growing increasingly alien, fatuous, smug, and corrupt, as well as the individual protagonist's being progressively stripped bare of heroic characteristics—are often portrayed together. The masterpieces doubtless are James Joyce's *Ulysses* (1922) and Robert Musil's *Man without Qualities* (1930–43). An exemplary instance in miniature can be encountered in a passage by Flannery O'Connor, which might be designated "Mrs. Shortley and the Peacock": "[Mrs. Shortley] stood a while longer, reflecting, her unseeing eyes directly in front of the peacock's tail. He had jumped into the tree and his tail hung in front of her, full of fierce planets with eyes that were each ringed in green and set against a sun that was gold in one second's light and salmon-colored in the next. She might have been looking at a map of the universe but she didn't notice it any more than she did the spots of sky that cracked the dull green of the tree."[22]

One can hardly assert that bird and woman have met at all. On the one hand, Mrs. Shortley does not even see what is in front of her face. She cannot respond to beauty, to terror, or to meaning. There is, in fact, something almost dreadful about her unhealthy and permanent indifference, insensitivity, and isolation. On the other hand, when it is viewed and appreciated, the peacock's tail seems ambivalent and unnerving. It might well be taken as emblematic of nature, of the creation, of beauty. But the feathered scene transcends the beautiful and turns ominous: for pictured in the bird's fanning tail are a shimmering, changeable sun and "fierce planets" with lurid eyeballs. We confront a living "map of the universe," and we begin to recognize the eerie sensations produced by the unnatural, the grotesque. As if to punctuate the scene with approval, the "spots of sky" flash and ominously "crack" against the nearby tree. Mrs. Shortley sees nothing, whereas we have apparently seen too much. The natural unaccountably metamorphoses into the unnatural and fractures our complacency.

Doubtless the reader might well commence to wonder how people for more than a century could continue to smile upon all these crass, demeaning and disturbing topics. One might well object that our dire situation is no laughing matter. So it would seem. We could reply by punning, saying that we seek to laugh ourselves into stitches or, further, to laugh ourselves to death. But moderns could perhaps best respond by quoting Byron:

> And if I laugh at any mortal thing,
> 'Tis that I may not weep; . . .
> 'Tis that our nature cannot always bring
> Itself to apathy.[23]

16 Dark Comedy

We are not yet reduced to apathy, and therefore we still react to violence violently. Hence we choose to confront our gods and devils with a ritualized and cathartic blast and guffaw as rejoinder and counterstatement. One thinks of Robin's irrepressible burst of laughter at the moment of catastrophe in Hawthorne's "My Kinsman, Major Molineux." A deliberately articulated human response is, after all, on this side of life and outside the confines of madness. We could do much worse. For in spite of all the sick and deadly substance of contemporary art, it is still within the precincts of sanity that we persist in making our stand. In the words of Edgar in *King Lear:*

> To be worst,
> The lowest and most dejected thing of fortune,
> Stands still in esperance, lives not in fear:
> The lamentable change is from the best;
> The worst returns to laughter.[24]

2

Satiric Gothic, Satiric Grotesque

Let us begin by considering the origins and meanings of the word *grotesque*. Maximillian E. Novak doubtless oversimplifies when he suggests that the grotesque stems exclusively from "the rendering of skeletons, demons, witches and ghosts," but he is certainly correct in urging that the "serious grotesque" is significantly utilized in the eighteenth-century gothic novels. Responses to the word *gothic* have clearly varied over the ages; in the late eighteenth century, the gothic represented the mystically mysterious architecture of the long-ago medieval period all too often visible only as "ruins," its ghosts "haunting" the Age of Sensibility that sought to exercise pent-up emotions and to indulge in thrills, sighs, and titillations.[1] The gothic also represented the awesome and threatening powers of Catholicism; the Church had once been universal in its sway and fearful in its persecutions and in supplying visions of hellfire. But the gothic also indicated the barbaric invasions of Eastern hordes and served perennially as an object lesson to human pride: man's highest attainments in civilization could at any moment come tumbling down as had the grandeur that was Rome. A near-apocalyptic tide of barbarism could initiate "dark ages" when least expected. Sir William Temple and Jonathan Swift often appealed to the cyclic nature of history, calling attention to culture's decline and to the potential reinfestation of society by savages.[2]

Particularly as an antidote to Enlightenment optimism, neoclassicism, and rationalism, the theory that heralded dark irrationalism as an inevitability generated in the spectator an ambivalent *frisson* and *Schadenfreude:* one could tremble at the black uncouth heart of darkness in man and his penchant for bringing civilization down with an axe and at the same time feel justified smugness in repudiating excessive optimism and naive rationalism. But the optimism prevailed throughout most of the nineteenth century, with the full blossoming of the idea of progress to ripeness. To be sure, many back-benchers of the opposition—Browning, Baudelaire, Hawthorne, Melville, and, later, Dickens, Twain, and Flaubert—expressed their objection to progressive idealism by utilizing features of the gothic vein.[3] But with the twentieth century the ideal of inevitable progress came terribly crashing to the ground, shattered by monumental world wars, revolutions, indeterminacy, atomic energy, the Freudian id, and the Holocaust. In the present century, then, the gothic and the grotesque mate and become the dominant imagery of our era.

The term *grotesque* originally referred to a specific art of the grotto. In the fifteenth century the remnants of Nero's first-century Domus Aurea, or Golden House, were discovered and excavated beneath the baths of Trajan and of Titus. The bizzare wall paintings in the palace represented elaborate knots and festoons of floral decorations, designs oddly transforming into snakes, satyrs, mythological animals, as well as human figures or parts of human appendages. Hence, an art that unconscionably mingled and interfused human, animal, vegetable, and mineral in eerie and nightmarish fashion (the atmosphere in the darkened crypt generated some of this mood) became but one more exotic mode or style—*la grottesca*. The style flourished in the work, over the years, of Bosch, the Brueghels, Raphael, Velázquez, Hogarth, Callot, Goya, and Dali.[4]

The grotesque, however, does not merely come down to us from the eerie etchings in Nero's house. Much evolves from early Roman dramatic and public practice—in mimes, in the Saturnalia—that celebrated nonrationality and laughter and was thoroughly incorporated into the medieval period in popular folkways stressing ambivalence, jollity, and release. Mikhail Bakhtin terms it the "carnival grotesque."[5] But despite its twofold overtones—exhilarating exaggeration and the ominously extraterrestial—the grotesque was always understood to be excessive, requiring boundaries and regulation lest it burgeon, "break out," or get out of hand.

Such an effete and incredible art was not merely the invention of the supposedly decadent Neronian age. Art has always wavered in cycles betwixt the classical and the romantic, betwixt the idealized humanistic and the imaginative sub- and suprahuman sublime. Egyptian fantastic art was subsequently replaced by the formalized sculpture of the Greeks of the fifth and fourth centuries B.C., and these extremes in conception have continued to manifest themselves alternately throughout history. Indeed, even in so-called classical Augustan Rome, ca. 1 B.C.-A.D. 10, the irrational creations of a baroque art were popular, and Vitruvius complained about popular tastes that preferred

monsters rather than definite representations taken from definite things. [In architecture nowadays] instead of columns there rise up stalks; instead of gables, striped panels with curled leaves and volutes. Candelabra uphold pictured shrines and above the summits of these, clusters of thin figures seated upon them at random. Again, slender stalks with heads of men and of animals attached to half the body. Such things neither are nor can be, nor have been.[6]

We might add that the so-called staid era of ideals and order in Augustan Rome produced one of the masterpieces of grotesque art, Ovid's *Metamorphoses*—a now-witty, now-awesome catalog of human transformations into godhood, into animal and vegetable creatures.

Doubtless the popularity of insidious nonrational art led Horace in his classic *Ars Poetica* to depict such profusions in one of his most striking images: "If a painter wishes to join a horse's neck to a human head and to place varied plumage on limbs brought together helter-skelter so that a woman beautiful in her upper parts should terminate hideously in a black fish," who could avoid laughter, Horace queries. For such a portrayal, he adds, would be similar to a chaotic book "whose meaningless ideas will be shaped like a sick man's dreams." And yet, after all, with a bestial flourish, Horace merely describes with some contorted variation a species of mermaid. And classical art (in Homer, in Virgil, in Seneca) had profusely delineated and proliferated hydras, sphinxes, pig-manufacturing Circes, gorgons, Polyphemuses, Stygian birds, and bewitching sirens.[7] The standards of classical tradition, however, incline it to label such art (in Stoic terms) as deviant from right reason, from normality, and from rigorously harmonious mathematical form—in short, to label grotesque art "unnatural." And such have been, down the ages, the repeated grounds for censure of Blakean monsters and all such visionary and opium-induced ambulations down the road of excess.

Yet not only the violation of harmony, symmetry, and proportion characterizes the grotesque. Mere association of this ludicrous and effete art with the name of the mad tyrant Nero lent it more macabre qualities of the ominous and the berserk. In addition, its location in a darkened crypt suggests that it was an underground artistry. Man alwways associated the underworld with the shadowy, the chaotic, and the unnatural, and the popular imagination regularly peopled Hades and Sheol with monstrous creatures (one thinks of the triple-headed Cerberus), devils, and demons. Even the dead acquired attributes of the unnatural, conceived of as becoming haunting spirits and ghosts. As early as the *Odyssey*, Homer depicts the shades of the slaughtered suitors as fluttering and flying, gibbering like bats as they descend to the underworld. Hence the grotesque is repeatedly associated with gross unnatural distortion and calls to mind the fearful, the unearthly, the nightmarish, and the demonic. At its mildest, the *grottesco* style may merely be employed lightly and frivolously, of course, as a decorative, filigreed, and mannerist wallpaper art; but exploited intensely, the scenes of the grotesque can cultivate a strange and strikingly ominous atmosphere—as in the artistry, say, of *King Lear* or of Büchner's *Woyzeck*.[8]

As we move further into the period of the last four hundred years, we more and more encounter man's psyche turning inward upon itself and assessing its own functionings. Sir Philip Sidney in the 1590s had already modified Horace, suggesting that art need not follow nature; what counted was the imagination's improvement upon the natural.[9] Thereafter, Europeans became increasingly concerned with evolving and formulating the concept of the self; thinkers explored man's imaginings and profoundly probed the irrational, the lunatic, the subliminal, the id, the stream of consciousness.[10] In such a climate, the grotesque mode and many features of the gothic novel become more serviceable and more relevant as a means of representing the "dark side" of human nature. Over the past two centuries, one need only recollect powerful works of art developed in this vein: the jaundiced images of Baudelaire, the ironies of Laforgue, the Dostoevskian Underground Man, the dark settings in the later novels of Dickens, the "power of blackness" expressed in Hawthorne, Melville, and Conrad, the supernatural forces in James, German expressionism, the dadaist and surrealist movements, the theater of the absurd, the black humor novels of the 1960s, the genre of the dystopia—all utilizing the gothic and the grotesque with vitality, potency, and shock.[11]

It is for such reasons that an artist like Pirandello, around 1910, joined a theater movement in Italy called "the theater of the grotesque"; his essay on *Humor* had called for a mixture of tragedy and ludicrous absurdity, and his great plays subsequently fragmented the drama, exploring a strange mixture of multiple points of view.[12] Thomas Mann detected a similar strain of comic vigor mingled with threads of ugliness and horror in the novels of Conrad, and he generalized that "the striking feature of modern art is that . . . it sees life as tragicomedy, with the result that the grotesque is its most genuine style." Further, such a grotesque "is the genuine antibourgeois style."[13] Mann is surely right: much literature and art in our era is indeed devoted to the traumatic grotesque. Tennessee Williams fully concurs with Mann's assessment. So much modern literature embraces gothicism and morbidity, he explains, because it raptly conveys "a sense, an intuition, of an underlying dreadfulness of modern experience"; indeed, it is this "Sense of The Awful which is the desperate black root of nearly all significant modern art." Accordingly, such art utilizes "Symbols of the grotesque and the violent."[14]

Of course, since much of the grotesque manner appears startling, demonic, disorderly, and depressing, it is not surprising that its deployment has frequently discomfited and annoyed the popular audience. Moralists particularly object that such art lacks piety, joy, and affirmation. And neoclassicists frequently protest, as Horace had done, that grotesquerie violates the canons of ordonnance and of form. We wish, however, to remind the modern audience that grotesque art has always been a weapon in the hands of the classicists who seem so stridently to disapprove of its use. Horace himself was not averse to introducing ghosts, witches, transformations, and disorderly arrangement and conduct into his epodes, satires, epistles, and odes. The satirist usually fosters the grotesque as a mirror held up to chaotic and distraught generations, and grotesquerie has been a dominant feature in major satiric art—in Lucian's *Lucius; or, The Ass,* in Juvenalian jeremiads, in *Reynard the Fox,* in Rabelais, Cervantes, Montaigne, von Grimmelshausen, Jonson, Pope, and Swift.

Hence Montaigne with studied aplomb cultivates in his writing the "Crotesko" painter's "fantasticall pictures, having no grace." Indeed, he claims that his own loose essays are grotesques: "What are these my compositions in truth, other than antike workes, and monstrous bodies, patched and hudled up together of divers members, without any certaine or well ordered figure, having neither order, dependencie, or proportion."[15] As ironist and paradoxer, he claims an innocence that produces chaotic matter, just as Horace had insisted that he could not achieve classic or epical status and had to settle for only *sermones* or "chats" in his lowly writings. Yet such a naive pose allows him to attack much questionable opinion and conduct in his own day with seeming impunity.

Alexander Pope maintains a like-minded naïveté when he allows his persona, Martinus Scriblerus, to extol wretched modern poetry. Scriblerus's manual, the *Peri Bathous,* actually attempts to aid aspirants in the writing of bad poetry; Scriblerus recommends that poets avoid common sense and strive for "a most happy, uncommon, unaccountable Way of Thinking." The neophytic bad poet should "consider himself as a Grotesque painter, whose works would be spoiled by an imitation of nature, or uniformity of design. He is to mingle bits of the most various, or discordant kinds, landscape, history, portraits, animals, and connect them with a great deal of flourishing, by heads or tails, as it shall please his imagination, and contribute to his principal end, which is to glare by strong oppositions of colours, and surprise by contrariety of images." Yet for all of this irony, Pope himself is an absolute master of chaotic and discordant modern creations, his masterpiece being that grand dilapidated and defective epic, *The Dunciad* (1728–43).[16]

In a similar manner, modern satire has been especially fond of utilizing the absurdities of perverse gothic underground men entrapped in their entropic universe. Such satire gains poignant force from shattered and ominous images of demonic disarray. Doubtless our century of warfare, bloodshed, and mass communications has earned the violent public art (one thinks of Picasso's *Guernica*) it has inspired. Being necessarily selective, we will examine five influential modern writers of this grotesque art—Kafka, Faulkner, Beckett, Grass, and García Márquez.

Franz Kafka, one of the seminal influences in twentieth-century literature, generated a fiction of inexplicable trials, persecutions, and dismemberment. His medium was especially effective for its internal contradictions—the patient, rational analysis of the wildly irrational. "A Common Confusion" well illustrates his method. Its genre is close to a logical problem frequently encountered in course texts in algebra and plane geometry. All is neatly labeled, *A, B, C, D*, and one expects in such a genre that the alert arithmetical student will do some paperwork and provide a solution. Yet Kafka's "problem" is insoluble: different characters operate forever in different "sets"; time is forever different in each character's world. As a result, Kafka's creatures dwell on different planes and can never meet. Mathematics and the world it seeks to measure and regulate have run out of control.

Much the same occurs in "A Hunger Artist," in which an emaciated artiste starves in public for a living. Opposites suddenly conflict—a man may be a creator of nonconsumption, a composer of starvation. This generator of sterility lives in straw and a cage, like a beast; the apex of his achievement becomes synonymous with self-destruction. And all around this immobile, decaying carcass swirls a public senselessly committed to violent changes in taste. Even more grotesque is "The Metamorphosis," wherein Gregor Samsa, the bourgeois office clerk, is inexplicably converted into a gigantic insect.[17] He continues to rationalize like a middle-class human, while behaving like a bug. And almost inadvertently his family, which cannot cope, slowly and ineptly bruise, batter, and starve the creature to death. Paradoxically, his demise triggers joy and relief and is the means of his sister's "transformation" into vigorous and healthy female adulthood. Kafka, of course, powerfully exemplifies the existential absurd: the universe has betrayed man, but man's perverse values have also led to his betrayal of himself.

One of William Faulkner's best novels of the comic-grotesque is *The Hamlet* (1940). All his novels, to some degree, are inhabited by obsessed maniacs, desperate little men, and maimed leaders, but *The Hamlet* concentrates them all together in an especially rich abundance.[18] The novel satirically portrays the triumph of vice and folly. The southern white-trash horde of Snopeses proliferates on the land like mink, overpopulating and inundating rural Yoknapatawpha County with criminals and halfwits. Good men are conned, deceived, robbed, driven mad, and the implacable Flem Snopes, silent and intransigent, irrevocably takes over in Frenchman's Bend. Common sense is driven out, and the only kind of love in evidence is bestial and perverse. A climactic vision conjured by Ratliff, the sewing machine salesman, portrays Flem Snopes as outmaneuvering Satan and taking the underworld as his prize. Such a grotesque operator is intended to be seen as the new comptroller of a universe gone awry. William Faulkner has simply up-ended the romantic tall tale, converting it into a lyrical (and epical) account of the triumph of civic savagery.

Another master, Günter Grass, is best known for his monumental metaphor for the German war years in *The Tin Drum* (1959). Perverting the Bildungsroman, this novel offers in a sense no "development" at all. Its protagonist is the stunted dwarf, Oskar Matzerath; with full intellectual growth at birth, he elects to stop growing physically at the age of three and is magically capable of shattering glass with his voice. Symbolically beating a tin drum throughout, he subsequently becomes a mad dwarfish leader of street gangs. Oskar, believing that he is destined for some messianic goal, represents the rise of Nazi power and the chaotic destructiveness of the war years. He is at once barrenly infantile and sexually potent, a brilliantly creative destroyer surrounded by a world of brilliantly greater destruction. His loudly beaten drum is the thunder that represents the militant jungle magic of primitive man and that throughout this novel, as one critic observes, "calls the world's tune."[19]

An additional masterpiece of grotesque satire is Gabriel García Márquez's *One Hundred Years of Solitude* (1967), which treats the panorama of eight generations of the Buendía family, from the founding of the remote village of Macondo in the Colombian jungle until the town's destruction by hurricane. The Buendías have a penchant for obsessive and singular behavior: they lust violently, inaugurate senseless civil war, crave magic and secret rituals, and retire frequently in dread silence or madness, inchoate in the face of destiny. Their lives are infested by unearthly drives and incomprehensible signs: magical hieroglyphic texts, madness, visitations by ghosts, massive loss of memory, incredible assaults and inundations by birds, butterflies, and droughts, unheard-of fecundity and proliferation of domestic animals. Throughout their entire history, they are haunted by the attractions and fears of incest. The original Buendías (married cousins) had migrated to and founded Macondo in an attempt to escape the curse of incest: an offspring that would manifest a little pig's tail. At the novel's close, before the town is demolished by storm and flood, an aunt and her nephew, violating this taboo, do indeed manage to beget a little pig-tailed son—as if this were the fated and desired completion of an entire family's fantastic quest. We are assaulted by a near-mythic tale of a civilization's rise, decline, and apocalyptic demise, but it is a uniquely modern myth, without any evident heroes or virtues, suggesting a sick land without standards or noteworthy achievements—in short, the jaundiced realm of our own modern history and consciousness.

Doubtless the greatest purveyor of grotesquerie in our century is Samuel Beckett. His panoply of novels perhaps best dramatizes modern man's boredom, claustrophobia, and withdrawal inward—to a barren lunatic terrain. The earliest hero in his short stories, *More Pricks Than Kicks* (1934), is Belacqua, named after the sloth in Dante's Purgatory. Subsequent figures exceed him marvelously in lethargy and inertness: Murphy in voluntary isolation in his rocking chair, Watt endlessly devising "possible" rational strings of explanations for trivial everyday events, Molloy maniacally pondering the probable arrangements for his sixteen suckingstones in four pockets. Inevitably, Beckett's characters are more and more constricted and physically confined: Vladimir and Estragon wait interminably; Lucky and Pozzo exchange roles as master and slave, horse and buggy; Molloy is reduced to traveling by bicycle, then to crutches, then to crawling, moving toward paralysis; Macmann (in *Malone Dies*) rolls in a circle of mud and rain; the speaker of *How It Is* is a captive in lukewarm mud in the dark; Nagg and Nell (in *Endgame*) appear legless, in garbage cans; Winnie (in *Happy Days*) is buried to her chin in the desert sand; and the Unnameable appears armless and legless, his torso stuffed in a jar in front of a Parisian restaurant. Many such mutilated victims have nothing but writing, or tapes, or endless talk to keep them going—but there is always the threat of total insanity, final annihilation, acts without words, silence. Beckett's clowns and tramps eternally metamorphose into victims. He is clearly a master of comic small talk, with its incessant repetitions and elongated lists, of parody of learning, of obscene puns, and his satire pushes his readers closest to the abyss.[20] For here, his fictions seem to tell us, lies man in his human condition: solipsistic yet paralyzed by ignorance and the absurd. No one has been able, more comically or horribly, to dig down further into man's intellectual grotto. Perhaps Beckett takes us as far underground as we can bear to go.

Horace, in conceiving his hideous mermaid-beast, spoke of the inventions of a "sick man's dreams." In its shocking way, the modern grotesque appears to postulate that such a sick man's brain is possibly the lowest common denominator of the human condition itself. Normally the middle class is perfectly content with touches of the grotesque in comedy, or with threads and frills of the odd in the decorative arts. The Victorians were placidly fond of garish furniture, elaborate and wildly ornate lamps and screens and wallpaper, or of sofas whose arms and legs were transmogrified into eagle's talons, elaborate vines, or lion's claws. But in the persistent grotesque the themes of unworldly upheavals and transformations and near lunatic disarray threaten to overturn the bourgeoisie's own world of sanitary and sanctimonious normalcy and diurnal mediocrity. Baudelairean flowers of evil, mystifying (and sinister) symbolist imagery, surrealism's mayhem, Jarry's murderous Ubu puppets, Büchner's insane half-wit Woyzeck, Čapek's invading newts, Golding's pig-hunting child-savages, Céline's journeys into the heart of darkness, Burgess's slang-ridden menacing street gangs, and Ionesco's evolving rhinoceroses present pervasive scenes of malice and distortion, far more disturbing to conventional expectations and dissatisfying to citizens bent upon the pursuit of happiness, quietus, and relief. Yet it is upon that rough road that the many classic satirists increasingly have determined to propel a nervous and unwilling readership. Generating a paradox, we can assert that classical satiric artists find for themselves a happy medium for their message in the gothic and truncated extravagances of anticlassical artistry. Nowhere is such a practice more in evidence than in the creations of twentieth-century art.

Part II. Stratagems

Part II of this study explores prominent methods that the grotesque satirist employs to shock the reader by manipulating, undercutting, and even dismantling conventional literary form. Satirists have always sought to parody and to lampoon traditional literary and popular genres—romance, apologia, Bildungsroman, confession, detective mystery—and grotesquerie continues such practice. But grotesque satire seeks to go one step further, hoping to startle its readership by boldly shattering broadly accepted decorum and even elementary formal usage. Furthermore, it tends to wreak this havoc and perform this mayhem with some glee and a great deal of insidiousness.

Chapters 3-9 consider the chief ways that satirists distort, fracture, and subvert the plot and other standard apparatuses of fiction. The conventional hero-protagonist decays; the author is mocked or else intrudes upon his fiction, breaking down verisimilitude; normative language and diction are skewered; and the machinery of smooth and harmonious plotting is battered or expunged. By such means, the authors of the grotesque capture attention, keep the reader off balance, and call into question the basic clichés and assumed paraphernalia of writing and of fiction-making, thereby upsetting the habitual lassitiude and passivity of typical readers. Such satiric fiction, as Donne noted of the "new philosophy," calls all in doubt.

3

Degrading the Hero

One point that has been driven home to audiences of modern literature and film is the death of the hero, even of heroism itself. Carlyle may have exalted heroes and hero-worship in the nineteenth century, but our era champions the antihero. Thackeray subtitled *Vanity Fair* "A Novel without a Hero" in 1848, and the modern era has increasingly contributed to the hero's demise. In his place lurch his faulty replacements: criminals, bumblers, toadies, cowards, outsiders, and buffoons.

In fact, every society always contends with a radical protesting minority that seeks to question, alter, and replace the regnant society's mythologies and idols. Such rebels of course have their own goals and agendas, but they tend primarily to emphasize revolt—accentuating the traditions and standards that they renounce and against which they rebel. Such opponents debunk the traditional heroes of conventional culture only to extol the newly proposed replacement—the "contrary" culture.

Hence, the term counterculture might appear to be new in the last decade or so, but the concept and what it stands for are as old as the hills, for a counter-society is a deliberate opposite, a negative mirror-image, in the sense that Baudelaire's *Les Fleurs du mal* grow in the rotting garden plot across from the bed of Christian lilies. A counterculture is contrapuntal, engaged in a music-making that plays off against the prevailing themes of dominant cults and mores in precisely the same way that the Greek παρῳδία (parodia) suggests a counter-music that mimics and plays beside the traditional ode. Because such a deviant culture takes its definition and being from the accepted society but constitutes a wild divagation, it tends to flourish with a kind of deadly zeal and serves (often even unconsciously) as purgative saturnalia for the civilized soul.

In this sense the counterculture represents the reverse side of a civilization's single coin and functions, like Freud's "wit" and "humor," as an aggressive creative attack upon that part of the society or self that is sublimated and projected. We must remember that Freud believed such an overleaf or underside absolutely necessary for a civilization (and its discontents) to survive.[1] Some lively underbellied countercultures of the past immediately come to mind: the Elizabethan preoccupation with the criminal "underworld," for instance, and, related to it and spreading from Spain in the sixteenth century, the picaresque literature of roguery.[2] More recently, we have become increasingly aware of the Sade-like nether side of nineteenth-century priggishness and rectitude that cultivated pornography and perversion, the alter ego of a prim society.[3]

Lionel Trilling suggests that perhaps society always contains built-in "alienation," a bipartite dissociation of sensibility of what may be named "the two environments." In that sense, he reminds us, a significant "counter" in the seventeenth century to the gay courtier and suave cavalier existed that was just as "modish and faddish" as is our youth cult today:

It is necessary [that we] recognize the part a mode or a fad may play in the history of culture. The English middle classes of the sixteenth and seventeenth centuries fell prey to a fad of Bible-reading and theological radicalism. It is hard for us to imagine how these Puritan predilections could once have impassioned many minds, but before they passed beyond our comprehension, they changed the social and cultural fabric of England and helped create the social and cultural fabric of America.[4]

Similarly, Velma Richmond proposes that such a "characteristic cleavage" always exists within a culture and follows McLuhan in noting "correspondences between popular medieval and contemporary thought," such as "a view of hippies and Cathars [or Albigensians] as similar counter-cultures in their rejection of conventional civilization."[5] In a certain sense, of course, the entire monastic and mendicant movements of the Middle Ages constituted islands and fortresses of radicals withdrawn from the dominant barbarian and feudal social norm.[6] Later, to be sure, the earthy Provençal singers and the lusty heretical Church fathers themselves seceded from the sacred font and created the vulgar secular lyric hymns of the Goliards and the *Carmina Burana*.

One of the most pressing causes for the development of a counter-culture (and one with which we, in our century, are surely familiar) occurs in reaction to the creation of massive international and metropolitan civilization. Hundreds of cities, in such an expansive society, cultivate stability and sameness. There is significant population growth and the breakdown of inbred coherencies, local ties, and rural roots. Oswald Spengler describes this eventuality as the advent of the "World-city": "In place of a world, there is a *city*, a *point*, in which the whole life of broad regions is collecting while the rest dries up. In place of a type-true people, born of and grown on the soil, there is a new sort of nomad, cohering unstably in fluid masses, the parasitical city dweller, traditionless, utterly matter-of-fact, religionless, clever, unfruitful."[7] Just such an engrossing culture evolved in the Hellenistic era, that witnessed the breakdown of the πόλις (polis) and the sudden spread of Greek culture, after Alexander, throughout the Mediterranean world. Isolation was the lot of Hellenistic men, who had become the lonely crowd, as Timon of Phlius (fl. 250 B.C.) wistfully remarked: "As the individual walked through the streets of the great cities, he was lost in the crowd, become a simple number in the midst of an infinity of human beings like himself, who knew nothing about him, of whom he knew nothing, a man who stood alone in bearing the weight of life without friends, without reason for living."[8]

The Cynics constituted the most notable group of intellectual "dropouts" from that Hellenistic society. All philosophical schools, in some sense, derive from Socrates, his humble demeanor, and his devotion to ethics or to the individual's moral conduct. The πόλις (polis) was already threatened by the Peloponnesian War; increased international trade fostered cosmopolitanism; and tribes, sects, and local religious practices were already commencing to disintegrate. Hence it is not simply that "Socrates first brought philosophy into the field of ethics . . . [but that] all philosophy was becoming practical," that is, concerned with the newly emergent and disestablished individual.[9]

Balding, disheveled, uncouth, simple in his habits, Socrates appeared never to work, spending his time instead incessantly (and naggingly) questioning others and debating. Humbly he sought clear ideas and often discovered a lack of clarity in others. Socrates left behind no writings, no systematic philosophy, only the legacy of ceaseless interrogations and conversations; he saw himself as the "midwife" of philosophy—forever bringing forth ideas out of others. The silent majority perceived such a casual flouter of metropolitan conventions as the nagging "gadfly" of Athens. Yet he was strikingly successful with the youth, for he attracted about himself an ardent band of young disciples—aristocrats and conservatives, agnostics and atheists, socialists and anarchists. And from him a dozen philosophical schools evolved.

The most theatrical and revolutionary of the youthful enthusiasts were the Cynics, or Dog-Philosophers, so called after their gathering-place at the Cynosarges, or "white dog", a gymnasium outside the walls of Athens. But they were also associated with dogs because of their overt shamelessness and audacity. The first of the Cynics was Antisthenes, a pupil of Socrates' who intensely extolled virtue by emphasizing the cultivation of freedom from wants, cares, and desires. Indeed, Antisthenes initiated the famous Cynic habit of dress—the doubled cloak (for all weather), the large and simple wallet, and the humble staff. And particularly did that cloak, the τρίβων (tribon)—tattered and worn—become the emblem and symbol of Cynic shabbiness. Antisthenes' follower, in turn, Diogenes of Sinope, went farther still and mocked, excoriated, and fulminated against the conventions and appurtenances of civilization itself. Calling himself the Dog, he stood upon street corners and barked, snarled, and snapped obloquy at startled bourgeois passers-by.[10]

In fact, Diogenes did more than antagonize and harangue the crowd. Once, at a banquet, when the genteel guests playfully threw their bones to him, Diogenes commenced playing the dog in earnest, romping and cavorting, until he finally lifted a leg and did on them a dog's business. For Diogenes advocated an anarchic "absolute freedom in speech, absolute fearlessness in deed"; he contended that "a great deal of theory may be upset by a small amount of brute fact." In the most flagrant sense, this is what he meant when he spoke of living "life in accordance with nature."[11]

Indeed, Diogenes cultivated a life-style of conspicuous abstinence and exigent eccentricity. He insisted upon leading a mendicant's life, always appearing barefooted, always extravagantly unshaven and unbathed. And paradoxically, together with an immoderate poverty, he advocated extreme individualism; he recognized no distinctions of birth or class, no restrictions of place, person, or ceremony.[12] Thus, he considered marriage supererogatory and extolled random free love, maintaining that one may engage in intercourse—with anyone of either sex—at any time, in any place. To add to such shocking opinions, he frequently put theory into practice. Diogenes even advocated "that incest and cannibalism may be justifiable in certain circumstances."[13] Such early Cynics took to giving "soapbox lectures" and created free street-corner "happenings," as if they were conducting "open universities" and classrooms-without-walls. They mixed paradox and insult with an everyday colloquial and conversational manner; they were wits and anecdotists as well as masters of the tirade hurled to the four winds of heaven. Later Cynics, such as Menippus and Bion, perfected the diatribe, the satire, and what was later to become the informal "essay."[14]

Diogenes, always the crackerjack outrager of social norms and ace performer, is remembered for marching along the streets with a lighted lantern in broad day, proclaiming that he was searching for an honest man. He even renounced a simple dwelling place in Athens and, to everyone's astonishment, took up residence in a large public earthenware tub or enormous wine jar (πίθος, pithos) in the Metroum of the Ceramicus, or market district. He observed, Diogenes claimed, how the snail lived, carrying about with it its own house—and he would aspire to no more.[15] Moreover, he early asserted that he was a κοσμοπολίτης (cosmopolites)—a citizen or patriot of no single nation or state, but a free inhabitant of everywhere. Thus was Cynicism assuredly an "unconventional philosophy" and, as one critic observes, a distinctive counterculture "involving a rigorous, practical critique of social traditions."[16]

One of the more surprising moves of these early Cynics was their pronouncing Heracles (or Hercules) as their hero, patron, and archetype.[17] Heracles, doubtless the most famous of the strongmen, had been an early Doric deity and long accepted throughout Greece as a national hero. Already in the fifth century he had been adopted for every sort of role—in religion, in epic, in tragedy. He even was made to serve in comedy as a figure of farce. Such a national Hercules was already being transformed into an ethical ideal among the intelligentsia. But this was hardly the case with the "unabashedly anti-intellectual" Cynics, who brazenly and shockingly celebrated merely his "labors" and physical strength.[18] For them, Hercules was the ideal of coarse and pristine brawn, and they particularly lauded his primitive and savage garb—the lion skin and the enormous Neanderthal club. Once again, the Cynics, with a masterful flare for the actor's pose and the melodramatic gesture, succeeded in undermining traditional culture and religion with their own avatar. For Cynics sought to agitate, scandalize, and appall common public opinion—and they succeeded well enough. Diogenes baldly insisted that in his tub he lived exactly like Heracles, preferring liberty over all things.[19]

Such strategies should be familiar to us today, for we have witnessed the era of the beatnik, of Britain's angry young men, and of the hippie. We have beheld the Berkeley Free Speech movement and rather impatiently abided the snarlings of the Panthers, the ablutions of the Jesus Freaks, and the public's adoration of the already apotheosized Beatles and the Rolling Stones. We have also remarked the recent fashion of converting the tenement and the broken-down homestead and hovel into the commune. Ours, too, has become a period subject to outrageous paradox and vociferous rhetoric: R.D. Laing praises the sanity of the schizophrenic, Herbert Marcuse celebrates revolution; and Norman O. Brown fragmentedly adores love's body.[20] Now we are growing accustomed to the concept of the "performing self" and to the shameless, flowery, and whorish language of Tom Wolfe and the New Journalism. Even our punk rock groups, discomaniacs, cinema and comic book heroes are becoming overtly "freakish" and downright ugly.²¹ One need merely reflect upon the popularity of Miss Piggy, Telly Savalas, the Hulk, and the Thing.

Beyond all such ugliness, tatters, and noise persists a serene and cynical regard for stylishness and attention-getting mannerism. The τρίβων (tribon) or threadbare cloak ultimately symbolizes, for the modern as for the ancient Cynic, what Yeats called "the foul rag-and-bone shop of the heart." As one critic observes, "Within our own time, rags have had a widespread vogue among the young, partly as protest against straight society, partly from a sense that being grubby is a way to be natural and therefore perhaps next thing to holy. . . . Living in a different world, sensual, imaginary, and presumably better, the [protester, the dropout, and] the addict advertise by costume or behavior [their] contempt for this common and commonplace globe." Given such an intense preoccupation with faded denim and tattered dungarees, with rags and filth, the modern almost becomes kin thereby to ancient religious hermits. "In thus acting out a disdain for middle-class decorums, rags may express an aloofness almost *dandy* in its sense of extreme style."²²

Such styles and fashions in history definitely recur. Indeed, in the late 1960s, perhaps it was no accident that a so-called children's television cartoon series regularly celebrated the Herculoids. It was a program full of ugly little monsters, "in which the abominable creatures who are the title characters are nonetheless the saviors and protectors of humanity."²³

Above all, one important fact should be patently clear: in our era conventional heroes have been brought among the lowest of the low. In his novel *The Maze-Maker*, Michael Ayrton reduces the classical hero Theseus to the level of thug. Daedalus describes him with acid precision:

[Theseus is] a relative of mine. He has become very celebrated and is much admired for his treachery to Ariadne, . . . for slaying the Minotaur, with her help, . . . [and] for his accidental—if it was accidental—destruction of his own father by negligence in the matter of the color of the sail, and other heroic acts. Perhaps the most famous of all his exploits is the victory he achieved over a group of women, a large number of whom were killed in battle with him. Altogether, my kinsman Theseus . . . was a murderous hero, which is the common kind. . . . This must be accepted, for killing, like so many destructive activities, is unavoidable to the uncreative. It is their principal demonstration of power.²⁴

Meantime, Eliot's Sweeney, Waugh's Paul Pennyfeather, Chaplin's tramp, Kafka's neurotic nonentities in jeopardy or on trial, as well as

James Thurber's and Woody Allen's schlemiels all undermine normative herohood. John Barth's febrile protagonist in *Giles Goat-Boy* (1966) can hardly manage to stumble along the heroic track, a track that has, by the way, been reduced to a muddy community college mall. More appositely, who does not remember Ford Maddox Ford's "good soldier" or Jaroslav Hasek's "good soldier Schweik"? Who can forget Faulkner's violent sharecroppers, Grass's warrior freaks, or García Márquez's surrealistic crazies? Indeed, there has been, if anything, over the ages, some species of degeneration; for whereas the Cynics could resuscitate a Hercules, we have nothing to show for our pains other than Dirty Harry, Rambo, Underdog, Mighty Mouse, and mutant turtles. Surely, much has already been written about the antihero in the twentieth century as tactic and as dominant theme.[25] It is enough here to remark that the antiheroic remains the quintessential ingredient of satire's caustic grin and grimace. Our debunking literature is full of him.

4

Debunking the Author

Not content merely to undermine other people's icons and heroes, the satirist is particularly alert to debunk authors—other writers certainly, and even himself. When pomp and pride are being forced to take a fall, no one is safe or exempt. For, after all, who is not pleased to preen and praise himself? Jonathan Swift, in one of his major satires, affirmed that "WHOEVER hath an Ambition to be heard in a Crowd, must press, and squeeze, and thrust, and climb with indefatigable Pains, till he has exalted himself to a certain Degree of Altitude above them."[1] He so much appreciated this imagery of "king of the mountain" as being man's characteristic way of life that he repeated it many years later in one of his best poems:

> WE all behold with envious Eyes,
> Our *Equal* rais'd above our *Size*;
> Who wou'd not at a crowded Show,
> Stand high himself, keep others low?
> I love my Friend as well as you,
> But would not have him stop my View;
> Then let me have the higher Post;
> I ask but for an Inch at most.[2]

Every man, no doubt, has inflated pretensions, but learned men are distinctively more articulate in framing their own "advertisements for themselves," as Norman Mailer would term them. Here is one leader's self-devised titles, according to the gospel of Evelyn Waugh: "Seth, Emperor of Azania, Chief of the Chiefs of Sakuyu, Lord of Wanda and Tyrant of the Seas, Bachelor of the Arts of Oxford University."[3] Even the redoubtable Swift himself, despite his apparent demise, nevertheless manages to affix a host of abbreviated titles after his name in the "Verses on the Death of Dr. Swift, D.S.P.D." It is precisely after those who would puff up their reputations that the satirist courses in eager pursuit.

Other vices deserve any satirist's attention, to be sure, but pride—particularly the unwarranted or excessive pride of a learned man concerning his intellectual ability and attainments—draws some of satire's sharpest assaults. The Parson in *The Canterbury Tales* delivers a long sermon about it. He warns that pride is "the general roote of alle harmes" and gives an extensive list of other sins that spring from this evil root. The list includes not only the remaining six mortal sins but sixteen lesser sins ranging from "Inobedience" to "Veyne Glorie." Actually, "no man kan outrely telle the nombre . . . of harmes that cometh of Pride," says the Parson.[4] In *An Essay on Criticism*, Pope sounds a similar warning:

> Of all the Causes which conspire to blind
> Man's erring judgment, and misguide the Mind,
> What the weak Head with strongest Byass rules,
> Is Pride, the neverfailing Vice of Fools.[5]

As Gilbert Highet points out, "Satire vaunteth not itself and is not puffed up, but God help those who vaunt themselves."[6] The satirist shows no mercy for the litterateur (or pretender to wit, culture, and learning) who believes that he is superior to other men because of his high I.Q., his university education, or his published writings. In the eyes of the satirist, such false pride ignores the reality of man's dual nature. According to the satirist, man always must remember that he is neither beast nor angel, but remains

> on this isthmus of a middle state
> . . . .
> In doubt his Mind or Body to prefer;
> Born but to die and reas'ning but to err.[7]

Thus, the artist who thinks of himself as an ethereal being producing great masterpieces through divine inspiration and the scholar who considers himself a cerebral being concerned only with erudite theories are ridiculous because they have forgotten their human state. The satirist has only scorn for those who believe that they are unlike other men.

Chaucer's Parson suggests that the remedy for the sin of pride is "humylite or mekenesse," and satirists through the ages have worked enthusiastically to restore proper humility to those whose pride has led them astray.[8] The errant litterateur finds himself attacked from all sides: his work is belittled; the honors that he holds dear are so exaggerated that they become ludicrous; his physical appearance is caricatured unmercifully; and, through the satirist's process of discussing him in physiological or mechanical terms, he finally is reduced to the subhuman level of a beast, a vegetable, or a machine. The satirist shows no mercy.

One of the methods that the satirist uses to deflate the pride of learned men is directed especially toward authors. Unlike the romantic, who elevates the work of the writer by suggesting that his words are so important that they will last eternally, or at least "so long as men can breathe, or eyes can see," the satirist devalues the writer's efforts by emphasizing their unimportance and ephemerality.[9] So the satirist demolishes the romantic's "winged words," attaches them firmly to a page, and then depicts the ignominious fate of that page.

When Juvenal advises his readers that certain writing deserves to be consigned "to some dark nook, / . . . for only worms will give it its due look," he sounds the satirist's twofold theme: the author's words will go unread, and the pages on which the words are written will serve some purely utilitarian purpose. Persius's *adversarius* in *Satire* 1 enlarges on Juvenal's suggestion that books frequently become merely food for worms: "Do you mean to tell me that any [author] who has uttered words worthy of cedar oil [that will preserve the manuscript from moths] will disown the wish to have earned a place in the mouths of men, and [will disown the wish] to leave behind him poems that will have nothing to fear from mackerel or from spice?"[10] This passage implies that every author would, if he could, cherish the idea that his work will survive to all eternity; he aspires to escape from moths, and more particularly he yearns to escape that ignominious fate whereby his forgotten pages serve as fish-wrapping or as confetti for the crating of spice. But the satirist loves nothing better than to puncture the pride of authors by picturing the real utilitarian uses most literature will be put to. And the satirist's implication is clear: the page as product is more meritorious than anything the scribbler can write upon it.

Horace similarly confides that he does not wish to be celebrated by bad poets in ill-written verse, lest he wind up—together with such scrap paper ("chartis ineptis")—in the marketplace as tissue for wrapping frankincense, pepper, and perfume. Indeed, such an inglorious and ludicrous fate for trivial authors and their manuscripts was a favorite topic of the satirists. Catullus envisions the outpourings of Volusius as serving for fish-wrappers, and Martial repeatedly stresses that trashy writings will provide wrappers for incense, pepper, pies, and fish in public kitchens and stalls.[11]

What is attractive to the satirist is the alacrity and the absurdity of this not-so-tragic fall. As John Lyly phrased it, "We commonly see the booke that at Christmas lyeth bound on the Stacioners stall, at Easter be broken in the Haberdashers shop."[12] The dates here are sacrilegious, introducing by comparison an embarrassment: the book that is born at Christmas fares altogether differently from the Savior; at Eastertide the book has "fallen" into bits and pieces upon the marketplace. Unlike the Savior, such a book shall never rise again. Oh, what a falling-off was there. *Hic transit in gloria mundi*: today's best-seller is tomorrow's pillow for pantaloons or parcel for stinking fish.

Such a trajectory is the perfect exemplum for pride. "All is vanity," in the classic words of the preacher. "What profit hath a man of all his labour which he taketh under the sun? One generation passeth away, and another generation cometh." And there is nothing new under the sun, nothing of vain, moiling man that is even to be remembered: "There is no remembrance of former things; neither shall there be any remembrance of things that are to come."[13] T.S. Eliot reduces the life cycle to an incongruous and absurd repetitive triad:

Birth, and copulation, and death
That's all, that's all, that's all, that's all,
Birth, and copulation, and death.[14]

In fact, this general mortification of vanity is, if anything, exacerbated in our more "modern" ages by the increasing worship of speed, of immediacy, and the introduction of evanescent best-sellers and top-forty hits that usually triumph and disappear within several months. In the *Dunciad* (a poem entirely devoted to disappearing modern fashionable dull poetry), Alexander Pope mentions "Each Cygnet sweet of Bath and Tunbridge race," and the annotations of Martinus Scriblerus confirm that such poets are indeed dying swans: "There were several successions of these sorts of minor poets, at Tunbridge, Bath &c., singing praise of the Annuals flourishing for that season."[15] But already these persons are and ought to be nameless.

Swift exaggerates this volatile tendency in his satire upon modernity, *A Tale of a Tub*. There, the modern persona objects to posterity that the horde of immediately known and fine writers suffers dreadfully because its "never-dying works" "are devoted to unavoidable death": " 'Tis true indeed, that altho' their Numbers be vast, and their Productions numerous in proportion, yet are they hurryed so hastily off the Scene, that they escape our Memory, and delude our Sight." This transition from high to low, from freshness to darkness and ignominy, is startlingly rapid and described with almost biblical relish. Brand-new works are in a few hours utterly lost: "I enquired in vain, the Memorial of them was lost among Men, their Place was no more to be found."[16] The concept that modern works of trash shall somehow receive rapid transit to the void is frequently reported (as here in Swift) with an almost intense religious relish: the enemies of culture (like the enemies of the Lord) shall receive their just comeuppance. Indeed, their demolition or demotion is but a species of cosmic irony, whereby fate and the deity levy suitable punishment upon upstart pieces of writing noteworthy only for their bad taste. If there is a perdition for sinners among men, then it is only appropriate that the vile and the offensive among books should likewise be allocated to their underworld, a site where moths devour their innards and decaying fish become enfolded with them in an interminable embrace.

Most satiric and comic authors foster this vein of debunking in a light, amusing manner. Rabelais repeats the now-familiar thought that manuscripts become food for vermin when he reports that "the rats and moths, or (that I may not lie) other wicked vermin, had nibbled off the beginning" of "The Antidoted Conundrums." And Swift in the *Tale of a Tub* laughs at the supposed author who wrote in 1697 but whose manuscript was not published until 1704. After such a protracted period of time (by the standards of modern wit and fashion) the work is essentially incomprehensible, and the manuscript virtually worn away, as its editor observes: "The Title Page in the Original was so torn, that it was not possible to recover several Titles which the author here speaks of."[17]

Rabelais also presents another possibility, whereby the pages of the written work might be utilized (if not for reading) superstitiously as relic, nostrum, poultice, swab, or bandage: "There are . . . others . . . who when they are suffering intensely from toothache, after having spent all they had on doctors without getting any relief, have been able to find no more effective remedy than that of placing those same *Chronicles* [of Gargantua] between two very hot cloths and applying them to the sore spot, sinapizing them with a little powdered dung."[18] The fact that these pages must be combined with heated dung in order to be effective even as a remedy for toothache devalues them completely.

For surely such works survive only to be employed in some wholly unliterary procedure. Under the pseudonym of Homer Wilbur, James Russell Lowell writes on this theme in *The Biglow Papers*, reminding journalists of the ephemerality of their work. "The wonder wears off, and tomorrow this sheet [of newspaper], in which a vision was let down to me from Heaven, shall be the wrapping of a bar of soap or the platter for a beggar's broken victuals." Once more, the satirist reminds all writers that the page of which they are so proud will soon serve a utilitarian purpose, and the wonder of the words that they so carefully arranged on the page will be wholly forgotten. Pope similarly speaks of those rare volumes "Redeem'd from tapers and defrauded pies": most writings have their pages confiscated to supply candlewicks or to serve as pie pan cushions, as window patchings, and as fish-wrappers. Swift likewise remarks that if one were to seek evanescent books, one might seek "oracular conviction" by being sent to "an *Oven*, to the Windows of a *Bawdy-house*, or to the sordid *Lanthorn*." Poor literary productions are absolutely destined to die the death and to be tortured and torn asunder to serve the most mercenary purposes. Only the book, Pope caustically remarks, that is burnt alive will retain the purity of its "maiden sheets; / While all [its] smutty sisters walk the streets."[19]

Hence, the lurid and sordid demise of pretentious books has been the satiric and comic theme of many an author. In part 1, chapter 9 of *Don Quixote*—one of the most influential books in Renaissance literature—we suddenly learn that the "manuscript" of this "history" has abruptly come to an end, leaving Quixote and his Biscayan opponent both standing with weapons held aloft, frozen on the verge of direct combat. The story remains imperfect, as the narrator tells us. After a diligent search, the would-be author, due to "Providence, Chance, or Fortune," discovers a boy offering to sell to a shopkeeper a parcel of manuscripts—in Arabic. Only at this moment does the befuddled reader learn that the history of the "Life and Miracles" of the Knight of La Mancha is indeed an "aged document," written in Arabic by the Arabian historiographer Cide Hamete Benengeli. How the tale of the addled modern would-be knight of Spain got to be told in Arabic in an "ancient" manuscript is anybody's guess. That leaves the current narrator reduced to being merely a translator. But we abruptly learn, too, that the narrator cannot read Arabic, for he hires a lad who, for very little cash, translates the whole of the new manuscript. Arab street urchins, it seems, can in such an atmosphere become authors overnight. The whole business of bookmaking and authorship is wonderfully called into question by such satiric strokes.[20]

Lawrence Sterne is squarely in this tradition: the inordinately sensitive Yorick uncovers "The Fragment" of a tale on waste paper used to overlay a print of butter. Inveterate snooper into quaint trivia that he is, Yorick finds this "old" manuscript to be in Gothic letter and in the French of Rabelais's era. Needless to say, the remaining sheets must be diligently sought, and they prove to have been "wrapt round the stalks of a *bouquet* to keep it together" and "presented [by his servant] to the *demoiselle* upon the *boulevards*." If anything, the manner in which Henry Mackenzie supposedly finds the manuscript that constitutes his novel *The Man of Feeling* (1771) is still more absurd: a sporting curate employs portions of the old manuscript piecemeal as "wadding" for his gun. Obviously, the manuscript as it comes to us is extremely mutilated and fragmented.[21]

Women are perhaps the most callous in dealing with *litterae*. In Congreve's *The Way of the World*, women find themselves "persecuted with letters" of admirers. Millamant candidly admits that she utilizes them "to pin up one's hair." Not, of course, with all letters. "Only with those in verse. . . . I never pin up my hair with prose. I fancy one's hair would not curl if it were pinned up with prose. I think I tried it once."[22] In *The Rivals*, Sheridan similarly strikes this lighter tone but conveys nonetheless an equally somber message about the fate of the written word. At first the attitude of the young ladies in the play toward serious literature seems encouraging; the ladies insist on keeping heavy religious volumes in the bedroom. Unfortunately, the ladies do not want the books for moral or intellectual improvement. The books are meant to convince older relatives that the young ladies are properly concerned about serious moral issues; even more important, from the young ladies' point of view, is the fact that the heavy books provide a steady supply of curling papers and a place to press wrinkled hairnets.

Lucy tells her mistress that one of the big books is "only *The Whole Duty of Man* where I press a few blonds, ma'am." The juxtaposition of the limiting adjective *only* with so large and weighty a subject prepares the audience somewhat for the discovery that the whole duty of man, in this case, is simply to smooth ladies' hairnets. When Lydia asks Lucy to "leave Fordyce's Sermons open on the table" before visitors arrive, Lucy replies, "O burn it, ma'am! the hairdresser has torn away as far as *Proper Pride*."[23] One doubts that pride is in any sense "proper"; and certainly the reference here to pride is indeed a two-edged blade. Most obviously, it cuts at the ladies' pride in their appearance, since they have allowed their hairdresser to use the pages of a serious religious work for the frivolous purpose of improving their coiffures. But the reference to pride is also intended to stigmatize the pride of authors who smugly suppose that their words will ever meet with anything approaching the thought and consideration that the authors themselves accorded them.

Moreover, such mutilation of authors is intended to be directed at hosts of such writers. At the end of his "Defense of Satire," Horace threatens, "If you aren't tolerant . . . a great host of poets—for we are more than half the world—shall come to my rescue and, like the Jews, we will compel you to join our crowd."[24] This view of the author as simply one of an enormous flock or shoal robs him of the heroic individualism and the superhuman solitary mystique accorded him by the romantics and makes him seem very ordinary—merely one carton in a carload. Such an author is no longer a separate entity inspired by a private muse, but rather one member of a herd that foolishly floods the world with more words than the world can (or ought to) absorb. Voltaire makes the same point in *Candide* (1759), when the naive Candide inquires of an abbé about dramatic productions in France:

> "Pray, sir, . . . how many theatrical pieces have you in France?"
> "Five or six thousand," replied the other.
> "Indeed! That is a great number," said Candide, "but how many good ones may there be?"
> "About fifteen or sixteen."[25]

Pope reduces the concept of overproduction to absurdity in his satiric mock manual, the *Peri Bathous* (1727). His scholarly mouthpiece, Martinus Scriblerus, provides a how-to handbook for the writing of bad verse and includes several "recipes" for cooking up plays and epics into the bargain. The implication is that there are so many cooks about (as well as poets), that everything commonplace should be done by trivial rules and instructions. Needless to say, the broth is spoiled—and so is the poetry.

Satirists continued throughout the Renaissance to assault the pride of authors with these combinations of ideas: first, that there are too many authors producing too many works; and second, that most of the works have little value beyond that of the paper on which they are printed. Indeed, the Renaissance made a point of celebrating the rise of authors and nationalistic pride. And the printing press certainly made works available—in excess. That was surely the topic satirists more and more came to stress during the later Renaissance and the Enlightenment. In making their case, satirists frequently turned scatological and satirically tart. For example, Quevedo's *The Life of the Great Rascal* ("The Swindler" or *El Buscón*) contains this proclamation: "AND CONSIDERING the vast harvest of roundelays, songs, and sonnets there had been these fertile years WE DO ORDAIN that all bundles of them found to be unsuitable for grocers' shops, be placed in privies without further appeal."[26] Naturally, the toilet became a favorite locale for the satirists; throughout the ages, separate sheets of paper obviously could be made to serve—to pun a little—a "fundamental" purpose in the outhouse. And furthermore, satirists love nothing better than to shock the audience into attention by flinging about some element of filth. This tradition is very old.

Catullus long ago debunked the writings of the would-be litterateur Volusius as *cacata charta*,—"shit paper." Aretino similarly dedicates his *Dialogues* to his monkey, reminding the reader that monkeys and great lords look much alike, and expects the worst, as he does of any work fawningly and obsequiously dedicated to some "great person." He candidly tells his monkey: "How, my Supreme Highness Bagattino (for that is how one addresses great lords who are worthy of such dignity as you), take these pages of mine and tear them up, for great lords not only tear up the pages dedicated to them but even wipe themselves with them, as I almost didn't tell you." Jonathan Swift consigned most proliferating works directly "to a *Jakes*, or an *Oven*."[27] Needless to say, the satirist implies that the toilet is precisely the place for wretched, stinking, fifth-rate productions (or "excretions") of mundane, bathetic writers.

Dryden, in "MacFlecknoe," scores the Augustan point that was frequently put forward: modern authors fill the world with overwriting and bad taste. He perfectly pictured what happens to "neglected authors"; their pages have inevitably (and deservedly) become "Martyrs of pies and reliques of the bum." And indeed, a great tidal flow of bad writing purportedly threatens the life of London society. Writings are everywhere: "Loads of *Sh*—— almost choakt the way."[28] Here the satirist portrays the complete devaluation of Shadwell's writings, while the punning double entendre on *sh*—— reduces the man to excrement. Not only does the public ignore the work itself while using its pages in nonaesthetic ways, but also the works themselves are devalued simply because of the vast numbers of writings that have inundated society. The number of filthy pages is portrayed as being so great in London's streets that Shadwell's "imperial" train can barely push through the detritus.

Alexander Pope's *Dunciad* simply enlarges that magnification of refuse. In book 4, after "Fame's posterior Trumpet [is] blown," a vast herd of dunces mechanically assembles:

> The gath'ring number, as it moves along,
> Involves a vast involuntary throng.
> . . . .
> There march'd the bard and blockhead, side by side,
> Who rhym'd for hire, and patroniz'd for pride.[29]

More and more fools join the throng until "crowds on crowds around the Goddess press, / Each eager to present the first Address." When the goddess calls for pedants, "Thick and more thick the black blockade extends, / A hundred head of Aristotle's friends." Finally, of course, so many fools glut the world with so many foolish words that Genesis is reenacted in reverse, the world is uncreated in a monumental satiric catastrophe, and "Chaos! is restor'd; / And Universal Darkness buries All."[30]

Matthew Hodgart asserts that the "basic technique of the satirist is reduction: the degradation or devaluation of the victim by reducing his size and dignity."[31] Thus, when a character in satire is described in terms usually reserved for portraying an animal, vegetable, mineral, machine, or madman, the character immediately relinquishes his human dignity and declines toward the level of the metaphor with which he has been associated. Critics frequently term such a satiric strategy *meiosis*, or "diminution" and "belittling."[32] Joseph Bentley terms this phenomenon "semantic gravitation," whereby words and images "sink" a character:

> A total, or unselective, image of an object would include all known facts about it—high . . . as well as low . . . —and the value attached to the image would . . . accord with its total reality. [Yet usually] unfavorable aspects of [an] image are suppressed . . . the resulting image . . . thereby [being] raised in value. Semantic gravitation [halts] the process of suppression . . . upon which high values depend. Satire . . . is . . . the technique of distorting reality by bringing previously excluded reality back into the picture.[33]

It might not be true that satire merely "reduces" by restoring "reality" or revealing the "whole picture," but satire certainly does diminish by seasoning liberally with degrading figures, with depressants. Surely the artist is most violently debunked when he and his writings are deemed synonymous with food, drug, and universal vacuity. That is one of the satirist's trump cards in his hand that contains, after all, many wonderful dirty tricks.

And what of twentieth-century satire? The modern satirist, like his predecessor, emphasizes the short life and inglorious fate of the written word. Some of what the modern satirist has to say on the subject sounds very familiar: an indifferent public remains unimpressed by the written word but finds practical uses for the paper on which it is written. In Orwell's *1984*, for example, posters are used to wrap sausages, just as poems and hack compositions were so employed for centuries in the satiric tradition. If anything, the deliberate destruction of words is exacerbated and augmented. In Vonnegut's *Breakfast of Champions*, the glut of writing that Augustan authors anticipated and dreaded has become so enormous that most words must be destroyed so that the pages on which they are printed can be recycled to make room for still more composition. In Libertyville, Georgia, trucks and trains bring in hundreds of tons of unwanted printed material every day so that old newspapers, magazines, and books can be pulped to make new paper. Reminiscent of Shadwell's paper-choked coronation route, Libertyville has "pieces of books and magazines and so on blowing all over town." In fact, there are so many books in Libertyville that "they used books for toilet paper in the jail."[34]

In addition, however, following the apocalyptic rumblings frequently sounded in earlier satire, particularly in the *Dunciad*, the modern satirist more strongly suggests the possibility of demolition, of massive, and even universal, destruction. To this he adds a new note: the word is not merely a victim of indifference or of overproduction; it is itself under direct attack. New, more absolute tyrannies are envisioned (and made plausible by modern history of the likes of Hitler and Stalin). Satirists throughout the ages have complained that careless poets or mindless scholars misuse words so that the life of language is endangered, but modern satirists frequently foretell that the word will fall victim to some deliberate or willful scheme to destroy it entirely. Librarians, authors, and especially books themselves are singled out for attack by the ruthless street gangs of the future in Anthony Burgess's *A Clockwork Orange*. And in *Animal Farm*, the bureaucracy inevitably deals with words—but only so that they might be shredded and destroyed: "Pigs had to expend enormous labours every day upon mysterious things called 'files,' 'reports,' 'minutes,' and 'memoranda.' These were large sheets of paper which had to be closely covered with writing, and as soon as they were covered they were burnt in the furnace."[35]

Like so much sawdust or so many splinters of wood, words here survive only long enough to be gathered in piles and incinerated. In earlier satires, words were destroyed because the material the words were written on seemed more important than the words themselves. But in *Animal Farm*, words are decimated because they are words; files and reports do not get consigned to the furnace because paper seems potentially dangerous in itself.

The fate of the word in such a socialistic, totalitarian state mirrors the fate of the worker. Both exist solely for the benefit of the government and its leaders; neither has value beyond an immediate utilitarian purpose; and both are expendable. In *1984* the destruction of words (and of men) continues, if anything, revealing more forethought and greater selectivity. Just as in *Animal Farm*, records are destroyed or altered in accord with current government policy, and the words are regarded as tools of the state rather than as reflections of truth or beauty. But here the government plans to eliminate the threat of rebellion by eliminating words that would enable people even to think about rebellion. Syme, who works on adjectives in the eleventh edition of the Newspeak dictionary, explains the process simply: "We're destroying words—scores of them, hundreds of them, every day."[36] Such official alteration of records and the transformation of truth should remind one of recent Soviet practice in the writing of history and of the ancient Roman habit of *abolitio memoriae*: those who offended the Senate were voted into oblivion with a decree ordering the destruction of all statues, monuments, or historic, civic, and private references to them. Names, people, concepts, words disappear suddenly and totally, overnight, like the victims in Arthur Koestler's *Darkness at Noon* (1941), or they are whisked away and convicted, absurdly, of they know not what, and executed, like Kafka's K in *The Trial* (1924).

Occasionally such destruction is merely a mild irony, as in Günter Grass's *The Meeting at Telgte*, in which a congregation of authors at a writers' conference aspires to devise a manifesto for peace, desiring to preserve their own compositions as emblematic of that which is truly German: "For . . . each of our rhymes, provided our spirit has fashioned it from life, will mingle with eternity."[37] Yet the novel concludes with their dream demolished, when the inn in which they meet, together with all their assortment of books, papers, and manuscripts, is consumed by fire.

Probably one of the seminal and most telling ways in which authors are debunked is achieved by a more intimate strategy. The author himself, his first-person persona, or his central protagonist is exposed and incriminated by what he says and does. Horace the satirist is interrupted by Davus, his own slave, who chastizes and lampoons Horace for committing a whole host of follies and vices.[38] In the *Satyricon*, Petronius's poet Eumolpus is revealed as a crazed artiste, a dull babbler of verses, but also as a vicious seducer of children; he is denuded by what he himself says and does. Petronius's orators, Agamemnon and Menelaus, are in precisely the same case: they are cheap hangers-on, leeches at other men's tables who nevertheless recite pious clichés about the general decline of virtue in the modern world. Lastly, Petronius's narrator, Encolpius, the "author" of the piece, is slowly revealed to be no more than a low-life drifter, an escaped slave, a cheap adventurer, and a wanton homosexual. In *Don Quixote*, the "author" is belatedly discovered not to be Cervantes but one Cide Hamete Benengeli, an Arab "historian"; hence the Spanish author-editor must employ a stable boy to translate the work, which he then passes off as his own. Swift's Lemuel Gulliver is author and reformer in *Gulliver's Travels*, but he is discovered at the close to be a reclusive madman and misanthrope, one who at his best talks only to horses, inhabits a stable, and dines upon straw. Such authors, it is implied, are only to be trusted if we ourselves are mentally unfit.

The modern era opens with two superlative Russian pieces that dramatize the fitful and frenzied voices of two intellectuals gone awry: Gogol's "Diary of a Madman" (1835) and Dostoevsky's "Notes from Underground" (1864). Much writing in the twentieth century deliberately questions the integrity or sanity of its authors and writer figures. Such is the case with the inept "love song" composed by Eliot's paralyzed Prufrock. And so it is with the two incompetent and neurotic psychiatrists impersonated by Thurber and White in *Is Sex Necessary?*, with the pathetically helpless writer of columns for the lovelorn in West's *Miss Lonelyhearts*, with the learned but pathological sex maniac and nymph-chaser Humbert Humbert in Nabokov's *Lolita*, with the incompetent literary critic whose lunatic essays compose Borges's *Chronicles of Bustos Domecq*. In short, key literary figures are analyzed and their defects uncovered in numerous major works in our century: the crazed sadistic teacher in Ionesco's *The Lesson*; the incompetent newspaper reporters in Evelyn Waugh's *Scoop*; the literary historian Roquentin who arrives at an absurdist intellectual impasse in Sartre's *La Nausée*; the effete and disillusioned poet Hugh Selwyn Mauberley who comes to grief in our society in Pound's poetic sequence; and the aging and distinguished novelist Gustave von Aschenbach who comes apart at the seams while on an Italian holiday excursion in Mann's *Death in Venice*. These writers simply do not have the values, the abilities, or the self-awareness and self-regulation to hold themselves together.

Not only, however, are individual artists portrayed in various stages of decadence or collapse. More devastatingly, a strong literary trend in our age deploys a savage and even cosmic irony, envisioning for the future regular "regression" toward some negative utopian state, in which mankind and his writings will be annihilated altogether. Such is the continuous theme of a number of novels of the future that have been termed "dystopias," a genre particularly fruitful in the twentieth century. A fiction might simply portray the destruction of a city, a society, or of all men and the planet, as in H.G. Wells's *The Time Machine* (1895), Karel Čapek's *War with the Newts* (1936), Kurt Vonnegut, Jr.'s *Cat's Cradle* (1963), Gabriel García Márquez's *One Hundred Years of Solitude* (1967), "Kilgore Trout's" *Venus on the Half-Shell* (1974), Nevil Shute's *On the Beach* (1957), Stanley Kubrick's film *Dr. Strangelove* (1963), Norman Mailer's "The Last Night: A Story" (1962).[39]

Even when man is not destroyed completely, there is little cause to celebrate. For at these times, such fiction portrays a future of incessant warfare, as in Evelyn Waugh's *Vile Bodies* (1930), John Hawkes's *The Cannibal* (1949), and Karl Kraus's monumental work *The Last Days of Mankind* (1922). Or, still more darkly, the future includes cannibalism as in Anthony Burgess's *The Wanting Seed* (1962) and in Barry Hannah's "Eating Wife and Friends" in *Airships* (1978). Sometimes the future includes prefrontal lobotomies for thinking men; see Ken Kesey's *One Flew Over the Cuckoo's Nest* (1962) and Eugene Zamyatin's *We* (1920). The possible total genocide by "purges" in the superstate are envisioned in works like Dobrica Cosič's "Freedom."[40] The most insidious image for this totalitarian/destructive trend may lie in Ray Bradbury's *Fahrenheit 451* (1953), in which, in the new superstate, firemen are ceaselessly deployed to scour the state with flamethrowers, burning and destroying all books—and any readers of books as well. It comes almost as a relief when this entire civilization itself explodes, terminated in a massive bombing attack. Such an intrepid rapine against books is at its most cosmic and debonair in Stanislaw Lem's *Memoirs Found in a Bathtub* (1971), in which, in the future, "the Great Collapse" occurs, caused by a "Hartian Agent" from "the third moon of Uranus": "Unwittingly brought back to Earth by an early expedition, the Hartian Agent set off a chain reaction and paper disintegrated around the globe."[41] Ironically enough, when a bathtub manuscript is relocated, excavated in such an age, we learn that man had gotten to such a state of spying and deceit, that written documents had already ceased to make any sense or pertain to any truth: writing and man himself have become magnificently superfluous.

Here we have approached the furthest reaches of irony against the pride of authors: what you have written will be exterminated, and indeed man himself, together with all his petty pride, is doomed to desecration and dissolution. Satirists in the twentieth century—perhaps with reason—have been especially fond of promoting that destructive vision. But they are hardly alone, for satirists have always implied that affairs are fatally scheduled to get worse. Evils and corruptions, Jonathan Swift remarked in an issue of *The Examiner*, should be discovered to posterity.

I should be glad the Authors Names were conveyed to future Times along with their Actions. For, although the present Age may understand well enough the little Hints we give, the Parallels we draw, and the Characters we describe; yet this will all be lost to the next. However, if these Papers, *reduced to a more durable Form*, should happen to live until our Grandchildren be Men; I hope they may have Curiosity to consult Annals, and . . . find out.[42]

Swift compellingly implies that his papers will not survive—even for several generations. For the satirist assumes that human behavior coerces history to degenerate; and a popular image with a great satirist like Swift postulates that history will prove cyclical, a wheel of fortune that, from the satirist's point of view, forever turns around—inevitably

50 Stratagems

downward. Swift likes the image of the Gothic invasion—a recurrent cataclysm inflicted upon civilization by the invasion of barbarian hordes.

> Censure, and Pedantry, and Pride,
>   Numberless Nations, stretching far and wide,
> Shall (I foresee it) soon with *Gothick* swarms come forth
>   From ignorance's Universal North,
> And with blind Rage break all this peaceful Government.[43]

Whose pride of place can then withstand such a tide? Indeed, the imagery of the Goths and Barbarians as imminent invaders and destroyers is very similar to the repeated image of books being reduced to a tissue of foolscap, tattered wrappers, and toilet paper: all these depict civilization coming apart at the seams, culture being torn into shreds, the virtual shards and "fragments" that T.S. Eliot in "The Waste Land" had wistfully "shored against [his] ruins." There cannot be any more potent antidote to pride than that.

5
Dislocating the Language

As we have seen, the satiric/comic artist deliberately seeks to undercut conventional audience expectations. His fictions demolish heroes and even pervert ideas of the noteworthy author and his enduring reputation. The satirist's implication, of course, is quite simple: his cynical vision proposes that in our defective society heroism is tainted or bogus and in our deteriorating era the pious aims, exalted motives, and self-congratulatory claims of artists are at best pompous and misguided, at worst entirely spurious. Doubtless we get the kinds of flaws and folderol that we deserve. Simply put, the satiric author will not permit us to continue to float securely upon a cloud of virtuous platitudes and grandiloquent delusions.

Perhaps, therefore, we should not be surprised to learn that the satirist similarly undercuts traditional ideas of staid diction, consistent or comely style, and lucid language. Overall, satiric plots regularly dramatize the triumph of folly or vice. Satiric form is most commonly anticlimactic, foreshortened, perplexing, defective—ending unsatisfactorily.[1] Hence the audience distinctly feels the absence of resolution and catharsis and is therefore not infrequently perplexed, frustrated, and let down. As such a recipe for disappointment, satire is that ancient *lanx satura* (literally a "medley," or "farrago," a mixed dish of foods), a provender so distasteful and cluttered that it causes aesthetic heartburn or outright indigestion.[2]

All this clutter and disarray results from the fact that the satiric artist renders an "imitation" of the excessive, the imperfect, and the negative; his work may often be laughable and diverting, but it is always somehow discomforting—providing not merely Dickensian M'Choakumchild, but M'Choakumeverybody. Hence, as a necessary part of such an imitation, the satirist, like the parasite, attaches himself to virtually any literary form or forms.[3] And this kind of inclusive imitation specifically applies to language, to thought, and to style.[4] The satirist frequently imitates the ignorant man; just as he can imitate faulty action, so can he also imitate the action of the faulty imitation.[5]

And he accomplishes these imitations of the defective with a simulated naïveté that requires, in fact, considerable artistry. In such a manner, we might say that Lucian creates a historian who writes a very poor and incredible *Vera Historia;* Horace (in *Satire* 1.5) composes a "newsletter" so poorly managed that it produces not one single piece of important news. Seneca's *Apocolocyntosis* and Byron's *Vision of Judgement* are poorly managed formal literary apotheoses; Chaucer's *Sir Topas* is very bad metrical romance. Similarly, Gay writes wretched pastorals and dislocated opera; Swift composes poor philosophical treatises and turgid astrological predictions; Dedekind (in the *Grobianus*) devises a miserable manual of human conduct; Lytton Strachey (in *Queen Victoria*) produces commonplace celebratory biography; and Nathanael West generates in *Miss Lonelyhearts* a monumentally incompetent writer of advice columns for the lovelorn.

Needless to say, many readers and critics have taken the satirist at his word, and have presumed that the satirist is the master of bad style, disjointed structure, corrupted thought. Paradoxically—in spite of the fact that most critics do not think so—satirists are normally delighted if their debilitating imitative romances, novels, or treatises are taken for the real thing. Amusingly, Jonathan Swift produced in "A Famous Prediction of Merlin" (1709) a black-letter "prophecy," supposedly printed in 1530, that indirectly advised Queen Anne to marry. Swift would have been, I am convinced, perfectly content to have learned that this imposture deceived Dr. Johnson and came to be included, later in the eighteenth century, in the *Typographical Antiquities* of the British nation.[6] If the reader misunderstands the satirist so far, then the satirist has demonstrably perfected his negative utopia and has imitated very well indeed. Such readers (or misreaders) are members of the vulgar "mob," excluded from participation in the long tradition of satiric imitation; they respond inadequately to the satirist's art and become at a stroke inherent parts, inhabitants, of the negative utopia the satirist pictures.[7]

Recently, for instance, a critic bitterly complained that Joseph Heller's *Catch-22* was "intolerably sentimental." Both Heller and Yossarian, he believes, emotionally overrespond and fail ultimately to use reason.[8] Yet we might well inquire why one must apply the standards of reason to *Catch-22*'s world at all, since the novel not only zestfully delineates warfare's universal irrationality but also mimics in its language and thought the same irrationality. Who can lay down laws and proclaim that the satiric author cannot fashion whatever story and devise whatever linguistic surface he desires?

For the satirist is concerned with the perfection of his imitation; he is "maker" of types of perfected falsehood, the constructor of the ideally inept. It is not his business either, as artist, to provide maps, telegrams, explanations, *cartes d'entrée*. Like Evelyn Waugh in Edmund Wilson's phrase, the typical satirist "never apologizes, never explains."[9] You must take his witty, mangled, ironic, creative art, or you must leave it alone. Naturally, the satirist is not entirely disappointed in his own powers, surely, if he discovers that his foolish audience mistakes his foolish imitation for grave reality; for the satirist's imitation (and indictment) is precisely that something has gone wrong with contemporary manners, morals, and taste.

Obviously, the satirist's production contains a strong element of playfulness and fun.[10] Yet there is ever present in his pages a moiety as well of dreadful earnest. C.S. Lewis once observed that "it is a very old critical discovery that the imitation in art of unpleasing objects may be a pleasing imitation."[11] But the unpleasant remains the unpleasant still, and satire successfully commingles the comic and the gross into a kind of witty grotesque. Much literature and criticism has been mightily attracted to its crazy realm. And indeed, the monstrous and the far-fetched have always found a way of being particularly alluring to the satirist, and what is "indecorous" to pastoral or to tragedy is well suited to satire.

In this chapter, we are most concerned with the manipulation of language and style. For crippled language and turbulent style precisely mirror the defective world. "Wheresoever, manners, and fashions are corrupted, Language is. It imitates the publicke riot. The excesse of Feasts, and apparell, are the notes of a sick State; and wantonesse of language, of a sick mind."[12] Candidly, the satirist has an incredible ability to isolate the fleet, the fake, and the ephemeral in language within vast mausoleums. By so doing he merely seeks to outdo the prevalent outpourings of charlatans, humbuggers, and propagandists who placidly manipulate and cauterize language to further their ruthless, selfish, and destructive ends. Hence, the satirist's imitative practice is much akin to the enshrinement of drivel in temples of marble and gold.[13] What better way to preserve, display, shock, and expose the diseases of our works and our words?

In a demented fairy tale, entitled "The Peach in Brandy," Horace Walpole tells of a stillborn fetus of a royal heir that is retained in a pickle jar. Alas, the archbishop mistakes it for a peach: "He gulped it all down at once without saying grace. God forgive him!" Thereupon the five-year-old princess cries out, "Mamma, mamma, the gentleman has eat my little brother." The ambiguities of language here are rife: perhaps the archbishop should say grace before daring to eat a peach; but then, the assertion that he ate the baby "without saying grace" insanely implies that one could feast upon babies—if only one followed appropriate ritual observances first.¹⁴ Much the same observation about the stretches of language applies to the little girl's announcing that the "gentleman" has eaten her brother; cannibalism, to be sure, puts a severe strain upon the common acceptation of the word *gentleman*.

The satirist is always busy shuffling and redefining our everyday words, dropping them nicely into a newer slot. Evelyn Waugh does this, for instance, with the words *war* and *peace*. Once, Wenlock Jakes, Waugh's famous American reporter whose presence anywhere betokens the "news centre of the world," was sent to cover a revolution in one of the Lowland Countries. By some slight accident, he arrived in the wrong nation. All was quiet, but he immediately cabled home a thousand words of "colour":

Well they were pretty surprised at his office, getting a story like that from the wrong country, but they trusted Jakes and splashed it in six national newspapers. That day every special in Europe got orders to rush to the new revolution. They arrived in shoals. Everything seemed quiet enough, but it was as much as their jobs were worth to say so, with Jakes filing a thousand words of blood and thunder a day. So they chimed in too. Government stocks dropped, financial panic, state of emergency declared, army mobilized, famine, mutiny—and in less than a week there was an honest to God revolution under way, just as Jakes had said. . . .

They gave Jakes the Nobel Peace Prize for his harrowing descriptions of the carnage.¹⁵

Even an orgy can serve as the occasion for dislocated meaning. On shipboard, Tyrone Slothrop in *Gravity's Rainbow* finds himself in the midst of an orgiastic party. People of all conceivable races, colors, and creeds are panting and plugging into random orifices; octogenerians as well as children spontaneously participate. One young woman wields "an enormous glass dildo inside which baby piranhas are swimming." "A C-melody saxophone player has the bell of his instrument snuggled between the widespread thighs of a pretty matron"; he is playing "Chattanooga Choo Choo." All this seems perfectly in order—except that the matron is wearing sunglasses: "Yes, sunglasses at night, this is some degenerate company Slothrop has fallen in with all right," the author assures us. The orgy is commonplace, matter-of-fact, but sunglasses are avant-garde and "degenerate."¹⁶

Commonly, the satirist dislocates his readership by dropping a solitary bolus of absurdity, into his paragraph. Such is Mark Twain's strategy in this purple passage from "A Double-Barreled Detective Story":

It was a crisp and spicy morning in early October. The lilacs and laburnums, lit with the glory-fires of autumn, hung burning and flashing in the upper air, a fairy bridge provided by kind Nature for the wingless wild things that have their homes in the tree-tops and would visit together; the larch and the pomegranate flung their purple and yellow flames in brilliant broad splashes along the slanting sweep of the woodland; the sensuous fragrance of innumerable deciduous flowers rose upon the swooning atmosphere; far in the empty sky a solitary esophagus slept upon motionless wing; everywhere brooded stillness, serenity, and the peace of God.[17]

Twain was always proud of that "esophagus"; he had thrown it up casually, and most of his readers had swallowed it down. He was particularly delighted, however, that two professorial types had written to inquire about it. Needless to say, of course, the entire passage is a tangle and a jangle of confusion: pendulous bushes of flowers in the "upper air," wild animals visiting together up there, amazingly "deciduous" flowers, the "swooning atmosphere." And hovering above them all, sound asleep upon a "motionless wing," floateth a very humanoid esophagus. What we encounter, then, in this sleepy parodic dreamworld, is the sudden, lightning appearance of nonsense, or, if you will, of the comic grotesque.

The nonsense need not be restricted to single words or isolated occasions. Particularly interested in capturing that vapid bit of fashionable fluff—the popular hit song—Aldous Huxley describes a popular cabaret dance in the roaring twenties in *Antic Hay*:

They are playing that latest novelty from across the water, "What's He to Hecuba?" Sweet, sweet and piercing, the saxophone pierced into the very bowels of compassion and tenderness, pierced like a revelation from heaven, pierced like the angel's treacly dart into the holy Teresa's quivering and ecstasiated flank. More ripely and roundly, with a kindly and less agonising voluptuousness, the 'cello mediated those Mohammedan ecstasies that last, under the green palms of Paradise, six hundred inerrable years apiece. Into this charged atmosphere the violin admitted refreshing draughts of fresh air, cool and thin like the breath from a still damp squirt. And the piano hammered and rattled away unmindful of the sensibilities of other instruments, and banged away all the time reminding everyone concerned, in a thoroughly business-like way, that this was a cabaret where people came to dance the fox-trot; not a baroque church for female saints to go into ecstasies in, not a mild, happy valley of tumbling houris.

At each recurrence of the refrain the four negroes of the orchestra, or at least the three of them who played with their hands alone—for the saxophonist always blew at this point with a redoubled sweetness, enriching the passage with a warbling contrapuntal soliloquy that fairly wrung the entrails and transported the pierced heart—broke into melancholy and drawling song:

> What's he to Hecuba?
> Nothing at all.
> That's why there'll be no wedding on Wednesday week
> Way down in old Bengal.
>
> "What unspeakable sadness," said Gumbril, as he stepped, stepped, stepped through the intricacies of the trot.[18]

Here is amassed a gorgeous melee and cacophony of image and sound: the Christian saint, the Mohammedan paradise, and the Indian song; the instruments of "compassion and tenderness" juxtaposed with a "hammering," "rattling," and "banging" piano; ecstasy and sweetness counterpointing the businesslike mechanical stepping of dancers to the fox-trot. The vocabulary, too, provides a miasma of conflicting dictions; that which is "meditated," "warbling," "quivering," and "ecstasiated," somehow affecting the "bowels," the "entrails," "the flank,"—all wonderfully "transporting the pierced heart" to some indeterminate destination.[19]

But the song's refrain itself properly deserves most of our attention. It is a typical "popular" lyric, concerned, as so many pop tunes are, with the failures of everyday love. Still, there are more serious matters. The metrics are uneven, even violently askew (as in the third line). And, we might logically want to know, if Hecuba is wholeheartedly uninterested in the young gentleman, why has a wedding been scheduled in the first place? There is, of course, no answer. But most important, to be sure, is Huxley's allusion to Shakespeare's *Hamlet* in this idle ditty.[20] The player, in reciting the tale of the death of Priam at the hands of Pyrrhus and of the conflagration of Troy, was actually able, assimilating Hecuba's point of view, to blanch and to weep; Hamlet later chastizes himself for responding less fully, although Hamlet has the actual "motive and cue for action." Seen in this light, the popular jazz song contains a still-greater plethora of confused motives and ideas. Shakespeare's actor at least sympathizes with the downfall of a major culture; Huxley's dancers and blackamoors can only confuse the epical and the tragic with the trite modern tango of the She loves me, she loves me not. Like Eliot in "Sweeney among the Nightingales," Huxley by this amalgam reveals that noble suffering and passion (in the tradition of, say, Agamemnon and Christ) have been eroded, drained of significance, trivialized. Such a fox-trotting monkey-culture shuffles without motive among the ashes and ruins of a once-meaningful civilization. The wretched song is nothing less than a broken farewell to the past.

Petronius, too, is capable of ringing changes upon a conventional scene—the patching-up of a love-quarrel between two jealous homosexual contenders for the favors of the boy Giton. The scene commences, as might be expected, with melodramatic fervor:

With the tears streaming down my face, I begged Eumolpus to make his peace with me too. After all, I reminded him, it was simply not in the power of a lover to master his transports of jealousy. For my part, I solemnly promised neither to say nor do anything in future which could possibly give him offense. Only let him, as a poet, that most humane of all humane vocations, cure himself of his scabrous anger, yes, efface even the scars of it from his mind. "Reflect," I cried, warming to the occasion, "how on the rough barren uplands, the winter snows lie late and long. But where the land, tamed by human love, glisters beneath the plow, the frost falls light and vanishes away in the twinkling of an eye. So too with the anger in our hearts; it strikes deep where the spirit is harsh and gross, but glances lightly away from a civilized mind."[21]

The argument has the clarity of mild sludge: I cannot (nor can anyone) control my jealous rage; I will, however, promise "solemnly" hereafter to control my jealous rage; and you must control your jealous rage. Then follows what we normally designate as the "epic simile," reduced and made Farmer Brown humble. At first glance, the analogy appears lucid enough: snow is like anger; both fall heavily upon barren highlands; yet neither is encountered in cultivated human valleys.

But there are several difficulties with this comparison. First, anger is usually equated with heat, not with cold. Moreover, snow always falls more heavily in the uplands, whether human cultivation exists in the lowlands or not. Further, snow does occasionally fall heavily upon the lowlands. And finally, anger may, but snow does not necessarily, "strike deep" upon the hill country. For a moment, the falling snow, the anger, and the sharp plow all confusedly interfuse, and the elaborate figure trembles and shakes. The speaker is, after all, an emotional fairy, who moves from tears to elaborate discourse in a matter of seconds; he is the would-be orator, "warming to the occasion," as he says, the rhapsodic rhetorician delighting in cliché and debate. Whatever the stimulus, the response is only partially rational and definitely risible.

Most of the passages cited represent complex amalgamations (and parodies) of a host of literary kinds: back-to-nature primitivism, the detective story, the quest romance, the popular song, the melodramatic lover's quarrel, the oratorical disquisition. It should remind us that satire is never so happy as when it is savaging a half-dozen genres. Northrop Frye calls our attention to the fact that the ironic or satiric mode represents "the literature of experience"; this mode is one of the last to fully mature in any civilization. Consequently, it is an extremely self-conscious and aesthetic mode, borrowing from all the past literary kinds, mocking conventions, systems of reasoning, and aesthetic forms themselves.[22] Thereby it becomes a sophisticated, learned, and cultural literary kind. It delights in flights of ratiocination or in soaring aesthetic constructs that somehow come tumbling to the ground. The analyses and pronouncements of the "formal" literary critic and *raisonneur* in *The Pooh Perplex* provide a perfect example: "what, in essence, is the end purpose, the teleology, of poetry or poesis? It is, of course, to take the building blocks of language, combined with the glue or mortar of experience, and to join them in whole meaningful structures which, upon noesis on the part of the trained critic, prove analyzable or decomposable into their constituent elements."[23] This passage is amusing because it jumbles together the vocabulary of Aristotelian philosophy, contractor's cement, and children's glue. The mixture is awful, but it sticks. Mumbled and patched together are the vocabularies of infant and professional. And of course, the trajectory of such a passage's "thought" helplessly progresses from compilation to decomposition.

Upon occasion (though seldom enough, alas) such a reductive and prescriptive philomath will even concede that his "difficult" thoughts and mathematical conceptions travel at a goodly pace—beyond his own ken. Such is the case with the "hypothecator" at one point in Swift's *Tale of a Tub*: "The present Argument is the most abstracted that ever I engaged in, it strains my Faculties to their highest Stretch; and I desire the Reader to attend with utmost Perpensity; For, I now proceed to unravel this knotty Point."[24] What follows is an apogee, a brace of asterisks, a *desunt nonnulla*. But your average philosophaster stumbles along, never once conceding his learned ineptitude.

The satirist most often creates a persona who is frantic with ideas and activity—one who wonderfully dramatizes the Chaucerian concept of "bisinesse," a kind of empty officiousness and hyperefficiency, what Dryden designates as "Pangs without birth, and fruitless Industry." E.M. Forster observes that "obviously a god is hidden in *Tristram Shandy*, his name is Muddle. . . . Muddle is almost incarnate." Delightful and true as this observation is, we must not forget for one moment that muddle bears two faces, the false face of laughable folly, as well as the grim satanic mask of vice. Thus Henry James speaks with awe about an evil power in the universe, what he calls "the *constant* force that makes for muddlement."[25] The satirist dramatizes such a fuddled and bemuddled archetype.

Updating Bacon in her chapter on the "idols of the laboratory," Susanne Langer analyzes the failures of the social sciences through undue emphasis upon mathematizing, physicalizing, methodologizing, objectifying their data. But the greatest sin among the infant sciences remains their susceptibility to jargon—the creating of a "language which is more technical than the ideas it serves to express."[26] Undoubtedly, satirists have known this for centuries and have provided literature with hundreds of pompous buffoons and dangerous lunatics spouting their own particular jargon—divines, physicians, lawyers, scientific projectors.[27] The twentieth century cheerfully adds psychologists, sociologists, economists, Freudians, Marxists, educators, and literary critics to the heap.

Let us examine the simplicity and diversity of a number of such busy voices in the satiric tradition. We will commence with the "fools," and then move on to more complex, even demonic, types. First, let us consider the anonymous naïf in the prologue to *Lazarillo de Tormes*, the first picaresque novel (1554):

I think it fitting that anything so outstanding—perhaps never before heard of nor seen—should come to the attention of many and not be buried in the tomb of oblivion, for it is possible that somebody who reads of it may discover something there to please him, and those who do not make too profound a scrutiny may be entertained.

And concerning this idea, Pliny says that every book, no matter how bad it may be, may contain something of profit. In the first place, all men's tastes are not the same; what one person eats ruins another. And so we see that many things held by some to be of little worth are not so regarded by others. My point is simply that nothing should be lost or ruined; on the contrary, if a thing is not too loathsome, it ought to be imparted to everybody, especially since something fruitful may be got from it, and that without any harm.[28]

This passage accomplishes a full circle of apologetics. The author proposes at once that his work is "outstanding," yet he incessantly thereafter proffers apologiae and the "humility topos" as counterpoint: a "few," and "somebody" (who doesn't scrutinize too carefully), might find it entertaining. People "may" and possibly might find a work pleasing. Thus, such a work cannot "ruin" everyone. Therefore (and here the logic marvelously breaks down), if a work is not too hideous, it should be imposed upon everyone—particularly since it is harmless. The remainder of the prologue is of a piece—absurd, tautological, diligent, and inane. Nothing can halt the incessant stream of broken logic that carries all before it, like a flood. The speaker's is an idiot voice of the apologetic, the aggressive, preface, of a kind that we encounter all too often: solipsism *über alles*, what Keats called the "Wordsworthian sublime."

60 Stratagems

A similar case of incredible exaggeration occurs in the only instance extant of a *cante-fable*. The supposed knight Aucassin, imprisoned by his intransigent father, laments his more-than-divine Nicolette, filling his isolated cell with "wailing" and moan:

> Nicolette, white lily-flow'r,
> Sweetest lady found in bow'r;
> Sweet as grape that brimmeth up
> Sweetness in the spiced cup.
> On a day this chanced to you;
> Out of Limousin there drew
> One, a pilgrim, sore adread,
> Lay in pain upon his bed,
> Tossed, and took with fear his breath,
> Very dolent, near to death.
> Then you entered, pure and white,
> Softly to the sick man's sight,
> Raised the train that swept adown,
> Raised the ermine-bordered gown
> Raised the smock, and bared to him
> Daintily each lovely limb.
> Then a wonderous thing befell,
> Straight he rose up sound and well,
> Left his bed, took cross in hand,
> Sought again his own dear land.
> Lily-flow'r, so white, so sweet,
> Fair the faring of thy feet,
> Fair thy laughter, fair thy speech,
> Fair our playing each with each.
> Sweet thy kisses, soft thy touch,
> All must love thee over much.[29]

As medieval plaint, this passage is utterly astounding. Its matter is pilfered from tales of saints and martyrs, telling of the "miracle cure" of a Christian pilgrim. But the "sickened" pilgrim is healed by exposure to the holy relics, in this case, the female body. Whatever the stretch of imagination, this tale is sacrilegiously outrageous and is somehow to be perceived as Aucassin's "complaint." As the instigator of a new religion, he alone conceives of the virtue of Nicolette as a woman of holy parts. For a moment we are shocked by the blatancy of this sacrilege; but upon second thought concerning such a spoof on the religious cult of women, we are richly rewarded and amused.

To turn from the supposedly sublime to the blatantly ridiculous, here is Mikhail Zoschenko describing the insignificant, the everyday, the inane. His own "voice" mimics this material, and his style becomes casual, childish, trivializing:

Here's an incident that happened in Arzamas. As it now turns out, there's a felt factory there. . . .
Here's what happened in that factory.
During their lunch hour five girls got together and started fooling around and babbling all kinds of stuff and nonsense. Well, naturally—that's the way young girls are. They have just finished working. Now they're having a break. And, of course, they felt like joking a little, laughing, and flirting.
Besides, they are not professors, dried-up pedants, interested only in things like integrals and so on. They are simply the most ordinary kind of girls, from eighteen to twenty years old.
So that their conversation was rather of a frivolous nature than possessing a scientific foundation.
In short, they were discussing the boys they liked and which one of them would like to marry.
There's nothing bad about that. Why not talk about it? The more so that it was their lunch hour. And even more so that it was a splendid spring day. The end of February. The first, so to speak, awakening of nature. Sunshine. Madness in the air. Birds chirp-chirping. You feel light-hearted and joyous.[30]

Such prose reeks of the prosaic, the commonplace, the everyday mundane. There is no truck with intellectual or scientific or highfalutin stuff. There is never a touch of poetry—just plain, down-to-earth chirp-chirping. Such prose almost becomes soporific and idiotized. There are dozens of paragraphs and loads of minor digressions, and the syntax breaks down toward the close into mere sentence fragments. Here is an everyday joe, a writer of the people.

Zoshchenko clearly establishes this ethos, and it permits him to mock almost anyone who is the least bit serious, intellectual, businesslike, or official. He is for pikestaff-clear simplicity and naturalness. And who can dislike nature? Moreover, what Hugh McLean calls Zoshchenko's artistic method—"a combination of irony, ambiguity, and camouflage"—stood him in good stead.[31] He published for some twenty-five years under the Soviet regime before he was "officially" denounced, and even after that, he managed to survive. His doubletalk and mock idiocy prevailed.

Equally successful in finding a unique voice is Ezra Pound's "Portrait d'une femme." Pound had been toying for a number of years with personae, and this quiet, denunciatory voice seems just right for the occasion. The lady, like Victorian London itself, has become a veritable museum of assorted imperial spars, snippets, savings, and wares:

Great minds have sought you—lacking someone else.
You have been second always. Tragical?
No. You preferred it to the usual thing:

> One dull man, dulling and uxorious,
> One average mind—with one thought less, each year.
> Oh, you are patient, I have seen you sit
> Hours, where something might have floated up.[32]

One finds the seeming contradictions of content and style at once striking. In effect, the poem constitutes a scathing denunciation of a woman as tirelessly second-rate; and if anything, it gains in potency exactly because what is close to invective and curse is delivered in restrained and measured tonelessness. That such things could be said, and said with an aloofness that borders upon indifference, is the source of the poem's impact. And it almost gives us a foretaste of the heartless center of twentieth-century thought and approach: cold and calculating "analysis." Yet in the poem, this works for the good, for the central imagery throughout is of a floating and emasculated Sargasso Sea of tidbits and pieces. Therefore the speaker himself is incriminate and, in effect, "belongs." He too is but one further exhausted ware and oddment fished from an emotionless sea; his tired and satiated listlessness is but one further "trophy" awash and paid to her in fee. The poem is powerfully conceived, faultlessly realized. The voice of its satirist/victim is one of its achievements.

One of our finest modern ironists, Henry James, felt powerfully that he lived in a decadent, materialistic era. "The condition of [the English upper class]," he once affirmed, "seems to me to be in many ways very much the same rotten and *collapsible* one as that of the French aristocracy before the revolution—minus cleverness and conversation; or perhaps it's more like the heavy, congested and depraved Roman world upon which the barbarians came down." James felt this particularly acutely about the weekend at the country house: "The gilded bondage of the country house becomes onerous as one grows older, and then the waste of time in vain sitting and strolling about is a gruesome thought in the face of what one still wants to do with one's remnant of existence."[33] What, then, are we to make of James's specifically country-house novel, *The Sacred Fount?* Critics are not certain. Yet in this novel, Newmarch definitely is just such a country house. Vapid partyings, strollings, and smokings and the shadow of random liaisons and covert, polite fornications compose the totality of bland and banal aristocratic English life. But the sights are perceived through the eyes of an intellectual idealist, a narrator whose feverish, plodding, near-hallucinatory quest for secret "enchantments" and magical "systems" of fairy-tale bewitchments allows us to see through the glass of Newmarch's triflings, but darkly. His fantastic imaginings and almost Herculean ratiocinations becloud the scene of the country house, casting upon it the glitter of the Arabian Nights somehow interfused with the deadly tractates of Kant or Leibnitz. James's "torch of consciousness" enlightens (and indeed enflames) everything but the truth: the Newmarch of modern barbarians and their way of life are gratuitously mechanical, maudlin, and mindless; and such a culture is deadly, unconscious, and effete.

The narrator met Gilbert Long at the outset of the long weekend, and the narrator's intuited sense that Long has vastly improved in his intellect and acuity launches the spinning of an enormous cobweb of a system to explain Long's newfound sensitivity by attributing it to a fresh liaison. Moreover, the narrator comes to believe that Long is conscious of this new power; for the narrator, in fact, all events vibrate with monumental significance. Thus, on many occasions, he interprets the meaning of a look, of a receding back as someone leaves a room, and even of the "fixed expressiveness" of someone he cannot see.

We long to actually hear the conversation of this supposedly rejuvenated guest, although we only encounter people through the cerebral fog of the narrator's analyses, perceptions, and hypothecations. At last, however, more than midway through the novel, we are given a summary of the presumably astute after-dinner discourse between the narrator and Long. We have been waiting for it, with baited breath and exacerbated anticipation.

I fear I can do little justice to the pleasant suppressed tumult of impression and reflection that, on my part, our ten minutes together produced. The elements that mingled in it scarce admit of discrimination. It was still more than previously a deep sense of being justified. My interlocutor was for those ten minutes immeasurably superior—superior, I mean, to himself—and he couldn't possibly have become so save through the relation I had so patiently tracked. He faced me there with another light than his own, spoke with another sound, thought with another ease and understood with another ear. I should put it that what came up between us was the mere things of the occasion, were it not for the fine point to which, in my view, the things of the occasion had been brought. While our eyes, at all events, on either side, met serenely, and our talk, dealing with the idea, dealing with the extraordinary special charm, of the social day now deepening to its end, touched our companions successively, touched the manner in which this one and that had happened to be predominantly a part of that charm; while such were our immediate conditions I wondered of course if he had not, just as consciously and essentially as I, quite another business in mind. It was not indeed that our allusion to the other business would not have been wholly undiscoverable by a third person.

So far as it took place it was of a "subtlety," as we used to say at Newmarch, in relation to which the common register of that pressure would have been, I fear, too old-fashioned a barometer.[34]

64 Stratagems

Here we have all the placid, egocentric, self-serving complaisance that we have come to expect from such a speaker. But what is amusingly anticlimactic is the topic of their conversation. They had been speaking, as usual, about the day's "special" social charm. They had been speaking about each person present at Newmarch. They had been engaging, in short, in one further bout of idle chatter, vulgar and violent gossip, and boastful self-congratulation. Moreover, their minds race so furiously ahead with tattle and guesswork that they frankly do not listen to one another.

James manages to suggest in this tortuous novel with its insidious prose that the "sacred founts" of classical mythology are dry, that the days of magic and excitement have grown dark, and that the march of the barbarians has indeed come again. The final irony is that this narrator quests for a subtlety and a significance in civilized life that are no longer anywhere to be found; at the last, he himself has been drained of inspiration—at an empty fount. In romantic terms, James's narrator, then, is an artist, without the beautiful. Thus, he is no meaningful artist at all. Despite his intense self-reflections, he lacks awareness and consciousness. The audience is expected to perceive many facets of what the narrator cannot.

In that sense, like all art, satiric art intends to broaden self-awareness. T.R. Edwards proposes that "though satirists understandably claim that they mean to reform the world by exposing its confessed vices, it seems more realistic to consider their art as descriptive drama, expressing the *inner* counter-workings of benevolence and malice, hope and despair, through which ethical self-consciousness defines itself."[35] The satirist's creation of a host of languages and voices serves precisely to sharpen our awareness of logical, ethical, and aesthetic questions themselves.

We cannot do better than by concluding with a modern master of a whirligig of conflicting voices, Vladimir Nabokov. In his character of Humbert Humbert, Nabokov presents us with a virtual ferris wheel and Tilt-a-Whirl of conflicting attitudes and misguided schizophrenic selves. For at one time or another (and often simultaneously), Humbert portrays for us dozens of specific selves: the intellectual, the European of a genteel tradition, the artiste, the sensitive lover, the visionary, the confessor, the psychopath, and the vulgarian. Nabokov's handsome ability to capture such a string of creatures and to allow us to perceive the myriad changes this character effects on language and style surely ought to impress us.

Somewhere beyond Bill's shack an afterwork radio had begun singing of folly and fate, and there she was with her ruined looks and her adult, rope-veined narrow hands and her gooseflesh white arms, and her shallow ears, and her unkempt armpits, there she was (my Lolita!), hopelessly worn at seventeen, with that baby, dreaming already in her of becoming a big shot and retiring around 2020 A.D.—and I looked and looked at her, and knew as clearly as I know I am to die, that I loved her more than anything I had ever seen or imagined on earth, or hoped for anywhere else. She was only the faint violet whiff and dead leaf echo of the nymphet I had rolled myself upon with such cries in the past; an echo on the brink of a russet ravine, with a far wood under a white sky, and brown leaves choking the brook, and one last cricket in the crisp weeds . . . but thank God it was not that echo alone that I worshiped. What I used to pamper among the tangled vines of my heart, *mon grand péché radieux*, had dwindled to its essence: sterile and selfish vice, all *that* I canceled and cursed. You may jeer at me, and threaten to clear the court, but until I am gagged and half-throttled, I will shout my poor truth. I insist the world know how much I loved my Lolita, this Lolita, pale and polluted, and big with another's child, but still gray-eyed, still sooty-lashed, still auburn and almond, still Carmencita, still mine; *Changeons de vie, ma Carmen, alons vivre quelque part où nous ne serons jamais séparés*; Ohio? The wilds of Massachusetts? No matter, even if those eyes of hers would fade to myopic fish, and her nipples swell and crack, and her lovely young velvety delicate delta be tainted and torn—even then I would go mad with tenderness at the mere sight of your dear wan face, at the mere sound of your raucous young voice, my Lolita.[36]

First, we must juggle our way among three time periods while reading this passage. The present-day "now" occurs in prison. The manuscript tells of Humbert's rediscovery of Lolita in 1952, three years after he had lost her, this *rencontre* in the drab Eastern town of Coalmont. And there is the nontime of an eternal Lolita—the realm of the perennial nymphet—that is an unrecapturable past. Humbert has engaged in this elusive quest virtually all his life. We are jiggled and bumped in and out of these time spans, often with sudden hops and boggles.

Far more important are the mixed voices of Humbert the lover. First they exhibit a flickering tone of distaste for the banal reality of Coalmont and the "afterwork radio"; then, the repulsive "reality" of the pregnant Lolita, now age seventeen, with a flying detour to A.D. 2020. Then suddenly dawns the epiphany: he loved her. With this the voice launches into an echo of a standard romantic froth of the past, the alliteration of the "russet ravine," the imagery of the "far wood" and the last solitary cricket. Humbert comes to an abrupt halt; for he did not cherish merely the euphoric dream. No, with an allusion to Verlaine's verse (and the man's love for Rimbaud), Humbert now perceives that he actually rejected selfishness and vice, which he "cancels," as if they never existed. Then he bows rhetorically to a hypothetical hearing: the court can mock him, gag him, even "half-throttle" him (here the "half" is a considerable mathematical sacrifice); still he will "shout" of his love. Then he returns suddenly to the ugly present and the "polluted" Lolita. Then he is off, off again on allusive flight, reciting lines from Prosper Mérimée's *Carmen*. As suddenly, he makes another devious but comical turn into an alley of concrete possibility: Where can they flee to? Ohio? A portion of Massachusetts? But the Humbertian mind rushes onward: "No matter." Now we encounter the towering tragic language of a Shakespeare: even should she be rent and deracinated (and he is particularly sensitive to the corruption of her vital sexual parts), Humbert confesses, he would "go mad with tenderness" at the sight of her rather course face and the sound of her ugly voice.

With furious pyrotechnics, then, in a brief space we have been catapulted across oceans of thoughts, whimsies, romantic backwashes, and literary references and allusions; and we have been especially aflow in a tide of climaxes and reversals, tossed upon waves of rhetoric. And all this display merely lets Humbert assure his audience that he finally realizes that he truly loves Lolita and would "go mad with tenderness" even at the sight of her decaying carcass. Can we believe in this tender loving care? Had not Humbert come to Coalmont with his "chum," expressly bent upon murder, mayhem, and revenge? Has he not taken a dozen detours, rushing off in his vocabularies and dictions in seven or eight directions together? Rather, has he not in fact, by throwing on so many coats of language, ultimately laid himself bare? For Humbert is revealed at the end to be an "unaccommodated man," "a poor, bare, forked animal." He is, but he is no better than he should be. "The best-laid schemes o' mice an' men gang aft a-gley." But they are most often neither the best plans, nor laid by the best of men. Satire like this, with a virtuoso display of language and style, carries us far along to the higher reaches of art.

6

Gaming with the Plot

Clearly, the satirist is eager and willing to tamper with, loosen, and even overturn the fundamental conventions and foundation-stones of fiction-making. He will snicker at or debase the hero, mock or taunt the author, and parody or pillage language and style. He naturally, therefore, also plays with traditional plots. In his hands, narratives all too frequently turn into games. Now, as Geoffrey Hartman has observed, there is an "almost universal . . . acceptance of the element of playfulness in art."[1] Our awareness of such "playfulness" and "gaming" has particularly deepened and matured since the appearance of Johan Huizinga's influential *Homo Ludens* in 1938, and, subsequently, numerous studies have explored gamesmanship in life and in art.[2] I am particularly interested in calling attention to the increasing utilization, throughout the present century, of gaming as a central theme, metaphor, and preoccupation in modern literature, and especially in identifying some of the causes of this heightened usage.

In writing about Ring Lardner's successful portrayal of the gaming American—in baseball, in boxing, at the card table, etc.—Virginia Woolf in 1925 commented, "It is no coincidence that the best of Mr. Lardner's stories are about games, for one may guess that Mr. Lardner's interest in games has solved one of the most difficult problems of the American writer; it has given him a clue, a centre, a meeting place for the divers activities of people whom a vast continent isolates, whom no tradition controls. Games give him what society gives his English brother."[3] I would go even further than Woolf and suggest that games lend poignancy to much in almost every nationality in the twentieth century, since artists in most nations have sensed a break with almost all in the past that we term literary tradition. Literature in our period has responded to this isolation, this breakdown in coherence, by cultivating themes of exhaustion, decadence, and ennui, and particularly by parodying past traditions—by generally playing games.

To borrow a tetrahedronic manipulation from Northrop Frye, primitive literature was generally perceived as being cosmic, magical, and religious; Renaissance literature was understood to be cultural and especially expressive of national destiny; and nineteenth-century literature was comprehended as performing public service while also providing "entertainment" and comic relief. To complete this narrowing of context, the twentieth century has slowly been reduced to comprehending its literary art as pretense, as pose and posturing, as melodramatic excess, as nearly demonic lunacy and nonsense.[4]

To the twentieth century mind, the torch of the Enlightenment has gone out; the utopian dreams of the nineteenth century have turned "sour," yielding a fetor.[5] Darwinian "natural selection" appears to be nature's jesting evolutionary game of randomness; Freudian psychology exposes the incessantly overflowing stream of consciousness in a fundamentally irrational psyche; and the indeterminacy, relativity, and quantum mechanics of modern physics suggest to modern authors an end to normative conceptions of space, time, and progressive linear narrative.[6] Game analysis and probability theory literally spill over from mathematics into art. For many critics, the so-called inventive zest and creative thrust of the early "modernist" artists—Proust, Mann, Eliot, Pound, Joyce, Picasso, Stravinsky—appears to have petered out.

Equally important, the fin de siècle mentality, as we enter the modern period, deals a death-blow to historical eras and chronological traditions in art. For the first time, mass communications, rapid transit, historical rigor, and archaeological vigor lay bare and render uniformly accessible hundreds of techniques, styles, and conventions from the past. The many "phases" of Picasso's artistry and the innumerable personae of Pound's poetry demonstrate the advent in our art of this universal traditionalism. Discussing painting, J.P. Hodin indicates that "Modern Art is cognition, the findings of which . . . are organized into a new visual order. Linking up with a tradition of its own choice, of universal significance and without limitations in time and thus breaking with the chronological tradition generally acknowledged in art history, it strives for a synthesis of the work of the individual artist."[7]

Harold Rosenberg designates this twentieth-century development as "the famous 'modern break with tradition' ":

Under the slogan, FOR A NEW ART, FOR A NEW REALITY, the most ancient superstitions have been exhumed, the most primitive rites re-enacted: the rummage for generative forces has set African demonmasks in the temple of the Muses and introduced the fables of Zen and Hasidism into the dialogue of philosophy. Through such dislocations of time and geography the first truly universal tradition has come to light, with world history as its past and requiring a world stage on which to flourish.[8]

This total awareness of all times, all styles, and all places in our century is rather grandly portrayed by the metadimensional intelligence and world view of Kurt Vonnegut, Jr.'s Tralfamadoreans.

Yet this "universalizing" of tradition has been by no means purely advantageous, for the embracing of all traditions renders us rootless and relativistic, with no distinct or coherent traditions whatsoever. Blending ourselves into all of the past gives us no distinctive perception—or understanding—of that past.

The barriers of the past have been pushed back as never before; our knowledge of the history of man and the universe has been enlarged on a scale and to a degree not dreamed of by previous generations. At the same time, the sense of identity and continuity with the past, whether our own or history's, has gradually and steadily declined. Previous generations *knew* much less about the past than we do, but perhaps *felt* a much greater sense of identity and continuity with it because of the fixity, stability, and relative permanence of their social structure.[9]

The uneasy sense of dislocation—infused with heady creativity—has been present and predominant throughout the twentieth century. One need merely recall the far-fetched mockeries of modernism inherent in Alfred Jarry's Ubu plays and philosophy of pataphysics, in dada, in surrealism, in the Beat movement, in the black humor novelists, and in the theater of the absurd to perceive a perverse and spoofing continuity in modern art's anxious laughter at itself. And such self-criticism is clearly in evidence when we consider this century's enormous predilection for and addiction to parody.[10]

It is true, of course, that playfulness and self-mockery are hardly new in literature. The Aristophanic agons are in some sense children's debates; Chaucer and Shakespeare are, upon occasion, masters of scrim, self-parody, and nonsense. From one perspective, as Ian Watt has reminded us, the early novel could be comprehended as a kind of civic and gamesome "trial," with the amassing of evidence, the presentation of testimony and exhibits, and the concern for verdicts looming large.[11] But the fact remains that what in the literatures of the past served as one of many possibilities has for the twentieth century become an overarching attachment and preoccupation. We are, as a result, increasingly beset by playfulness and nonsense games and by an expanding concern for far-fetched fantasy.[12] One need merely think of

70 Stratagems

the recent devotion to antistories, the increasing prankishness of self-consciousness among authors, and the growing tendency for writers to engage in what one critic terms "literary disruptions" of narratives.[13]

Furthermore, a growing number of fiction titles suggestively reveals this childish-seeming, rollicking, and sportive tendency: *In the Labyrinth* (*Dans le labyrinthe*, Robbe-Grillet, 1959); *Labyrinths* (Borges, 1964); "The Lottery" (Jackson, 1948); *The Collector* (Fowles, 1963); *The Glass Bead Game* (*Das Glasperlenspiel*, Hesse, 1943); *The End of the Game and Other Stories* (Cortazar, 1967); *Endgame* (*Fin de partie*, Beckett, 1957); *War Games* (James Park Sloan, 1971); *War Games* (Wright Morris, 1951); *King, Queen, Knave* (Nabokov, 1928); *Winner Take Nothing* (Hemingway, 1933); *Cards of Identity* (Nigel Dennis, 1955); *Criers and Kibitzers, Kibitzers and Criers* (Elkin, 1965); *The Universal Baseball Association, Inc., J. Henry Waugh, Prop.* (Coover, 1968); *End Zone* (Don DeLillo, 1972); *Cosmicomics* (Calvino, 1965); *Lost in the Funhouse* (Barth, 1968); *Cat and Mouse* (Grass, 1961); *Slapstick* (Vonnegut, 1976); *The Sandbox* (Albee, 1959); *Hopscotch* (Cortazar, 1963); *Catcher in the Rye* (Salinger, 1951); *The Ginger Man* (Donleavy, 1958); *Snow White* (Barthelme, 1967); *Wonderland* (Joyce Carol Oates, 1971); *Say Cheese!* (Aksyonov, 1989); *An Ice Cream War* (William Boyd, 1982); *The Chronicles of Doodah* (George Lee Walker, 1985).

Probably the best means for assessing this sporting and prankish trend is to observe more carefully a number of novels whose entire world view is ultimately gamesome. I have deliberately avoided the more renowned and conventional works, and I particularly have sought to draw my examples from the broad range of the whole century.

The nameless narrator in Henry James's too-often scanted novel *The Sacred Fount* (1901) spends a long and busy weekend at a country house party. He commences to evolve a "hypothesis" about a select number of the guests: an aging wife appears to have been "rejuvenated" by her marriage; she looks vastly younger, whereas her new, youthful husband has unaccountably aged. The narrator conjectures that a magical umbilical cord connects the two, an enchanted reverse-transfusion mechanism that fulfills the one while draining the other. Similarly, two presumed lovers appear to the narrator to be equally affected: the male becomes ebullient, articulate, and intelligent, while the female declines into silence and a mumpish stupidity.

Patiently the narrator assembles the particles of his evidence piece by piece to substantiate the miraculous alterations. At the close, in a confrontation with the rejuvenated wife, he is totally defeated and routed in argument: it is as if her "system" or "hypothesis" prevails over his own. Or is she merely fighting for her new life, laying down smoke screens, and attempting to conceal the wonderful transformations and metamorphoses from the prying outsider? More profoundly, might the narrator himself have fallen prey to the mystical transformations, himself being drained of energy as his artistic hypothesis flourishes and expands into life? James never provides an answer, but he tantalizingly suggests that the entire novel's world is somehow mysteriously alive with the consecrated (and even lunatic) logic of permutation, an overflowing of sacral supply and demand.[14]

A Scotland Yard man infiltrates an anarchist cell and indeed manages to become one of the seven great leaders (each named after a day of the week) of G.K. Chesterton's sweeping European conspiracy, *The Man Who Was Thursday* (1908). Slowly it is revealed that every single one of the criminal leaders is in fact a "plant," another disguised policeman. Like God, Scotland Yard represents the whole of creation, both law and order as well as its opposite—revolt, chaos, and scam. But then the first police agent awakens as from sleep and a dream, yet he is a new and more confident man after his imagined adventure. Are the police, we ask, but another version of criminality (or vice versa)? Does organized crime truly represent the civic order it supposedly seeks to overwhelm? Every man, in such a detective drama, is the absurdist player of innumerable roles, and the answer to the play of the roles, as in religion, is a mystery.

In Robert M. Coates's Work *The Eater of Darkness* (1926), Charles Dograr, newly arrived in New York from Paris, is plunged into a terrific murder story, made an accomplice to a malevolent fiend, sought and chased by all of New York's police, and trapped in a tower. All of this breakneck tale is recounted with the combined strategies of Dickens, melodrama, humdrum detective story, silent cinema, and surrealism. Then Dograr is finally whisked out of his nightmarish entrapment and set, smoking a cigar, walking down Fifth Avenue. An old beloved of his in Paris, also a storyteller, had been daydreaming about him: Had she written his misadventure? Was it a novel she had been reading? Had she "wished" him in and out of danger? All the stops are out, and there is no satisfactory solution. But Charles is safe and sound, returning to his beloved in old Paree. Who told the tale, and what, exactly, happened? No one quite can tell; suffice it to say that it is a tumbling, raucous, cliché-ridden story, stuffed with detours, false starts, footnotes, vignettes, and extras. Ultimately, all the fictional games are played for the reader's benefit—yet also at the reader's expense. The novel is a hilariously misconstructed hurricane of happenstance, adventure, and parody.

72 Stratagems

In a trifling contest, the narrator of Harry Mathews's novel *The Conversions* (1962) wins a golden adz from Mr. Wayl, the millionaire, and thereafter attempts to explain the mysterious carvings on its handle. Indeed, the millionaire's will promises to bequeath all his wealth to the one who can answer three mysterious questions about the adz. Tempted by this enormous prize, the narrator travels all over the world, collecting evidence about a secret society of gypsies, yet he increasingly comes to see that great quantities of this evidence have been fabricated by the millionaire himself. His seeming benefactor has devised a vast conspiracy merely to frustrate a would-be heir and drive him into considerable debt. Mathews's entire quirky, fictional world is doubly fictitious, since the dead millionaire is another creator. Appendixes expand the fiction by giving additional scholarly "data" concerning bogus documents.

In Thomas Pynchon's tale *The Crying of Lot 49* (1966), clue by clue, Oedipa Maas discovers a comprehensive sixteenth-century mail conspiracy that still persists and even thrives in California—and possibly throughout the United States. How could such a massive underground postal service exist out of sight? Is it a sign of America's decay, the promise of the rise of a rival, life-giving system, the demonic invention of the dead businessman Inverarity, or a huge paranoid conception proliferating within Oedipa Maas's own brain?[15] Once again, a metaphysical detective is set to work, uncovering a "plot" that may or may not be real, one that is sinister and ambiguous, involving the novel's entire fictive world.

Martin Amis's story "Insight at Flame Lake," in *Einstein's Monsters* (1987) describes our present-day world: the proliferation of media communications, the acceleration of horrible news and its torments: "This morning at breakfast I was fanning myself and scratching my hair over some new baby-battering atrocity in the newspaper and I said—Is it just me, or the media, or is there a boom in child abuse? And Dan said, 'It's exponential, like everything else these days.' Himself a hostage to heredity, Dan naturally, argued that if you abuse your children, well, then they will abuse theirs. It adds up. In fact it multiplies."[16] Dan's response seems cool, scientific, learned. But his commentary is anything but consoling: we live in an era of child abuse, and therefore each generation will experience a multiplication of instances. Disconcerted, we reflect that such mathematical, incremental growth can only lead to infinity.

Dan himself, we learn, is a mere thirteen year old, but a fully developed schizophrenic, a madman on a summer vacation that ends

Gaming with the Plot 73

with his total breakdown and demise. More disconcerting still is the suggestion that all the generations since 1945, the happy birthday of the atomic bomb, have been increasingly infected by fear, frustration, and mania about destruction. Both bombs and offspring are equally "Einstein's children" in Amis's five short stories. Like a self-fulfilling prophecy, madness, violence, and destruction are calmly, steadily, statistically, mechanically, on the upswing. In these tales, the sphere of inclusiveness placidly broadens, and there is no escape.

All the works that I have singled out for review overtly detail the superimposing of an external "plot" or framing device that controls, alters, and manipulates the fictional world and entraps the central characters in its toils. Plot—the traditional construct by which an author shapes fiction—becomes synonymous with some sort of conspiracy within the novel, an arranging of affairs that the characters attempt to discover and from which they attempt to escape. The characters, in short, seek to avoid and to transcend the confines of fiction. And the author himself is sympathetic. From the point of view of nineteenth-century determinism, plot and author alike are equivalent to the rigorous "plan" and the person of a monstrous manipulator of events, a kind of "President of the Immortals," whom we encounter in Hardy's *Tess of the d'Urbervilles*. From the point of view of twentieth-century ideals of randomness and experimentation, authors and characters alike may be seen as fascinated by entrapment and yet desirous of evasion and liberation. They seek to elude incarceration in chronology or in the narrow bounds of the recent European novelistic tradition.

Fantasy provides one means of escape into a worldwide and civilization-long perspective. For fantasy and myth can leave behind the conventions of rationalism, realism, fiction as distinct from history, and specific spatial and temporal order and constraints. Science fiction has permitted just such freedom and flight, and it is no accident that this genre has proved so popular and abundant in our century. A good example of such a flight can be observed in a novel by Stanislaw Lem, a recent master of science fiction.

The Cyberiad (1967) catapults the reader completely into a universe of robotics; human beings are absent altogether or so scarce (and weak and slippery and scummy) as not to be believed in. Trurl and Klapaucius are ingenious inventor-robots, "constructionists," along the lines of Abbott and Costello. Trurl is the true near-hero of these pieces, and he is a genuine mixture of Daedalus, Panurge, and Woody Allen. Some of his inventions are perfections; some are perfect disasters. As if we were in the realm of medieval robot-romances, the separate and disjunct tales tell of individuals' sallies from an automated round table out into the universe of galactic oceanic voyages to do battle with dragons, pirates, evil kings, scamps, and fools. Increasingly, as if literary time were moving backward, we find ourselves in a world of a thousand and one Pyrite Hoplites, with overtones of allegory, exemplum, parable, and Aesopic fable becoming more and more prominent. Increasingly, too, there are tales within tales, like nests of boxes, until it is suggested that perhaps Trurl himself is but another creature captive in another frame of stories.

The finale abandons Trurl altogether, and we commence a Cyphroeroticon, a kind of space operatic *Decameron*, that is incredibly truncated, consisting of but a single tale. Indeed, the reader is caught in some in-between species of time, encountering tales from the far-distant future that are nonetheless so fragmented and disorderly that they seem to be epical, ancient futurist documents that have come down to us in mythic, vaticinating, and incomplete form. Past, present, and future are thereby handsomely juxtaposed and intertwined, and the reader is left suffering from a kind of multipressured time warp and culture shock.

Like Lem, Italo Calvino ranges, in his brief cluster of tales (*Cosmicomics*, 1965), across the history of the universe. His nonhuman characters (formulae, light, cells, dinosaurs) swirl along through the creation's seemingly endless displays of élan vital, motion, generation, and evolution. Similar voyages outside the bounds of the novel, outside the borders of particularized time and space, can be observed in John Barth's retelling of myths in *Giles Goat-Boy* (1966) and *Chimera* (1972). Barth's well-known ambivalence leads him to rob such plots of conventional and forthright conclusions and of certainty and definite signification. His characters and the tacit or implied meanings of his tales directly oppose clarity and certitude. Other fictions, like those of Borges, break down distinctions between story and essay, metaphor and fact, while authors like Robbe-Grillet (consult *Le Voyeur*, 1955, and his screenplay of "Last Year at Marienbad"), Robert Coover (*Pricksongs and Descants*, 1969), and Jonathan Baumbach (*Babble*, 1976) eliminate the linear story and, fusing event, libidinal imaginings, and probability, tell stories with multiple sequences and alternate finales.

Perhaps most noteworthy has been the tendency of a growing number of writers to dissolve the barrier betwixt authors and their creations, allowing authors to break into their own fictions and characters to break out. Such a practice is by no means altogether new, but it has been a practice alien to the bourgeois tradition developing since Defoe. Becoming the darling of the middle class, this mode called for aloofness of presentation and extreme verisimilitude; the result of such ideals slowly drove authors out of their fictions, while their stories increasingly reveled in "realism." In modern fiction, the sanctity of such verism is called into question or openly taunted.

In our own century, Pirandello's story "The Tragedy of a Character" (1911), subsequently transformed into his major drama *Six Characters in Search of an Author* (1921), most memorably reverts to authorial intrusiveness. The author-narrator complains of characters who "break into" his fiction and move about at will, beyond the control of the "author." One such character in his tale clamors to get "in." André Gide, in *Les Faux-Monnayeurs* (1925), enriched this experimental procedure by having himself and his character Edouard simultaneously at work upon a novel called *The Counterfeiters*. Bits of "journal" for the novel naturally turn up in the novel itself, and Gide includes, in an appendix, his own "journal" for the novel.[17] In this novel Gide frequently becomes an intrusive commentator, offering assessments, evaluations, asides. Technically, this work has been considered an innovative landmark, and it has influenced subsequent fictions in this country.

Other authors, like Ronald Sukenick in *Up* (1968) and Steve Katz in *The Exagggerations of Peter Prince* (1968), have regularly and obtrusively introduced themselves into their fictions—and have even introduced one another into them. But characters are also interested in getting out of their own constrictive tales, and one might recall in this respect Kurt Vonnegut, Jr.'s *Breakfast of Champions* (1973). There, the author enters the novel and visits the scene, only to be fearfully frightened by Kazak, one of his own maniacal creations. Nevertheless, in a more generous mood, the author magnanimously promises "freedom" to characters like Kilgore Trout, because they have rendered him years of faithful fictional service. Pathetically, the aging Trout can only think to cry out for a single benefaction: "Make me young, make me young, make me young!" With that, the novel comes to a close. It is a paradoxical and tense moment when a character meets his maker. For one thing, Vonnegut hears something of his own father's voice from the past in that beleaguered cry. And aside from all the wizardry that this authorial deity might be able to supply, nothing can prevent Kurt Vonnegut, Jr. (and his father of long ago) from implacably growing old, old, old themselves. For a moment, then, author and character are akin, identical in their helplessness inside somebody else's creation. And the shock of their confrontation and even assimilation of identities is, of course, managed by art.

All the fictions that I have described may be zany, ambivalent, and incredibly experimental in their explorations of fantastic content and form, but they are nonetheless amazingly aesthetic receptacles, assimilating echoes from dozens of popular cultural forms and literary traditions. Such works help to facilitate the breakdown of normative spatial, temporal, and linear narrative conventions. Instead, in an atmosphere in which recent trends and movements in art have been replaced by a kind of achronological universal traditionalism, as J.P. Hodin and Harold Rosenberg have suggested, these literary works mix together elements from fable, quest romance, dream sequence, expository writing, detective story, spy thriller, "tales of ratiocination" (Poe's phrase), science fiction, surrealism, melodrama, cinematography, and cartoon. Such fictions accordingly are gamesome and gamey indeed—open-ended and growing by an aggressive osmosis and fusion. As literary creations, they are far from being "exhausted" or benighted; rather, they are distinctly sportive, fertile, healthy, and irrecusable. For the once-narrow "fragments" of past civilizations that Eliot "shored against [his] ruins" have in more recent fictions recombined, mushroomed, become large and substantial—until they compose the whole shebang.

7

Further Intrusion and Obstruction

We have been reviewing the ways authors disturb normative literary conventions and, as a result, shake, riddle, and roil readers out of their ordinary expectations and ho-hum responses. We have considered how the conventional hero is downgraded and debased, how even authors are implicated or impugned, how language is manipulated to imitate or expose sentimentality, sanctimony, chicanery, and cant, and how games and ploys are utilized to tarnish, subvert, and displace traditional "realistic" plots. Continuing in the same vein, this chapter considers further strategies authors deploy to break down traditional fictions and to sully or destroy the reader's "willing suspension of disbelief." As a matter of fact, the incidence of intrusions and obstructions is, in twentieth-century literature, steadily on the increase—but these traditions have been accessible for centuries.

Yet so frequently has recent literary work been associated with experimentation and novelty that it has been given a niche of its own and designated rather grandly as "postmodern fiction."[1] Jerome Klinkowitz perceives a whole new world of literary forms being created since the late 1960s that is unique, especially in its uses of what he terms "literary disruption."[2] And it is quite true that recent writers do strive to be disruptive in their fictions.

Numbers of authors of late have flagrantly "jostled" or "toyed" with their own fictions, quite often disrupting the fictional narrative with a variety of inept scene changes, with abrupt alterations of mood, tone, or theme; often mocking the fictionality of the fiction by permitting it to be invaded by elements of news, autobiography, anachronism, hearsay, history, divagation, parody, and just plain detour that debunks the sacrosanct "forms" of literature—or even by creating a fiction that is blatantly absurd, far-fetched, peculiarly naive and jejune, and awkward. A second species of disruption, achieved by the author's breaking somehow into the fiction *in propria persona*, intruding other "voices" and particularly some species of the author's own distinctly nonfictional voice into the story's framework, also shatters staid conventions and dislocates normative expectations.[3]

The former kind of disruption, wherein fact is confounded with fiction and the narrative surface is flurried by deliberate ineptitudes and dislocations, can be clearly observed in the fictions of William Burroughs, in Alain Robbe-Grillet's novels and screen plays, in Robert Coover's *Pricksongs and Descants* (1969), in Italo Calvino's *Cosmicomics* (1965), and in the tales of Richard Brautigan, Thomas Pynchon, and John Barth. Jorge Luis Borges frequently confounds fact and fiction in his short stories, as in "Tlon, Uqbar, Orbis Tertius," in which an actual encyclopedia is puffed with fictional pages. In "Three Versions of Judas," scholarly footnotes, precise biblical citations, and respectable theologians are interlarded with fictional names, blasphemy, and fanciful debates. In "Pierre Menard, Author of Don Quixote," Borges ponders the statistical probability of a second author's identifying totally with Cervantes and recomposing *Don Quixote*. What Borges does best is to catapult the world of meditation, of ratiocination, of fact and data—the proper domain of the essay, the treatise, and the report—out of its context, implying that reasoning and data are themselves wildly fictitious. Occasionally, too, Borges creates the persona of a critic who himself writes defective meditations and askew critical essays.[4]

Vladimir Nabokov also is a master of mixing scholarship with fiction. His novel *Pale Fire* (1962) interfuses a poem, a scholarly annotated edition of that poem, and the wildest vagaries, imaginings, and meanderings of a demented annotator all in a single creation. But such disruption need not merely consist of the intermingling of the fictional and the discursive. Gabriel García Márquez, in *One Hundred Years of Solitude* (1967), frequently obtains powerful effects simply by injecting a sudden overdose of imagery into the narrative mode, so that the excess will reduce the whole to the incredible, the fantastic, the absurd. This is done, for example, in the narrative of the secret liaison and love affair between Meme Buendía and the apprentice mechanic Mauricio Babilonia. Improbably, their regular trysting place is the family's bathhouse, and the mechanic-lover is everywhere accompanied, we are informed, by an enormous horde of yellow butterflies.[5] That is doubtless the greatest calling card invented since the cow bell.

Kurt Vonnegut, Jr.'s *Slaughter-House Five* (1969) carries such narrative disjunction to an extreme. His tale of everyday humdrum Americans on earth is regularly interrupted by a gigantic leap in space-time to other scenes upon the distant planet Tralfamadore. Indeed, such disruption might even include the intrusion into fiction of the "paperchase" world of bureaucracy and tabulation. Donald Barthelme suddenly halts his distorted retelling of *Snow White* (1967) to interject a reader questionnaire, that contains such queries as

    1. Do you like the story so far? Yes ( ) No ( )
. . . .
    5. In the further development of the story, would you like more emotion ( ) or less emotion ( )?
. . . .
    8. Would you like a war? Yes ( ) No ( )
    9. Has the work, for you, a metaphysical dimension? Yes ( ) No ( )
. . . .
    14. Do you stand up when you read? ( ) Lie down? ( ) Sit? ( )[6]

Since our dry quotidian world is already vastly cluttered with letters to the editor, with revenue reports, with public opinion surveys, why shouldn't these materials invade our periods of relaxation, our worlds of fiction? In any event, almost all the stories selected by Jerome Klinkowitz and John Somer in the collection *Innovative Fiction* (Dell, 1972) contain some sort of far-fetched use of imagination (causing a reductio ad absurdum) or a tampering with the boundaries between nonfiction and fiction. These disruptions are similarly self-evident in the anthology edited by Philip Stevick, pointedly entitled *Anti-Story* (Free Press, 1971).

The latter kind of disruption, in which the author in some manner breaks into his fiction in his own person, can be found in John Barth's *Chimera* (1972), in Kurt Vonnegut, Jr.'s *Breakfast of Champions* (1973), and in the esoteric fictions of such writers as Ronald Sukenick, Raymond Federman, and Jonathan Baumbach.[7]

In Barth's tale, Bellerophon in ancient mythic Greece recovers a manuscript in a bottle that refers to Napoleon, to Maryland, to very modern notes for a revolutionary novel concerned with a character Bray (to be met in Barth's novel *Giles Goat-Boy* [1966]), and to a series of novels that are in fact fictional continuations of books earlier written by Barth himself. In Vonnegut's novel, the fictional character Kilgore Trout at the close has a pathetic encounter with Vonnegut himself. And in Ronald's Sukenick's *Up* (1968), Sukenick himself is a character in his own novel, but he also arranges for the appearance of novelists and friends. We encounter (on a scrap of paper) a dedication "To Steve Katz here briefly on a special guest appearance from his own novel."[8]

Even more strikingly, seven-eighths of the way through William H. Gass's supposed novel, *Willie Masters' Lonesome Wife* (1968), the reader is jogged awake from what he had taken to be a flurry of prostitute's monologues, fornications, asides, changing typefaces, footnotes, fabricated skits, and metaphorical meanderings by what appears to be, on a fresh page, sudden, pithy, and disconcertingly direct communication from the author himself to the reader:

YOU'VE
BEEN
HAD

haven't you, jocko? you sad sour stew-faced sonofabitch. really, did you read this far? puzzle your head? turn the pages this and that, around about? Was it racy enough to suit? There wasn't too much plot? . . . Nothing lasts.[9]

As if to make the matter of authorial intervention clear, Kurt Vonnegut, Jr., once affirmed, "I want to be a character in all of my works. I can do that in print. . . . I have always rigged my stories so as to include myself, and I can't stop now."[10] If such self-intrusion can be said to promote "disruption," then surely we should consider a great many recent authors subversive and disturbing.

The point that needs stressing, however, is that such "literary disruption" is by no means new to the literary scene. It appears to be too often assumed that "modernists" (see Conrad and James) were conservative, staid, and conventional, whereas more recent authors are "unshackled" and liberally "experimental." It is not so. Yet if we are to believe Jerome Klinkowitz, the "post-contemporary" innovations began precisely "with the publishing season of 1967–68," inaugurating, in America at least, a "radical disruption of [the genre of fiction's] development."[11] We should counter that such novelty is not so innovative or neoteric after all, and with the preacher we might affirm that "there is no new thing under the sun. Is there any thing whereof it may be said, See, this is new? it hath been already of old time, which was before us."[12]

We should recall that in fifth-century Athens, Aristophanic comedy regularly utilized a chorus that does conventionally "break into" its dramatic fictions in the voice of the author during the play's parabasis. Elsewhere in the plays, Aristophanes goes to considerable lengths to frustrate or fracture dramatic illusion by injecting sudden references to the audience or to stage props.[13] Moreover, writers like Horace, Dante, and Chaucer complicated their fictions by inserting central characters bearing their own names. Voltaire could inject himself into his own fiction, as could James Joyce and Pirandello as well.[14]

In the same manner, the tradition of narrative disturbance is equally as old, notably evident in Menippean satire, particularly in Seneca's *Apocolocyntosis* (ca. A.D. 54) and in Petronius's *Satyricon* (ca.

A.D. 60).¹⁵ These works later influenced a great deal of fictional ploys, as in Erasmus's *Praise of Folly* (1509), More's *Utopia* (1516), and even Swift's *Gulliver's Travels* (1726). In fact, such strains of narrative disturbance appear in the first picaresque novel, *Lazarillo de Tormes* (1554), in Swift's *A Tale of a Tub* (1704), in Sterne's *Tristram Shandy* (1759–67), in Carlyle's *Sartor Resartus* (1833–34), in Dostoevsky's "Notes from Underground" (1864), in Gide's *Les Faux-Monnayeurs* (1925), and in Faulkner's *The Sound and the Fury* (1929) and *As I Lay Dying* (1930).

Surely, too, our "postmodern" fiction has derived much from the deliberate antifictions of the nineteenth-century French avant-garde literature, followed by works in the twentieth century of impressionist painters, expressionist playwrights, and particularly dadaist and surrealist writers. Assuredly, twentieth-century literature has been given a certain impetus by the mad, intrusive surrealist fictions of André Breton (*Nadja*, 1928) and of Louis Aragon (*Le Paysan de Paris*, 1926). Such disruptive fictions, together with the programmatic cubism of Picasso, certainly affected the writings of Gertrude Stein and, through her, a significant strain of American writing. Consider, for instance, the prose of William Carlos Williams, such distorted fictions as Robert M. Coates's *The Eater of Darkness* (1926) and John Hawkes's *The Cannibal* (1949), and the novels of Harry Matthews and Thomas Pynchon.¹⁶

When all is said and done, however, the great-great granddaddy of modern fiction, Cervantes' *Don Quixote* (1605–15), establishes an admirable convention and a most striking example of magnificent dislocation in part 1, chapter 9. Don Quixote and a Basque squire are abruptly left stranded in the midst of battle with swords aloft; they are frozen there, and the author intervenes in his narrative. We suddenly learn from him for the first time that the original manuscript of the book we are reading has been "lost" and that there are no less than three authors of the tale we have been blandly pursuing and taking for granted: one Cide Hamete Benengeli, the "historian," composed the original in Arabic; a low Arab peasant translator was hired for several pence to render the whole in Spanish; and our own "author" (at last), Cervantes himself, is thus a mere editor. Surely no such panoply of multiplying authors or such a disruption of narrative has ever more handsomely perverted and mocked the pious conventions of normative storytelling. Furthermore, we recall that François Rabelais, in *Gargantua and Pantagruel* (1532–52), posed as someone else, as the learned grand chronicler Alcofribas Nasier. With fiction given such jolts, starts, and disguises at the outset of the Renaissance, it is small wonder that artists in the subsequent tradition continued such innovation. It is at least clear that at the dawning of the novelistic tradition, invention, digression, and interruption were intrinsic in satiric literary practice and to a large extent even became conventional. Such disruptions certainly continued in the novelistic practice of Paul Scarron, Henry Fielding, and Laurence Sterne.

Recent authors, therefore, have simply been breaking away from the nineteenth century's special addiction to and reliance upon realism, and it should be no surprise that older conventions have been revitalized.[17] In fact, in our day, fantasy, science fiction, fictional biography, dystopia, parody, and satire are all hale, hearty, and zestfully thriving. Naysayers who regularly anticipate the death of the novel to the contrary, the possibilities for all kinds of fiction nowadays are enormous, and recent writers continue to tap and distill the rich resources of a broad, fluid, and hoary literary tradition. The best we can do is to wish them well.

8

Discordant Endings

Perhaps one of the most poignant means of inducing discomposure in an audience is by tampering with a story's climax and finale, a deliberate ruffling of a work's dénouement that we might jestingly designate as creating "the senselessness of an ending."[1] Since so many other disruptions have become normative, the desecration of conventional closings seems perfectly in order.

Ted Hughes created a terse and stark version of Seneca's *Oedipus* in 1968, successfully produced that same year by Britain's theatrical bad boy, Peter Brook. What is interesting is that Senecan theater has not been very popular since the Renaissance; it is a theater, like the Jacobean, of black moods, of bloodlust, of melancholy, of melodramatic despair and horror. The Senecan version of Oedipus is assuredly no hero in the Aristotelian sense; he appears to be a man worse than ourselves and one riddled by hesitancies, insecurities, passivity, and fitful self-doubt. The play is filled with morose black magical signs, prophecies, and portents of disaster, and a hapless Oedipus is merely swept along to his doom.[2] However out of favor Seneca may have been for several centuries, times and tides and tastes change. The lurid theater of Büchner's *Woyzeck* and of Strindberg, the excesses of Artaud and Jarry, and the new climate in our century heralding black humor and theater of the absurd have rendered Seneca altogether feasible—and even palatable.

But Hughes and Brook go one step further than merely revitalizing and refurbishing the lurid Senecan muse. Perhaps the most striking innovation they contribute is introduced at play's end: "The CHORUS celebrate the departure of OEDIPUS with a dance."[3] After the blinded and demolished Oedipus has been led away like a cripple, the members of the chorus suddenly let out a huzzah of jubilation and, accompanied by music and dancing, parade in masks, laughing in the theater aisles: "A large gilded phallus was carried like a totem pole down the aisle by choristers singing *Yes! We Have No Bananas*."[4] The tragic mood of balance and restraint, the hushed dismay of pained and reflective awe that besets an audience at the close of tragedy and even of disaster-melodrama is here rudely disbursed, and satyrlike raucous hooting and cavorting take their place.

Initially, this appendage to tragedy might seem uncalled for, disturbing, and out of place. But upon consideration, we must concede a certain suitability: for much of twentieth-century art obtains its raw power precisely by crossing the wires of comedy and tragedy and by crippling traditional decorum and Arnoldian "high seriousness" with injections of laughter, absurdity, sex, scatology, and panpiping mayhem.[5]

This is not to say that the deliberate violation of a genre's tone and decorum is unheard-of in classical antiquity.[6] Late Euripidean plays read more like comedy than tragedy; Aristophanic pieces often end ominously, threatening something worse than comic laughter, and the portion of the *Satyricon* that has come down to us shades off, toward the close, from picaresque and parodic high spirits into darker moods that accompany the newly introduced topic of cannibalism.[7] Mortal and grinning grotesquerie was a regular feature of the arts in the Middle Ages. In the Renaissance, too, stemming from the mixture of the serious and the comic in early mystery plays, are Marlowe's *Doctor Faustus*, Hamlet's grim graveyard humor, and Jacobean drama's scenes of slaughter. The romantics, also, cultivated a fondness for the demonic and the terrible.[8]

Particularly the modern era, however, deliberately and perhaps permanently intermixes comedy and tragedy. Especially is this true when a somber theme is suddenly trivialized and unaccountably lightened in a finale. A spurt of explosive laughter climaxes the key moments of Hawthorne's "My Kinsman, Major Molineux," for example, and a sudden influx of ironically brilliant, dawning sunlight concludes Ibsen's *Ghosts*. Kafka's "Metamorphosis" similarly concludes with sunlight, picnicking, and the celebration of the sister's physical vigor as she dances into healthy maturity after her brother's demise. In the final mad scene in Nathanael West's *Day of the Locust*, after the horror of the mass riots, poor Tod Hackett goes lightheadedly insane; we last hear the idiot voice childishly mimicking a police siren. In like manner, Carson McCullers's *The Ballad of the Sad Café* concludes with the grotesque and cross-eyed Miss Amelia Evans left a lonely recluse forever and the townspeople miserable and let down. Souls "rot" and peach trees "grow more crooked." Then, at this moment of final wretchedness, the author proposes turning, as relief, to a chain gang three miles down the road for consolation: the twelve prisoners are never lonely, because they sing and are conveniently shackled together. On such a ludicrous note of "solace," the story draws to a close.[9]

Almost equally disruptive is the finale of Tennessee Williams's play *Orpheus Descending*. At the most painful and penultimate moment, Lady Torrance is gunned down in her home by her sick and malevolent husband, Jabe. Her last words constitute another, seemingly frivolous non sequitur: "The show is over. The monkey is dead." Or consider Stanley Kubrick's film *Dr. Strangelove*, which concludes with the onset of an atomic Armageddon, yet accompanied by the cheerful whoops of the gung-ho Texan astride the first falling bomb as if at a gala upon a bronco (but he is riding backward). Pinter's *Birthday Party* moves rapidly toward doomsday celebration despite the festivities and childish toys, and Gabriel García Márquez's story "Big Mama's Funeral" swiftly becomes a hilarious epiclike extravaganza of drunken festivities and surrealistic hoopla. And strikingly, Donald Barthelme's tale "Views of My Father Weeping" is a "retrospective" of the son's responses to his father's suffering; a parody of a detective story in which the son, however reluctantly, is coerced by destiny, circumstances, and clues to plunge deeper and deeper into the routine "investigation" of and "revenge" for his father's murder, it nonetheless becomes simultaneously more and more absurd, ending abruptly with a comic disruption: the tale is truncated by a mere "Etc."[10]

Audiences are shocked at the close of Slawomir Mrozek's drama *Tango* (1965), when the young idealistic hero is brutally slaughtered and the murderer and the boy's uncle commence dancing to the music of "La Cumparsita" as the curtain falls. In fact, death and dying appear to be the appropriate topics for the violation of solemnity, as is illustrated by the finale of two recent satiric motion pictures. Blake Edwards's *S.O.B.* (1981) concludes with director Felix Farmer's funeral, an occasion for corpse-stealing and hilarious drunken orgy. Hal Ashby's *Being There* (1980) ends at a solemn funeral of a millionaire, from which the moronic Peter Sellers character wanders away in a daze, dawdles among some trees and shrubs like Charlie Chaplin, and then proceeds, like Christ, nonchalantly to walk away upon the water.[11]

Such deliberate violations of seriousness in a work's climax are, therefore, a striking and recurrent phenomenon of twentieth-century literature and constitute a kind of "literary openness" as R.M. Adams defines it: "A literary form . . . which includes a major unresolved conflict with the intent of displaying its unresolvedness." Or, in Thomas Mann's phrase, modern literature is most comfortable when confounding genres and tones, generating what he terms "the grotesque"; indeed, Mann predicted that the grotesque would grow to be the predominant mode in this century's literature.[12] He has been very largely right. Hence, the impish foolery of Ted Hughes and Peter Brook's finale to the Senecan *Oedipus* can be understood as anything but an aberration. In the present chapter we will briefly consider some of the reasons for and the meaning of intrusive comic spurts that frequently invade ultimate scenes at austere moments and in supposedly grave and serious works.

In the present century, we continue to share with the romantics the custom of debunking traditional literary decorum. It is also a commonplace that we have retained the romantic author's penchant for mocking the earlier Enlightenment's ideal of rationalism; Freud's ideas about the irrational psyche and the aggressiveness of humor, together with our experience of the brutal history of the twentieth century, have increased the degree and quantity of the nightmarish injected into our literature. After several generations, our response to science's principles of indeterminacy and randomness and to the existentialists' agonies over the absurd have become thoroughly domesticated. We virtually laugh now, however nervously, at ideas of fate and chance, disruptiveness and chaos. Then, too, the romantic's quest for a unique and exalted self has been dissipated and largely dispatched by disillusionment, and therefore more than ever we have discredited ideas of the hero. As a result of these factors, we tend to renounce ideas of tragedy; our major mode becomes mocking, parodic.[13] Unsurprisingly, therefore, our literature and other arts regularly intrude upon conventional seriousness with debunking laughter.

Perhaps no better concluding scene illustrates the intrusion of the comic/absurd upon potential tragedy than that devised by William Styron in *The Long March* (1952). Marine troops on maneuvers in the Carolinas are randomly ordered by their colonel on an overnight thirty-six-mile hike. The distance seems cruel and impossible to most of the officers, and before the ordeal the men have had little rest or sleep. Indeed, the setting for this hike is deliberately ominous; only the day before, several misfired mortar shells killed eight or more soldiers in a chow line, and death is made to seem hovering everywhere, militant, foreboding, and inevitable. The author's language throughout suggests as much, darkly hinting that "the end was at hand." Yet after a titanic struggle and after most of the troops have been allowed to drop out of the march as they falter and collapse, a remnant of the soldiers completes the hike. All our fearful expectations are anticlimatically disbursed and wafted away.

We have invested the greatest amount of our suspense in the figure of the rebellious Jewish captain, Mannix. He has all along thought the forced march a brutal exercise in sadism, but the colonel has especially designated his company as "soft," and Captain Mannix is as furiously determined to complete the march with his men as if their lives depended upon it. The captain also bears a grave handicap; a nail in his boot early in the hike rapidly tears into his heel, and although the nail is subsequently removed, his hobbled foot soon swells at the ankle to the size of a small balloon. Still he perseveres and limps onward. We clearly expect the worst. And yet, although court-martialed for insubordination, Captain Mannix simply completes the hike. Not only has our sense of tragic extremity failed to be fulfilled, but also the ludicrous and the absurd intrude as we watch the captain painfully staggering and lurching along the last part of the march:

Mannix's perpetual tread on his toe alone gave to his gait a ponderous, bobbing motion which resembles that of a man wretchedly spastic and paralyzed. It lent to his face too . . . an aspect of deep, almost prayerfully passionate concentration—eyes thrown skyward and lips fluttering feverishly in pain—so that if one did not know he was in agony one might imagine that he was a communicant in rapture, offering up breaths of hot desire to the heavens. It was impossible to imagine such a distorted face; it was the painted, suffering face of a clown, and the heaving gait was a grotesque and indecent parody of a hopeless cripple, with shoulders gyrating like a seesaw and with flapping, stricken arms.[14]

Our tragic appetite has been whetted, and the religious imagery is some sense suggests that the Jewish captain is near sainthood, possibly even fulfilling a version of the suffering Christ traveling along the Stations of the Cross. Yet all is scheduled for put-down: finally the flapping body seems ludicrous, the suffering parodic, and the martyr's face suddenly metamorphoses into that of a clown. The book concludes on such a ludicrous note. Bumbling toward the shower room clad in a towel, the captain encounters a black maid in the halls. She empathizes with him: "Oh my, you poor man. What you been doin'? Do it hurt?" She answers her own question: "Oh, I bet it does. Deed it does." Mannix exhaustedly drops his towel, and standing there in absurd birthday-suit nakedness, he can only repeat and mimic her dialect: "Deed it does."[15] They are the last three words in the tale, again tingeing the bitter with light comedy routine, suggestive of vaudeville blackface and travesty. Such comic disruptions do not, however, weaken this novel, dismantle its themes, or mitigate its impact—far from it. The reader is disturbed by the letdown, yet the suffering is not expelled; what the men have endured in a Marine camp is but an emblem of what all men suffer in the military—and even of what mankind suffers in a ruthless world. It is meaningless, ugly, enraging, and yet it is comedic.

88 Stratagems

A number of our practitioners and theoreticians in the twentieth century have called for large doses of extremities—pushing comedy toward disaster, smashing barriers between genres, preventing audiences from responding with a single complacent emotion or reaction. Hence, Artaud alleged: "Everything that acts is a cruelty. It is upon this idea of extreme action, pushed beyond all limits, that theater must be built." Ionesco concurred: "The essence of the theatre lay in magnifying . . . effects . . . farce . . . parody . . . back to the unendurable. Everything raised to paroxysm, where the source of tragedy lies. A theatre of violence."[16] Indeed, a group of scholars recently sought to distinguish a modern genre, based upon pronouncements like the ones we have just recorded, that might be designated "savage comedy."[17] Still, we must make a distinction here. We are not concerned in this chapter with comedy that abruptly or by stages metamorphoses into savagery or cruelty, but rather with tragic and painful acts that are toward the close modified by comic touches, with impact offset and somehow modified by the ludicrous or the flippant. Styron's work is not weakened by the final tapering off toward comedy. On the contrary, we are apt to believe that such fiction is psychologically right simply because reality seldom provides either humor or tragic suffering in undiluted form; all too often the two are—perhaps still more painfully and senselessly—intermixed.

Our age is somehow especially ripe for such ironic and multiple perceptions. After all, our civilization has long assembled and scrutinized its own history; we have witnessed eras of great hope and aspiration and equally terrible eras of squalor and defeat. We have come to expect the up-and-down wobble of historical events, and we are forced to confront such mechanical gyrations with more knowledgeability than we could ever have wished. All things, after all, that are incessant in their motion have a kind of humor as well as terror. Repetition pure and simple, from one point of view, is risible. And we dwell in such an era of jingles and repetitions. Even the vast interminable tortures of a Sisyphus rolling his stone, of the Danaïds eternally seeking to fill their perforated jugs, of Prometheus forever having his liver consumed by a predatory vulture—all these events once terrified the Greeks and tangibly constituted for them the idea of hell. Today such perennial motions are domesticated, perceived as "clockwork oranges," as the commonplace and everyday ludicrous and absurd machinery of nonproduction. We perceive ourselves as inhabiting such a hell, and we grimly grin and attempt to bear it. According to Richard Pearce, many of our major fictions are fully tinged with vaudeville, and men are dramatized not only as clowns but as clowns who have elected their clownishness—the case, say, with Oskar in Grass's *Tin*

Drum, or with Macmann, Molloy, and the Unnameable in Beckett's trilogy.[18] Hence in our time the rachitic laughter continues. Nowhere is it better displayed than in the disquieting conclusion of Evelyn Waugh's *A Handful of Dust* (1934), in which Tony Last, a country gentleman on an expedition in the South American wilds, becomes hopelessly lost in the immense jungle. There he is captured by a savage hermit and coerced—ever after—to read and reread aloud to his captor and interminable novels of Charles Dickens. It is hellish torment indeed—but one (as is so often the case nowadays) riddled with the senseless cacophony of laughter.

9
Infernal Repetition

Comic anticlimax in a work's finale, as we have seen in chapter 8, assuredly undercuts the fiction and aggravates the reader's expectations. As a matter of fact, authors of the satiric grotesque are just as apt to situate anticlimax everywhere in a plot, inserting a clutter of seemingly mindless repetitions in their narratives, arranging insidious circularities in their storylines. In fact, the most deplorable kind of plotting—frustrating for the reader, terrible for the characters—is the kind that engineers duplication, redundancy, reiteration. The same grooves, tracks, and scenarios inevitably recur, and the major character is inevitably stuck in it. This might seem comic and amusing at first, but at its worst it suggests a hellish eternal repetition.

One of the great ludicrous moments in literature occurs in Milton's *Paradise Lost*, when Satan makes his furious, resolute attempt at flight, after the Fall, across the immense distance from hell to the newly created earth:

> Flutt'ring his pennons vain plumb down he drops
> Ten thousand fadom deep . . .
>   [until] by . . . chance
> The strong rebuff of some tumultuous cloud
>   . . . hurried him
> As many miles aloft: that fury stay'd
> Quencht in a Boggy *Syrtis*, neither Sea,
> Nor good dry Land, nigh founder'd on he fares,
> Treading the crude consistence, half on foot,
> Half flying; behoves him now both Oar and Sail.
> . . . .
> So eagerly the fiend
> O'er bog and deep, through strait, rough, dense, or rare,
> With head, hands, wings, or feet pursues his way,
> And swims or sinks, or wades, or creeps, or flies.[1]

This hapless Satan is juggled and buffeted along what proves to be the greatest distance between two points. Furthermore, the increasing pauses and word lists and the breakdown of poetic rhythm toward the end imitate the dizzying, anfractuous, sea-sickening trip. Repetition and near-chaos amusingly spell disaster for the Evil One's affected decorum, presumptuous seriousness, and smooth sailing.

Similarly, Chaucer masterfully portrays his characters' "bisinesse": a kind of fevered and febrile flourish of activity that often gets such characters nowhere at all. One thinks of the marital manipulations and argumentative squabblings of the Wife of Bath, of the loud, avaricious, and boastful Pardoner, of the drunken Miller, a "stout carl" bagpiping away and fronting the procession, or of Chaucer himself, captive and hapless in an endless fit of rhyming about Sir Thopas. Perhaps the Canterbury pilgrimage in its entirety—set in constant motion in a meaningless direction—represents just such blustering activity. Certainly an excellent exemplar of such "bisinesse" is "handy Nicholas," the confidential clerk of "The Miller's Tale." In order to bring off a mere assignation and swift sexual encounter with the more-than-willing Alison and to beguile her carpenter husband, he must obsessively invent a fantastic scenario of Rube Goldberg–like eventualities: Nicholas must take to his bed at great length in mock illness, prophesy the Second Flood, and set the husband building and provisioning no less than three skiffs before he will consent to come at sexual congress. One has to chuckle at such a representation of intellectual and professorial types, who are driven to scamper about and hoist miles of hypotheses and entire grids of conjectures merely to be able to pronounce their arrival at "structuralism" or—worse yet—move along to the business of deconstruction.

Another handsome case of hyperactivity is Richardson's Lovelace, that monumental hellish rake who has to expend an infinitude of time and muster more ingenuity than the Creator merely to seduce the waspish, priggish little Clarissa. With incessant role-playing and frenetic vigor (not unlike Nabokov's demented Humbert) he roars about London, calculating and inveigling furiously: "Here have I been [he tells us] at work, dig, dig, dig, like a cunning miner, at one time, and spreading my snares, like an artful fowler, at another, and exulting in my contrivances to get this . . . creature absolutely into my power." Like a madman, he schemes to have prostitutes assume the guise of his sister, to have churlish hirelings dress as seamen, and he himself at one point hobbles about, posturing as a goutish old man. For indeed Lovelace is willing to convert all the world into melodramatic theater simply that he might stage his "production." As he unwinds his perpetual plot, he boasts and tootles: "Stand by, varlets—Tantara-ra-ra! Veil your bonnets, and confess your master!" He is hunter and player and orchestra in the pit. Elsewhere, he is a Proteus, a chameleon, an emperor, a veritable god during the protracted undertaking, as well as a Bacchanalian maenad: "*Io Triumphe! Io* Clarissa, Sing!" All, as he says, these actors are "engaged . . . so many engines set at work, at an immense expense, with infinite contrivance" to perpetrate his pitifully brief and solitary sexual emission.[2] But what an enervated discharge that is: the abandoned roué and omnifornicator is reduced to performing a rape upon the inert body of a sedated and senseless maid who is pinioned by a brace of whores. Of course, he is comical, terrible, and pathetic.

Such portrayals of enormous effort to little effect are a common feature of satire; they induce a furor and a flurry, only to accomplish a resounding anticlimax of the sort Dryden attributes to his lumpish MacFlecknoe: a puffed-up creature eternally infected by "Pangs without birth, and fruitless Industry." For satire recurrently dramatizes the action of a literary lame duck: enormous bustle, stir, and pother accompanied by minuscule and sterile achievement—what Horace nicely encapsulates in his phrase "Parturiunt montes, nascetur ridiculus mus": Mountains in labor, producing a piddling mouse.[3]

We observe in all the instances cited antitheses that are powerfully combined, stressing oxymoronic incongruity: violence, hunger, and locomotion juxtaposed with anticlimax, insipidity, inertia. Revolution is mated with ennui, furor with hebetude. Perhaps this mixture is the ultimate meaning of the preacher's "vanity of vanities," for in such a state, "all things are full of labor," but "man cannot utter it." All performance and endeavor are undercut, hailed as commonplace repetitions: "The thing that hath been it is that which shall be; and that which is done is that which shall be done: and there is no new thing under the sun."[4]

A tang of such ironic contradictions pervades all satiric busy idleness. It is the situation of ardent political souls like Manente degli Uberti, called Farinata, whom Dante encounters in the sixth circle of hell. Those who had been extreme activists in life are there fastened up to their waists or their chins in immovable sepulchres of fire. As a taunting temptation, because of their excessive earthly preoccupations, they are permitted dimly to perceive future worldly events, but nothing of the present. Yet it is precisely to the affairs of the present moment that they remain eternally devoted. In addition, the spirit of Farinata appears upright, aloof, gentlemanly—dignified and cool amid all that ludicrous heat—for he is still haughty, scornful, and factional, "as if he held for Hell a great disdain."[5] The audience response is intended to be a shudder, a touch of *Schadenfreude*, for what could be more powerfully absurd than a blind, flaming coffin-bound dignity in the underworld? Farinata is a wretchedly superfluous soul—so addicted to petty mortal affairs that he does not notice his eternal situation. Of course, we might say that this blindness is almost sublime; Farinata's myopic, geocentric vision obliterates for him his supernatural world, and it is that vacuum of insight that constitutes his perdition. But there is no helping some people; they are too dumb to know what in hell is going on.

The same idiocy prevails with Milton's hordes of fallen angels. While awaiting the return of their leader, confined in an unspeakable labyrinth of fire and ice, they can hardly help being assailed by boredom and "restless thoughts." Hence, like a rout of exigent children at a tedious party, they undertake a series of reckless "games": races, mock battles, song fests ("with notes Angelical"), and voyages of discovery (as if they were Columbuses, Balboas, Sir Francis Drakes).

> In discourse more sweet
> (For Eloquence [charms] the Soul . . .)
> Others apart sat on a Hill retir'd,
> In thoughts more elevate, and reason'd high
> Of Providence, Foreknowledge, Will, and Fate,
> Fixt Fate, Free will, Foreknowledge absolute,
> And found no end, in wand'ring mazes lost.[6]

It is a brilliantly laughable and shocking piece of news to learn that the eternally vigilant devils are reduced to fun and games, or that their "charming Souls" are merely lost in an obfuscating dither of discourse: "so many, / I had not thought death had undone so many."[7]

The underworld has a curious effect upon people; authors can hardly approach its precincts without turning ironic and satiric. Since the time of Aristophanes, Menippus, and Lucian, satirists have had a fondness for "dialogues of the dead."[8] The irony of these conversational set pieces can cut so many ways: the dead, given a fatal aesthetic distance, can tellingly reflect upon the futility of action among the living. Yet at the same time, the lively reader cannot but detect a certain irony in the fact that the dead appear to be so knowledgeable about living (and envious, too). In addition, there is revealed an eternal dichotomy betwixt *vita activa* and *mors contemplativa*, those who perform and those who interminably talk about it, activity and passivity.

Indeed, once one is permanently settled underground, philosophizing and chatter become superfluous, permanently called into question. And to be sure, such a lasting volubility combined with utter debilitation proves exactly that ironic mixture of flourish and fixity that we have been considering. Just such an uneasy combination is perfectly captured by those classic figures of myth in the underworld: Sisyphus perennially rolling his stone to nowhere, Ixion revolving upon his wheel of fire, Tantalus forever striving to obtain food and drink and yet forever famished and parched. These are the principle archetypes of the repetitious nonachiever.

The infernal principle need not, of course, always be present in satire, but it is an extreme boundary and a potent locale for dramatizing almost superhuman restlessness and eternal recurrence. Dryden's Achitophel is such a character, one who is, although alive, driven, warped, and stunted, as if by internal demons:

> For close Designs, and crooked Counsells fit;
> Sagacious, Bold, and Turbulent of wit:
> Restless, unfixt in Principles and Place;
> In Power unpleas'd, impatient of Disgrace:
> A fiery Soul, which working out its way,
> Fretted the Pigmy Body to decay:
> And o'r inform'd the Tenement of Clay.[9]

Sometimes the demonic realizes itself in a representative group. Thus, Jack and the choir boys in Golding's *Lord of the Flies* metamorphose into fiends of bloodlust, as the children's tentative civilization on the idyllic island regresses into barbarism. The devil or Beelzebub figure they worship on the mountain or perched atop a totem stick is in reality a demon within themselves that strives to emulate the atomic holocaust that the boys' elders have engendered in the outside world. Their vigor simply spreads strife and, like the fire that comes to rage on the island, is self-consuming.

Sometimes the demonic is symbolic and incriminatingly inclusive, representative. Hence Oskar Matzerath in Grass's *The Tin Drum* retains a dwarfed and stunted childish maturity that directly reflects the twisted, tormented, and chaotic political world of warfare in Nazi Germany. His guilt for his parents' deaths represents all Europe's guilt, and his final incarceration in an insane asylum suggests the insanity of an entire generation. Like the Mr. Kurtz of *Apocalypse Now*, Oskar is crippled as well as a crippler, a devilish avatar of a cursed and damned society. Oskar's multitude of picaresque misadventures, like his freakish sexual forays, merely dramatizes the fecundity of a proliferating and virtually all-pervasive evil.

John Hawkes's *The Cannibal* simply extends, if that were possible, Grass's evil vision to include three generations in Germany and three devastating bouts of warfare (in 1870, 1914, and 1939); the text's surrealistic density only intensifies the nightmarish reality of war's destructiveness. With ruthless irony, the novel concludes with the insane being once again "well tended" as the nation joyously prepares for a fourth consummation of world warfare. Again and again, the novel presents total war as a dark fruit devoutly nurtured only to produce an all-devouring fruitlessness, a species of self-consuming cannibalism.

Sometimes the demonic rears it head in a hauntingly, uncontrollably repetitious manner, almost becoming continuous. In D.M. Thomas's book *The White Hotel*, Frau Elisabeth Erdman was in her childhood disturbed by the sexual capers of her father with her aunt and distraught by the revolutionary violence of Russian strikers. These incidents help shape her subsequent hysteria, and her crippling fantasies about sex, violence, and catastrophes mysteriously and magically conjoined in an Alpine resort—of the sort that Freud himself can barely grasp or treat—persist. She cannot rid herself of her psychic disorders. Then, events come full circle once again: in Kiev in 1941 she is rounded up with thousands of other Jews for slaughter in a ravine. Two Ukrainian mercenaries, collaborators with the Nazis, murder Frau Erdman by raping her with a fixed bayonet. The reader is helplessly left to ponder the question Which is the more disabling, social reality or private neurosis? Who is truly sexually unbalanced in our world? Who is actually hysterical? Freud has often spoken of "projection," when a person projects internal psychic images and desires outward, into the physical world. But here we encounter a terrifying "injection," in which an international frenzy for sexual battery and the lust for violence infect and invade the individual conscience. Uneasily, the reader wonders Which comes first—man's general public malevolence or the individual's mental maladjustment? In any case, both seem to be segments of one cruel, demonic machine, each part fueling the other and generating a continuous and inevitable cycle of murder, rapine, and malaise.

Total warfare and incessant illness are infernal enough and are fitting topics in our bellicose century, as in Heller's *Catch-22*, Kubrick's *Dr. Strangelove*, or the conclusion of Waugh's *Vile Bodies*. And many a satirist pushes further, toward Armageddon and apocalypse for the human race, as in Pope's *Dunciad*, in Vonnegut's *Cat's Cradle*, in Čapek's *R.U.R.*, in Wells's *Time Machine*. Such blasted imaginings are surely related to the medieval and later preoccupations with the Last Judgment, the Dance of Death, and the torments of hell that we encounter in the paintings of Bosch, Brueghel, Hogarth, and Goya.

Frequently, modern works merely suggest the infernal at the personal level, as fictions end with some form of total defeat for the central characters—suicide, assassination, lobotomizing and brainwashing—as in Céline's *Journey to the End of the Night*, West's *Miss Lonelyhearts*, Zamyatin's *We*, Huxley's *Brave New World*, Orwell's *1984*,

Kesey's *One Flew over the Cuckoo's Nest*, or Lem's *Memoirs Found in a Bathtub*. For satire need not plunge all the way into the infernal pit; near approaches will serve satisfactorily enough. It is sufficient for characters to be driven, for example, into a towering insanity. One thinks of the grim portrait of Henry Armstid at the conclusion of Faulkner's *The Hamlet*, crippled, avaricious, perpetually digging and lusting for gold:

They had been watching him for two weeks . . . watching Armstid as he spaded the earth steadily down the slope of the old garden. . . . when . . . one . . . approached . . . Armstid climbed out of his pit and ran at him, dragging the stiffened leg, the shovel raised . . . and drove the man away. . . . he appeared to be not even aware of them where they stood along the fence, watching him spading himself steadily back and forth across the slope with . . . spent and unflagging fury . . . spading himself into the waxing twilight with the regularity of a mechanical toy and with something monstrous in his unflagging effort, as if the toy were too light for what it had been set to do, or too tightly wound. . . . the gaunt unshaven face . . . was now completely that of a madman.[10]

Similar incessant, repetitious, ambiguously "spent" yet "unflagging" lunacy (that is, concerning the monstrous regularity of the moon's changefulness) overcomes Gulliver, Woyzeck, Humbert Humbert, and *The Day of the Locust*'s Tod Hackett. Others are beset by immobility, inertia, and near paralysis, as if entropy had triumphed in their lives: Dante's Belacqua in the *Purgatorio*, Grimmelshausen's would-be hermit Simplicissimus, Goncharov's willfully bed-ridden Oblomov, Dostoyevsky's interred Underground Man, Ellison's Invisible Man, and certainly Murphy and some dozen others of Beckett's enervated personae. A classic case is James's John Marcher in "The Beast in the Jungle," a man whose destiny it is to have no destiny, a waiter and watcher who has nothing to do. As a modern exemplar of vacuous expectancy, he is akin to Musil's Ulrich, the man without qualities, swallowed alive in interminably irresolute committees.

More amusing is the character who is simply impotent, who lets everything all hang out and fall down, and who cannot get it up. The soul of all Sterne's zany "bisinesse" in *Tristram Shandy* and *A Sentimental Journey* is founded upon impotence or coitus interruptus pure and simple. The same persistent evil fate besets Encolpius in the *Satyricon*, and the same crippling modern disease plagues Prufrock. It is, surely, a debilitating effeminacy that unmans Gustave von Aschenbach, preparing him properly for the plague and for death in Venice.

Most often, such impotence, paralysis, and catatonia are only metaphoric, and many of satire's creatures are mere comic bumblers:

characters like Lazarillo and Candide, Waugh's Paul Pennyfeather, Thurber's oppressed males, and Kotzwinkle's Fan Man. If disaster did not exist, then these fools and naïfs would invent it; even with no roof over their heads, they would still bring the house down. Precisely like the horror-bound, their light comic brethren skip and bounce from mistake to mistake, anticlimax to anticlimax, pratfall to pratfall with patient placidity and sustained ignorance. They are going down—one, two, three times—but do not know the difference. Woody Allen's persona cannot even progress the length of a paragraph without several inevitable tumbles: "How can I believe in God when just last week I got my tongue caught in the roller of an electric typewriter? I am plagued by doubts. What if everything is an illusion and nothing exists? In that case, I definitely overpaid for my carpet."[11]

Allen's persona is exactly related to the erstwhile hermit in *Rasselas*, whose career orientation throughout his lifetime appears subject to cruel bouleversements and tergiversations; the poor, virtuous eremite has lived in solitude and retreat for years, attempting to secure himself from vice. He suddenly resolves, however, "to return into the world tomorrow" "with rapture": "In [an] assembly Rasselas [related] his interview with the hermit, and the wonder with which he heard him censure a course of life which he had so deliberately chosen, and so laudably followed.... One ... thought it likely, that the hermit would, in a few years, go back to his retreat, and, perhaps, if shame did not restrain, or death intercept him, return once more from his retreat into the world."[12] At such a rate, the religious recluse will be converted into a bouncing ball forever.

We can say much the same for the saintly Félicité (hardly the happy one) in Flaubert's "A Simple Heart." Whenever she exerts extreme effort, she is bound to be a loser. In fact, she steams along on the road like characters in Kerouac, expending incredible effort yet getting nowhere at all. She longs, for instance, to travel to the seaport to bid a last goodbye to her beloved nephew, Victor, about to sail away forever.

She put on her clogs and traveled the long twelve miles between Pont-l'Eveque and Honfleur.
When she arrived at the Calvary instead of turning left, she went right, got lost in the shipyards, and had to retrace her steps. Some people whom she approached advised her to hurry along. She went all around the ship-filled harbor, stumbling over the moorings.[13]

When she at last discovered Victor standing upon his ship, "she darted toward him, but at that moment the gangplank was raised" and the ship sailed away. Later, when her mistress's beloved daughter Virginie is dying of consumption and pneumonia in a distant monastery, Félicité strives mightily to make one last visit. The mother and doctor leave at once.

> Virginie had pneumonia. Perhaps her case was already hopeless.
> "Not yet!" said the doctor and both got into his carriage. . . .
> Félicité rushed into church to light a candle. Then she ran after the carriage which she overtook an hour later. She had jumped nimbly on behind, and was holding on to the straps, when she suddenly thought: "The courtyard isn't locked! Suppose thieves break in!" And she jumped off.
> At dawn of the following day, she went to the doctor's house. He had returned, but had left again for the country. Then she stayed at the inn, thinking some stranger would bring a letter. Finally, at dusk, she took the Lisieux stagecoach.
> The convent was at the bottom of a steep lane.[14]

Félicité knocks impatiently, and slowly the door opens: "The good sister, with a compassionate air, said that Virginie 'had just passed away.' At the moment, the tolling at Saint-Léonard's became louder."[15] And so, as Vonnegut would say, it goes. Everything Félicité undertakes is a near miss. Whether the satire is tragic or comic, the characters regularly—again and again—go bumpety-bump in their journey downhill.

The more frequently and grandiosely the action is repeated, the more discomforting yet amusing, the more curiously satisfying such deformed action in satire tends to become. As Bruce Kawin in *Telling It Again and Again* observes of "destructive repetition": "Say one word to yourself thirty times. . . . It loses its definition, becomes abstract and absurd." No matter how painful events might be in themselves, their multiplication renders them ludicrous, as one knows who has ever observed a laughing modern audience's response to grisly Jacobean tragedies. Knowingly, then, the satiric muse comes to us dressed in the accoutrements of a predictable superfluity: the measured rhythmic imprecations of the formal curse; the powder of expletives flying in *flyting*; the exuberantly excessive vocabulary and word lists in Rabelais; the parody of logic, treatise, and learning in humanistic attacks upon scholasticism; the crush of footnotes in the *Dunciad* and of all authorial superficies (apologies, dedications, prefaces, marginal commentaries) in *A Tale of a Tub*; the parade of courses and platters in the *cena*; the pageant of clothes, manners, and "polite conversation" in Restoration theater or at country house weekend parties in Peacock, James, Huxley, or McCarthy; and the crass itemization of materialistic possessions in satire of the bourgeoisie, as in Petronius, Flaubert, Fitzgerald, and Sinclair Lewis.[16]

Moreover, such repetitions usually appear locally, at the simplest level, in sentences and paragraphs, often giving satire the texture of staccato fragmentation. For satire thrives upon incremental form—the stichomythia of repartee and punch lines, the acerbity of noxious double entendres, the piling up of metaphors and other figures of speech, the production of numerous proverbs, sentences, aphorisms, and witty maxims. Many a satire even appears to be a temerarious compilation of bits and pieces: simulated recipes, mock laws, dictionaries of demented definitions, handbooks of misguided directions, how-to manuals, pseudocollections of tips, keys, and instructions. Among these, one thinks of La Rochefoucauld's and Nietzsche's Zarathustran maxims; the aphorisms of Lichtenberg and Stanislaw Lec; dictionaries like those of Flaubert and Ambrose Bierce; the seventeenth-century genre of "advice-to-a-painter" poems; manuals like Dedekind's guide to slovenliness, *Grobianus* (1605), and Swift's *Directions to Servants* (1745); anthologies like that of bad verse compiled by Wyndham Lewis and Charles Lee; and laws and principles propounded by the likes of Parkinson, Murphy, and Peter.[17]

Indeed, many other satires at the level of plot clearly reflect this rotating superabundance, as can be seen in cycles of quests and travels in *Don Quixote, Don Juan, Gulliver's Travels* or Céline's novels. Satire suits itself agreeably to the episodic series and to the refrain; a sturdy subgenre is surely the picaresque, as is the Menippean, that recurrently hobbles back and forth between verse and prose, between the author's own style and allusions and quotations that usurp the styles of others. Satiric characters, as well, do not surprise us when they appear and reappear, popping up in fictions like toast. Such include Eumolpus the reciting poet in the *Satyricon*, Falstaff, Pangloss, Waugh's Captain Grimes and Basil Seal, G.M. Fraser's Flashman. Parody is probably satire's strongest calling card; those familiar with the works and themes being imitated are constantly assailed by sensations of déjà vu, as the satire bobs back and forth, echoing and reechoing portions of the original.

Yet the pervasive, multifarious repetition so common in satire, that is tediously, frighteningly disturbing and funny, is not quite what Alvin Kernan calls going around in circles. Satire, as I have argued, tends to run us downhill; it's the pits. The repetitions and repeat performances merely deepen our sense of entrapment; the multiplication of cases of a single disease does not suggest fixity, but rather the eruption of an epidemic. Kernan, in postulating the "plots" of satire, metaphorically follows the extreme rhetorical figures proposed by Martinus Scriblerus in Pope's *Peri Bathous*: the "Magnifying," "Diminishing," and "Variagating" figures. "Variagation" Kernan associates with fixity, with overcrowding or "the mob tendency," and with circularity; in that sense, he perceives the fluctuating *Day of the Locust* as having "no plot" and Waugh's characters in *Vile Bodies* as traveling "in endless circles."[18]

But we had best be wary of Scriblerian discriminations, for despite the discernment of three motions—the rising, the falling, and the vibrating or jiggling—we must observe that Scriblerus's own volume is subtitled *The Art of Sinking in Poetry*. Despite his endless lists of different motions, the bad poetry he celebrates travels in no other direction but downward, into the bathetic, into the abstruse. Indeed, we might well perceive that the central irony of Pope's satire involves Scriblerus himself, who, although he lays on labels and distinctions like the gas, is himself the victim of a single fragmenting and falling action. Certainly, the most amusing redundancy of his "bisinesse" and crazy scholarship is his presumption to teach moderns the art of bad poetry, when all his cartload of terrible instances comes precisely from these moderns. Anticlimactically, they are the last people in creation to need such instruction; they have already mastered that art to hideous perfection. What could better constitute febrile ineptitude than the fervent teaching of a subject that the student already fully comprehends? Hence the *Peri Bathous* is a prince among the fallen angels of satire.

> From low to high doth dissolution climb,
> And sink from high to low, along a scale
> Of awful notes, whose concord shall not fail.[19]

Wordsworth's lines are all very well, so long as we note that his solitary "concord" is universal dissolution itself.

Whether it appears to elevate, submerge, or keep us afloat, satire always manages to send us to the bottom. For satire immerses us in oceans of terror and tepidity, stimulating its audience by a depressant. A piquant example is Gabriel García Márquez's story "Big Mama's Funeral," a paradoxical celebration of a holiday and a ninety-two-year-old oppressor's demise. With mounting mock-epic grandeur, the humble narrator treats us with religious zeal to everything in and about the village of Macondo. The camera in fact broadens upon an enormous panorama of petty politics, absolute corruption, and the populace's incredible squalor, gullibility, and superstition. The "carnival" simultaneously worships this perverse Virgin Mother's sanctity even as it regales the people's release from her barren and tainted domination. The narrative, a jumble of descriptions, lists, inventories, and name-droppings, progresses into the realm of sheer fantasy—and everything in its epic catalogs is thrown in, including the proverbial kitchen sink.

Only consider Big Mama's own deathbed tabulation of the possessions of her visible and invisible estate:

The wealth of the subsoil, the territorial waters, the colors of the flag, national sovereignty, the traditional parties, the rights of man, civil rights, the nation's leadership, the right of appeal, Congressional hearings, letters of recommendation, historical records, free elections, beauty queens, transcendental speeches, huge demonstrations, distinguished young ladies, proper gentlemen, punctilious military men, His Illustrious Eminence, the Supreme Court, goods whose importation was forbidden, liberal ladies, the meat problem, the purity of the language, setting a good example, the free but responsible press, the Athens of South America, public opinion, the lessons of democracy, Christian morality, the shortage of foreign exchange, the right of asylum, the Communist menace, the ship of state, the high cost of living, republican traditions, the underprivileged classes, statements of political support.
She didn't manage to finish.[20]

Instead, she expires—with a belch.

Furthermore, all the world comes to her funeral, from Scotland, from Asia, from the dunghill, from history: "the bagpipers of San Jacinto," "the rice planter of Sinu," "the shysters from Monpox," "the salt miners from Manaure," "the President of the Republic and his Ministers," the duke of Marlborough, and the pope—who concludes the grand ceremonies by himself flying bodily up to heaven![21] Through it all, the plentiful corpse of Big Mama, kept above ground for weeks and months of preparations and negotiations in 104° heat, is sublimely bubbling and rotting.

Yet we are hardly permitted, at the conclusion of these tumultuous and all-inclusive festivities, to feel that we have come full circle. True, the squalor remains, the low pedestrian garbage, detritus, and filth, the enslaved constricted inhabitants, remain. There is no new freedom or true release for anyone, since Big Mama's heirs will continue her corrosive reign, her perverse predominance in Macondo. But there will no longer be any obese, omnivorous, sanctified central figure of the likes of Mama, as before. The oppression will continue, but the populace will now have been robbed even of the tawdry grandeur of Big Mama's swollen, impotent, virginal presence, deprived of the distorted imaginary holiness and deluded pomp. The situation, if possible, is worse: there remains only the dull ache of a deeper misery and impoverishment.

Most frequently, satire is just such a saturnalia as was Mama's burial rite, a festival and a crazy panegyric—not the representation of disorder, but a parody of order itself. It celebrates the mockery of established order and constitutes a period of reversal and release. Its chaos is nonetheless orderly, making us, with all its details and repetitions and compilations, more aware of the vice and folly of the everyday world, a world to which, at the satire's close, we must return. That quotidian world of ours even Henry James—himself not averse to the satiric excursion—perceived all too clearly; "Life *is*, in fact, a battle. . . . Evil is insolent and strong; beauty enchanting but rare; goodness very apt to be weak; folly very apt to be defiant; wickedness to carry the day; imbeciles to be in great places, people of sense in small, and mankind generally, unhappy. But the world as it stands is no illusion, no phantasm, no evil dream of a night; we wake up to it again for ever and ever."[22] We may vacation from what we sense as our ironclad subservience to scientific laws, political malfeasance, the arms race, and a cruel fate. Consider the popularity of antiutopias, *A Clockwork Orange*, Vonnegut's fictions, and *Murphy's Law and Other Reasons Why Things Go Wrong!*[23] Nevertheless we still must return to these self-same inescapable tyrannies that we, at the outset, had fled; we must return to an increasingly circumscribing technology, to political ineptitudes, to threats of war, and to our own darkening fate.

One of the lunatic seven dwarfs in Donald Barthelme's mod retelling of *Snow White*, a character named Dan, explains that he and his brethren are busy, busy, busy manufacturing "plastic buffalo humps." There is no market for such useless and trifling dross just now, he acknowledges, but you never can tell. Society is, after all, addicted to the "sludge" and "stuffing" of modern mass production, and tastes are bound to change. Dan explains "that the per-capita production of trash in this country is up from 2.75 pounds per day in 1920 to 4.5 pounds per day in 1965. . . . I hazard that we may very well soon reach a point where it's a 100 percent." At that stage, we will have to learn "to appreciate its qualities." That's why Dan and his friends are producing buffalo humps: "It's that we want to be on the leading edge of this trash phenomenon, the everted sphere of the future."[24] Dan wants—and Barthelme wants—"to be on the leading edge of the trash phenomenon." Virtually every satirist would agree; as trivia, refuse, and wretchedness relentlessly continue to burgeon and multiply, the satirist vigorously lends a helping hand, continually building, amassing, and compiling the rubble, the dregs, and the sewage—for he is a visionary, ever aspiring to reach that ineffable 100 percent.

Part III. Themes

If the dark satirist is so attentive to crippling or unhinging his literary form and most artistic conventions too often taken for granted, then it should come as no surprise that he is equally devoted to content. Here, once again, it is his business and his pleasure to introduce subjects most often coyly scanted, topics stunning, repulsive, unpleasant, taboo. Chapters 10-14 investigate a sampling of such topics, including tedium and the soporific, the toilet and the bowel, cannibalism, hypermechanization, and the end of the world. Needless to say, other repellent and noxious matters are, for the brilliantly wayward and inventive satirist, quite ready at hand.

10

Ennui

Boredom, not one of the topics featured in romances or cherished in tales aspiring to be thrilling or action-packed, is a persistent theme of satire and the grotesque. For instance, one of the great moments in literature near the beginning of the modern period occurs in Jane Austen's *Emma* (1816) at the famed Box-Hill picnic and "exploration." Dances and outings, for the village and country gentry, occur seldom, and out of dullness, everyone is overly enthused about the upcoming "gipsy party" occasion. But for whatever reason, that occasion does not measure up to expectations; tensions mount, and the company is caught in a mean and sullen mood by what we would now term anomie and ennui. The result is an idle game and Emma's famous guard-down, offhand piece of surly curtness, when she insults the tedious but lovable Miss Bates. In a fit of the doldrums and victimized by what the eighteenth century called the spleen, Emma drops her honorable role as gracious gentlewoman, and a saucy other personality, a Mrs. Hyde, if you will, breaks out.

A similar moment is nearly effected by Dickens's professional tired man and snob in *Hard Times*, James Harthouse, Esq. The younger son of an aristocrat, he cannot inherit, but he has been educated and refined, for no good reason whatsoever. Flippant, haughty, faddishly lazy, indifferent, disinterested, he wanders aimlessly about the planet, enervatedly migrating from idea to idea, career to career. He "had tried life as a Cornet of Dragoons, and found it a bore; and had afterwards tried it in the train of an English minister abroad, and found it a bore; and had then strolled to Jerusalem, and got bored there; and had then gone yachting about the world, and got bored everywhere." Now he randomly falls in with industrialists and statisticians. What is more, he is absolutely without reason, principle, or interest. As for opinions, Harthouse languidly tells his new acquaintances, "I have not so much as the slightest predilection left. I assure you I attach not the least importance to any opinions. The result of the varieties of boredom I have undergone, is a . . . sentiment . . . that any set of ideas will do just as much good as any other set."[1] Emotionless, goalless, unaccountable, he can be a very unsocial and dangerous companion. In fact, his jaded posturings, half pose and half stark reality, prove attractive to others, and he almost manages to seduce Louisa, his employer's wife, in the course of the novel. And why not? There are no standards or values in his empty book. It is surely an irony that his name is Harthouse—for he is clearly a popular figure of the time, a man without a home, a man without a heart.

The conduct of both Emma Woodhouse and James Harthouse results from key moments of self-indulgence, born of frustration, absence of purpose or direction, and tedium; the two aptly demonstrate particularly romantic and modern moments. We get inklings of such outbursts lying just beneath the surface of the emergent individual self in Dryden's figure of Achitophel's "restless turbulence of wit"; in the *Tale of a Tub*'s modern who can write, seemingly interminably, upon nothing, but with his eye fixed upon the audience's mounting proclivities for yawnings and repose; in the *Dunciad*'s finale of the second book, in which Henley's sermons and Blackmore's poetry paralyze everyone with sleep; or in Voltaire's Senator Pococurante in *Candide*, who possesses everything but who (a deviant modern Faustus) is overcome by boredom, revulsion, and fatigue. We are but a step away from the *Langeweile* of Goethe's Werther, who, with nothing to do and nothing that he wants to do, expires in a suicidal vacuum.

Of course, the advent and proliferation of boredom, although a recent and peculiarly modern infestation, are hardly altogether new. The urbane Romans were familiar with an infectious lassitude and restlessness of spirit, taedium vitae, and the Church fathers in the Middle Ages were well acquainted with the sinful attractions of acedia and sloth.[2] But the Renaissance catapults us into the modern era— with its especial susceptibility to a bored and solipsistic exhaustion. The breakdown of a God-centered universe with its Great Chain of Being and the advent of the Baconian inductor and the Cartesian ego as *raisonneur* all shifted man's point of view, placing a new burden upon the "private eye," the singular individual. Both science and Protestantism stressed the self's, the conscience's, central role in the universe, a universe newly emptied of benign or deific companionship.

At the same time (say, in the Elizabethan era), accelerated urbanization increasingly confined "lonely crowds" together in little rooms and narrow thoroughfares. The emergence of the middling class contributed to the establishment of codes of mediocrity and more circumscribed standards of conduct, and the rapid growth of newspapers and transport simply transmitted those standards widely, letting everyone know more and more what they happened to be. The rise of democracies and republics merely "freed" men into the confines of uniformatarian fads, fashions, and popular opinions. The alteration and oscillation of public standards only served to remind the individual of life's instability and ultimately of indeterminacy and relativity.

As a consequence, man opted for the ideal of self-reliance at the same time that the self was insecure, changing, and largely unknown. An urban industrial society bequeathed time a new significance, and man was induced to live, as if a metronome sounded throughout his affairs, in the volatile realm of the present moment—but in a present moment of regimentation. As Lewis Mumford notes, a machine and clock society encourages an intense and extreme "regularity that produces apathy and atrophy—that *acedia* which was the bane of monastic existence, as it is likewise of the army"[3]

All such transitions have been taking effect over the past three or four hundred years with mounting decisiveness. It is small wonder that man's freedom seems constricted, his haste to no purpose, his solitude oppressive, his selfishness mean, his heroism blasted. Hence the modern is an organization man trapped in his own labyrinth, a narcissist stultified by the stunted invariable features he sees in the glass. Hurled inward upon himself and left to his own devices, he presents a case akin to that of the lonely traveler who complained to Socrates that however much he journeyed, he continued being disappointed. Socrates responded tartly: "Of course you're bored when you travel everywhere alone!—Look at the company you keep!"[4] Modern man, by insisting upon leaning on himself, has simply thrown himself off balance and fallen to the floor. Quite rightly, Baudelaire's view of his own romantic, tumultuous, and confused self is of the "Héautontimoroumenos"—the self-tormenting man.[5] The term might suitably apply to all the modern generations.

Reinhard Kuhn's recent study, therefore, of ennui in Western literature, *The Demon of Noontide* (1976), is of the kind long overdue. Yet excellent as Kuhn's book is, it does not particularly stress the nineteenth and twentieth centuries, and the truth is that we have witnessed a boredom explosion in the modern era.[6] Since Descartes, modern man has been motivated to focus upon the self as the apex and assessor of value. With the advent of the era of mass production, time and self have come to be valued insofar as they are made, produced, marketed, developed, manipulated, and sold: "Caught within the formidable pressures of time and the social world, the self is reduced to the status of what it can produce, accomplish, and achieve, or whatever terms may be used to designate this purely instrumental relationship."[7] Hence, in modern mythologies, the individual attempts to read himself into daydream scenarios of task-performance and success stories. It is significant, for instance, that only in the last two centuries have we witnessed the rise of pornography, which posits the male self as infinitely capable of an endless cycle of sexual performance and orgasm. Yet, because he is not a constant, not a perpetual-motion machine, man cannot simply continue indefinitely to be progressive, productive, successful. Therein lies his ultimate frustration and disillusionment: he cannot live up to his private mythopoeic dream, nor will his life unfold with heroic regularity and grandeur.

Rather, his life is a recurrent cycle of hope, anticipation, experience, and disillusionment, as Samuel Johnson repeatedly observed: "We desire, we pursue, we obtain, we are satiated; we desire something else, and begin a new pursuit."[8] His world is constituted, in short, by the paradox of precoital frenzy and postcoital longueur, as Shakespeare affirmed of "lust in action":

> till action, lust
> Is perjured, murderous, bloody, full of blame,
> Savage, extreme, rude, cruel, not to trust;
> Enjoy'd no sooner but despised straight;
> Past reason hunted; and no sooner had,
> Past reason hated.
> . . . .
> Before, a joy proposed; behind, a dream.[9]

Hence alienation, ennui, and despair proliferate. Man has elected to rely upon himself, and he fails to find his chosen topic continuously creative, reliable, or even interesting. As the crux of his modernity, contemporary narcissistic man elects to mate with and to marry himself.[10] Then follows the falling out of love, the sordid marital squabbles, and ultimately the breakup—or the breakdown.

John O. Lyons, in an important study of the self, suggests that the modern creation of a self-conscious, gesturing, melodramatic, and "performing self" emerged fully with the generation maturing in the 1760s.[11] But the modern self-aware individualist revolutionary, self-dependent, self-reflexive, has been taking shape since the Renaissance.[12] With the commencement of the romantic era, he assumes distinctive contours, questing for "spontaneous overflow," for "peaking," and even for orgiastic moments of immediacy and self-realization that all too often collapse into "dejection."[13] William Wordsworth is a case in point; the epic that romantic man aspired to recite features only himself: "A Traveller I am / And all my Tale is of myself."[14] Yet such a devotion and such a quest are destined to come to grief as the lonesome persona flutters and fails and his drama too frequently peters out.

What brought on this disillusion and despair in the romantic era? Curiously, George Steiner has hypothesized that the nineteenth century's "great ennui" was brought on throughout Europe by grand promises and "great expectations" of the French Revolution and by the apparent heroic stature of Napoleon and the excitement of war, troop movements, liberal political promises, change, and altercation that afterward came to nothing, leaving a resounding anticlimax as legacy to the remainder of the century.[15]

Steiner is only partly right: the Revolution did seem to make promises to European man. But the Renaissance also proposed reinvigoration, increased trade with the Orient assured luxuries, the voyagers' new frontiers seemed boundless, the Enlightenment guaranteed light, science assured panaceas, the idea of progress ensured advancement, the *Encyclopedia* prescribed and betokened knowledge. But the manufacturers shipped C.O.D., and their machinery made them fall short in quotas and in delivery. Thereupon commenced a general disillusionment that has deepened and grown more profound during the last two centuries. Promises engendered energetic explosions of anticipation that only became stoppered and suppressed. Hence, as Jacques Barzun remarks, "Byronic melancholy, which is to say almost all nineteenth-century melancholy, had its roots in energy repressed. Ennui, as bored young men have always discovered, is the product of enforced inaction or curbed desire."[16]

Yet, paradoxically, even the revolutionary self's desires were contradictory, negative, and self-destructive. In the nineteenth century, so sure did man become that life could not live up to expectations that we might take Villiers de l'Isle-Adam's drama *Axel* as a kind of archetype. At a key moment the lordly Axel de Auersperg obtains everything—a castle in the Black Forest, youth, vigor, and good looks. To top it off, he finds a fantastic treasure in gold and jewels and a beloved, the Princess Sarah de Maupers. Yet at that instant of realization, he turns his back upon life with high disdain: "Vivre? les serviteurs feront cela pour nous."[17] Let the peons and the domestics do the living, make and clean up the messes; the high soul is above reality, above corporeal existence. At the opposite extreme, and equally as viable, reclines the soporific and exhausted sensibility, damaged by life, as portrayed in Verlaine's "Langueur" (1883): "The lonely soul is sick at heart with impenetrable ennui."[18] In both cases, the self's suffering the torments of life is simultaneously exhibited with perverse pride as the artist's medallion and disease.

In fact, so conventional among the French poets became the reaction against life and hostility toward the bourgeoisie that it is the hallmark of art in nineteenth-century France.[19] André Gide observed that

"The major grievance against [the symbolist school] is its lack of curiosity concerning life . . . all of them were pessimists, self-abnegators, defeatists, 'bored with the gloomy hospital' [Mallarmé] that was for them our country (I mean: the world), 'monotonous and unjust,' as Laforgue said. For them, poetry became a refuge, their only haven from hideous reality"[20]

In the eighteenth and nineteenth centuries that disappointment was largely individual and private. The great romantic heroes—Goethe's Werther, Rousseau's confessional self, Chateaubriand's René, Sénancour's Obermann, Byron's Manfred, Sainte-Beuve's Joseph Delorme, Flaubert's Frédéric Moreau—all withdraw into the cradle of the self where they suffer acute mental torment, lassitude, and debilitation.[21] Only once in his career did Baudelaire attempt to exorcise such haunting personal guides: "Vanish therefore, false shades of René, of Obermann, and of Werther; flee into the haze of the void, monstrous creations of indolence and isolation; like the swine in the Lake of Gennesaret, go, plunge back into the enchanted forests from whence the fairy-tale enemies dragged you, sheep assaulted by romantic giddiness. The genius of action no longer allows you to dwell amongst us."[22]

But "the genius of action" does not prevail, and, like Hamlet, the poet retreats again into the world of hesitation, contemplation, self-contradiction, and bad dreams.[23] That is the *mal du siécle*, as Ruskin once confirmed: "On the whole, these are much *sadder* ages than the early ones; not sadder in a noble and deep way, but in a dim wearied way,—the way of ennui, and jaded intellect, and uncomfortableness of soul and body. The Middle Ages had their wars and agonies, but also intense delights. Their gold was dashed with blood; but ours is sprinkled with dust."[24]

Thus we are faced with the paradox that the intensely energetic nineteenth century, a period given over to the most daring explorations of self, discovered only decadence, decay, inertia, controversion, and loss of self. In any event, the remainder of the century witnessed the creation of great archetypal figures self-tormented by indolence and despairing fatigue. Here are the clear tones of Kierkegaard: "I do not care for anything. I do not care to ride, for the exercise is too violent. I do not care to walk, walking is too stenuous. I do not care to lie down, for I should either have to remain lying, and I do not care to do that, or I should have to get up again, and I do not care to do that either. *Summa summarum:* I do not care at all."[25]

"I do not care at all": these words ought to remind us of the triumphantly placid denial of Herman Melville's Bartleby: "I would prefer not to." They poignantly represent the individual's total withdrawal from society into the self. Huysmans's Des Esseintes, in *A Rebaurs* (1884), is a similar naysayer, the pale aesthete who turns night into day and contracts his sensibility until it quivers alone in his own apartments amid a detritus of odors, liquors, manuscripts, and flowers. Pater too addresses ideal sensualists, who are enjoined at the close of *Studies in the History of the Renaissance* (1873) to "burn with a hard gemlike flame"; but they might well burn themselves up. That is precisely the case with the notorious Oblomov, the title figure in Goncharov's 1859 novel; he simply withdraws vacuously and deliriously like an infant to a sofa and defies the realms of society and of time.[26] Still more invidious is the fate of Dostoevsky's renowned Underground Man, who burrows to the center of wretchedness to guarantee a specious, isolated, and imprisoned "freedom." And, not among the least, there is in James's "The Beast in the Jungle" (1903) John Marcher, a man who "marches" nowhere, who sacrifices his entire life egomaniacally to "waiting" and "watching" for the advent of his life, his destiny. But his destiny was to discover that he was moribund, defunct, a man without a destiny or a life. So much may be said for the avatars of the romantic self. The nineteenth century tracked the elusive self to its lair, and the beast that he proved to be was a poor, bare, forked, unaccommodated creature indeed.

When we turn to the great modernist writers of the present century, we encounter much of the same patterns of behavior—not only intensified but also expanded to include the authors themselves. Edmund Wilson remarked this expansion and this paradox in which (in Oscar Wilde's terms from "The Critic as Artist") life imitates art:

The heroes of the Symbolists would rather drop out of the common life than have to struggle to make themselves a place in it. . . . And the heroes of the contemporary writers . . . are in general as uncompromising . . . sometimes, indeed, the authors themselves seem almost to have patterned their lives on the mythology of the earlier generation: the Owen Aherne and the Michael Robartes of Yeats, with their lonely towers and mystic chambers, their addiction to the hermetic philosophy—and Yeats himself, with his astrology and spiritualism, his own reiterated admonitions . . . of the inferiority of the life of action to the life of solitary vision: Paul Valéry's M. Teste, sunken also in solitary brooding . . . and Teste's inventor, the great poet who can hardly bring himself to explain why he cannot bring himself to write poetry; the ineffectual fragmentary imagination, the impotence and resignation, of the poet of "Gerontion" and "The Waste Land"; the supine and helpless hero of "A la Recherche du Temps Perdu," with his application of prodigious intellectual energy to differentiating the emotions and sensations which arise from his passive contacts with life and with his preference for lying in bed by himself and worrying about Albertine's absences to getting up and taking her out—Proust himself, who put into practice the regime which Huysmans had invented for his hero, keeping his shutters closed by day and exercising his sensibility by night . . . Joyce's Bloom, with his animated consciousness and his inveterate ineptitude; Joyce's new hero [H.C. Earwicker] who surpasses even the feats of sleeping of Proust's narrator and M. Teste by remaining asleep through an entire novel; and Gertrude Stein who has withdrawn into herself more completely, who has spun herself a more impenetrable cocoon.[27]

In all such literature, authors and characters now participate, and Wilson detects a "sullenness, a lethargy, a sense of energies ingrown and sometimes festering." Moreover, he suggests that philosophers, mathematicians, and scientists reflect a similar "metaphysical hypertrophy," which he attributes to the general social and political environment.[28]

If anything, the spectrum of boredom in the twentieth century has been deliberately broadened well beyond the individual, so that major works scrutinize an entire exhausted society. As might be expected, such works are devised by the satirists. Thomas Mann's *Buddenbrooks* (1901), for example, surveys three generations of a family in decline and disintegration; increased aesthetic sensibility simply spells degeneration and extinction for the clan. Céline, in *Voyage au bout del la nuit* (1932), depicts an entire society of haunted, lost, indifferent individuals wandering aimlessly in the streets, seeking withdrawal, passivity, and isolation. Antonio Machado, in "Del passado efimero" (ca. 1912), depicts all of Spain as listless and impersonal, worn out, hypochondriacal, and unrepresentative:

> boredom; . . .
> This man is neither of yesterday nor of tomorrow,
> but of never; of Spanish stock,
> he is neither ripe not rotten,
> he is barren fruit.[29]

In the brilliant novel *Der Mann ohne Eigenschaften* (1930–42), Robert Musil portrays all of Austrian society idly and blindly "waiting for the end." As the whole world swings interminably and irrevocably toward world war, the Austrians blissfully plan a "Collateral Campaign" to honor the Jubilee year of the emperor Franz-Joseph in 1918—the year that will rather witness the destruction of Austria. In addition, the campaign will celebrate the leader as "the Emperor of Peace"—only moments away from total war. Ulrich and his entire society are conceived as listless, blind, detached. Appropriately, the responsibility for the planned honors is situated in a committee, and we witness the most beautifully stultifying motions and bureaucratic pseudoactivity drummed up incessantly, leading the committee nowhere at all.

In a recent review, Frederick Karl proposes that perhaps Kafka can better serve as exemplar of the modern age than Joyce since in the broadest sense Kafka's created universe projects a world enormous, allegorically vague, lost, unknown, confusing in its representation of time and space. Kafka certainly conveys the larger complexities that preoccupy twentieth-century man: randomness, indeterminacy, the sinister Freudian libido and unconscious, his animal addiction to aggression, relativity, sweeping paranoia, and preoccupation with decay.[30] Somehow, Kafka's "Hunger Artist" (1931) and "Metamorphosis" (1937) strikingly represent the dilemmas of the modern everyman. Gregor Samsa as insignificant clerk turns into insect and spends the remainder of his life in bed—(a drudge's paradise). But his alienation, confinement, decay, and subsequent death are a dehumanized torment. And similarly, the hunger artist is the perfect absurdist representative of negative achievement: the crowning glory of his art is inactivity, nonperformance, and this total abstinence is practiced in a cage. Paradoxically, the triumph of his "art" is simultaneous and synonymous with his self-destruction. But the fickle public has turned to other fashions and knows nothing of the artist's senseless nugatory passion for repression. So it is throughout Kafka's oeuvre: all his protagonists are mysteriously on trial, convicted, and passively unresisting, carted away.

As we move further and further into our own century and as our topic widens its sphere, we observe how many literary works become preoccupied with almost a total existential and surrealistic absurdity, dealing with *la nausée* in a mad, tedious, Sisyphean world from which there is no exit: "We have at last arrived at 'the age of assassins' which the poet Rimbaud predicted."[31] The literary realm reflects disaster with a vaudevillean panache, as is certified in Heller's *Catch-22*, Grass's *Tin Drum*, and the novels of Hawkes, Barth, García Márquez, and Pynchon. A whole genre of antiutopian or dystopian novels has grown up in this century presenting the destruction of society and even of the planet.[32] Science fiction too features an important strain of satiric novels, dramatizing absurdity and destruction at the planetary, galactic, and universal levels.[33] All this cataclysmic fiction is offered in the ho-hum manner, exaggerating frivolous Laforguian humor and irony to a fanastic degree. Seizing upon ideas in science, writers also utilize all the pessimistic concepts available—survival of the fittest, probability theory, indeterminacy, relativity, entropy—so that much literature pictures an exhausted universe unwinding and running down.[34] For "contrary to the confidence in our powers of technology and information, the prevailing image of man we find in modern art is one of impotence, uncertainty, and self-doubt."[35]

In such an atmosphere a thinker like E.M. Cioran goes further than Sartre and Camus: "Toute expérience capitale est néfaste." For him only two intellectual positions are tenable: if a man has any faith or hope, he is a fanatic, willing to turn violent and run mad. On the other hand, if he sees destroying time and the sinking world for what they are, he confronts the void and the spectacle of ennui: "Boredom reveals to us an eternity that is not the surpassing of time but its ruin; it is the infinity of putrid souls lacking in superstitions: an absolute plateau where nothing any longer hinders things from running smoothly to their own downfall."[36]

Surely the most remarkable artist dramatizing universal ennui and entropy after midcentury is Samuel Beckett. His fictions are chock-full of static, crippled, and abandoned creatures confined in rooms, cells, barrels, cans. Murphy is forever secreted in his rocking chair; Malone perennially lies prone, stretched out flat, as if for sleep or death. His inactivity leads to his dissipation, disintegration into nothingness. We recollect the endless figurative postures of waiting of Beckett's eternal denizens in *Waiting for Godot* (1952) that dramatize an almost fabulous torpitude. And we watch *Molloy* (1950), as the protagonist exhaustedly "listens" and hears that in the universe "all wilts and yields"; he hears "a world collapsing endlessly, a frozen world."[37] With Beckett we are almost at the outer extremity of universal catastrophe and immobility.

If we were to reduce our topic to farcical absurdity, we could incorporate it, as Donald Barthelme does, into a house of cards, a universe of games. The narrator of one of his stories is the perfect gamesman: he plays "Password, Twister, Breakthru, Bonanza, Stratego, Squander, and Gambit. And Quinto, Phlounder, Broker, Tactics, and Stocks & Bonds." He plays with Amanda:

"These games are marvelous," Amanda said. "I like them especially because they are so meaningless and boring, and trivial. These qualities, once regarded as less than desirable, are now everywhere enthroned as the key elements in our psychological lives, as reflected in the art of the period as well as—"

"Yes," I said. Then we played: . . . *Crise du Cinéma* . . . Zen Zen . . . Break the Ball . . . After the Ball Is Over. . . .

"Games are the enemies of beauty, truth, and sleep," Amanda said. The brandy was almost gone.

"There remains one more game."

"What is it?"

"Ennui," I said. "The easiest of all. No rules, no boards, no equipment."

"What is Ennui?" Amanda asked, setting it up for me.

"Ennui is the absence of games," I said, "the modern world at its most vulnerable."[38]

So it is, in an entropic world of Last Mohicans, last laughs, last tangos in Paris: not the bang, but the "whimper" that T.S. Eliot believed would splinter the world. It is more deadly now than it was in the nineteenth century, when Baudelaire looked for a personal yawn to swallow up creation.[39] For it has spread to the masses, has incorporated whole societies, and promises a much more infernal type of demolition. In 1978, in accordance with the trend among public relations experts and other high-minded U.S. officials of emphasizing holidays and spreading optimism, one could have observed that July 15-21 was officially designated "National Avoid Boredom Week." It is moot, however, to observe that bureaucracy will never be able to eradicate ennui from the modern world. Whether we like it or not, boredom looks as if it is here to stay.

11
Scatology

Ennui may be unpleasant, but it is mild enough as a subject and usually bearable. The fecal matter of bowels and bowls, however, is more unsavory and offensive, and in polite society it is treated as forbidden knowledge. For that reason, the satirist cheerfully opens the privy door and herds us in. And of course we do not wish in the slightest to wet our feet. Therefore, satire's business has ever been, where angels fear to tread, to inaugurate the unwary human reader's total immersion. Further, in the twentieth century, satire goes to even greater lengths to see that such unsavory matter is nicely compacted and heavily compounded. What is satirically grotesque about such a subject is obvious: proud, self-delusional man ever aspires to elevate himself and his dignity, whereas the satirist destroys such upward mobility by reducing man to defecating animal before our eyes.

Aldous Huxley once contemptuously remarked that characters in Henry James's novels appeared so genteel that one doubted whether they were capable of going to the bathroom.[1] But in most genres—epic, romance, tragedy, even comedy—no one ever does. Knights and private eyes, underdogs and overlords, kings and counselors rarely find time in fiction to eat, let alone secrete. The heroic and the middling modes endorse gentility; traditional decorum requires a moratorium upon topics intestinal or matters anal.

Indeed, the etiquette of polite society has always demanded restraint on a broad number of topics, particularly religion, politics, and sex. Alice and Kenneth Hamilton speak rather priggishly of sex, religion, and art as "the Three Great Secret Things," and Francis Bacon cautions against a too-great levity in conversation: "As for jest, there be certain things which ought to be privileged from it; namely, religion, matters of state, great persons, any man's present business of importance, and any case that deserveth pity."[2]

We must concede, however, that the erstwhile heroes of satire are not only slain, like St. George, by their dragons, but they are also afflicted by questionable smells and very bad taste.[3] Every satirist

Scatology 117

moves at once to break up furniture and to break in upon mores and conventions. Accordingly, religion, politics, and sexuality are the primary stuff of literary satire. Among these sacred targets, matters costive and defecatory play an important part. For what society normally considers low and sordid, as rhyparographic, are more frequently excretory than sexual. Many a man is willing to boast of his sexual prowess and caprice, but he is distinctly unwilling to tender public pronouncements about the size of his feces, the shape of his intestinal disorders, or the stature of his last bout with diarrhea. A man might be willing to look into another man's sex life, but not into his stool. To be sure, the "odors" of sweat, urine, and manure coalesce to confer upon the evacuatory portion of our privy lives the more objectional flavor. One critic conjectures that the word *smell* implies "bad smell," and society unites to repudiate stinks, owing to polite civilization's "cultural repudiation of decaying substances." Ladies and gentlemen do not discourse upon dung, just as the *Christian Science Monitor* does not mention death. In any event, satirists have ever been prompted to lure the unwary reader into the latrine, to force him to contemplate what one author fetchingly designates "the alvine dejections" of society. Augustan satirists, for instance, repeatedly invoked these unpleasant realities, as several recent studies have shown.[4]

Yet the satirist has had to pay a certain price for his lavatory strategies and manipulations. Swift's Celia poems have earned him the slander of literary critics and the almost prurient interest (and condescension) of psychoanalysts. And Swift has been dubbed as suffering from "the excremental vision," and even supposedly intelligent fellow satirists (who should know better), like Thackeray and Huxley, have openly rebuked him.[5] So seriously does society guard the portals of its private throne room that it will call the satirist sick, perverted, or even mad, for his spying at the keyhole or prying at the lock. One comic volume hardly misrepresents the "niceties" of advertising "tastes" on television.

Toilet cleansers: Demonstrations of toilet cleansers must not show a shot of a lavatory pan, but a toilet cleanser may be shown on a bathroom window ledge or being held above the actual toilet. This should not reveal any part of the toilet itself.
Toilet paper: Care should be taken when showing toilet rolls. They should not be shown installed.[6]

Precisely because of this continual fastidiousness, society is vulnerable to the satirist, who, more often than not, will plunge us up to our nostrils in curiously questionable and unpleasant fecal matter. He may have to pay for his aggressiveness by being slandered and misunderstood, but he nonetheless achieves several of his purposes—to rivet the attention, to shock, and to move his audience. The satirist may offend, but it is worth it. He frequently obtains a degree of power in his writing, and at his best, he will continue to be read. Hundreds have maligned Swift, but millions have read him. Camus once observed that "art can never be so well served as by a negative thought." Indeed, the ugly and the negative are, according to the satirist's prescription, mysteriously transmogrified into the affirmative. In Pope's words, "There is a real beauty in an easy, pure, perspicuous description even of a low action."[7]

As a matter of fact, from the earliest times, satirists have utilized scatological and bathroom humor. Aristophanes, always livid and nearly scandalous in his religious, political, and sexual references, is especially overt in *The Clouds*, which teems with imagery of sexual perversion and the "bum." Catullus debunks the vapid writings of Volusius as *cacata charta*, "shit paper."[8] Horace concludes *Satire* 1.8 with a "victory" of the god Priapus over the witch Canidia, as his wooden statue "cracks," emitting a wonderful wooden fart that frightens the witches away. Petronius portrays that virtual Hercules of the uncouth nouveau riche, Trimalchio, as one who, when playing volleyball, has slaves ostentatiously bearing a silver chamber pot for him to piss in. Later, at his protracted and almost sickening *cena*, he himself disappears in the midst of the courses, only to return, giving intimate details to the guests while they are eating concerning the status of his bowels and their particular disorders. The satirist Martial informs Ligurra that he is beneath Martial's satire or even notice. Instead, some basement and sottish poet is more suitable to scroll Ligurra's infamy—on the walls of a *cacantes*, or latrine.[9] In the age-old tradition of the paradoxical encomium, Francesco Berni (1497?–1535) writes a "chapter" of verses celebrating the urinal.[10] Sir John Harrington's well-known work *A Discourse on a Stale Subject, Called the Metamorphosis of Ajax* (1596) is half-way between a learned treatise proposing a new species of flush toilet and a vindictive Menippean satire. John Dryden's satire of Tom Shadwell in "MacFlecknoe" slowly reduces his corpulent victim to a vast pile of manure:

No *Persian* Carpets spread th' Imperial way,
But scatter'd Limbs of mangled Poets lay:
From dusty shops neglected Authors come,
Martyrs of Pies, and Reliques of the Bum.
Much *Heywood, Shirly, Ogleby* there lay,
But loads of *Sh*—— almost choakt the way.[11]

Major satirists have never, in fact, permitted us to forget the workings of the emunctories. Rabelais records how the youthful Gargantua, aged five, demonstrates his "genius" by his thorough research in the appropriate "means of wiping his bum." Like a good experimental scientist run slightly amok, he has tried everything—rose leaves, dill, beets, sheets, nettles, curtains, cushions, rugs, rags, cabbage, straw, oakum, wool, pillow, basket, slipper, hen, rooster, legal briefcase, coif-and-feathers. He concludes, learnedly, that nothing excels the neck of a plump and downy goose. Later, in one of the great urinary scenes of fiction, the gigantic Gargantua, arriving in Paris and surrounded by stupid, gaping Parisians, urinates so furiously and plenteously that he drowns 260,418 citizens, not counting women and children.

With Rabelais doubtless in mind, Swift permits his Lemuel Gulliver, in the land of the Lilliputians, to roll upon his side and make water that to the tiny natives appears to be a "torrent which fell with such noise and violence" about them. Subsequently, in the land of Brobdingnagian giants, the now insignificant Gulliver punctiliously insists upon removing himself "about two hundred yards" from his gigantic owners, hiding himself between two sorrel leaves to move his bowels. Surely such excessive care is unnecessary, for he is not bigger than an insect and perfectly obscure. But, true to form, Gulliver continues to overestimate his own importance and commences, like the typical voyager, to give a minute account of the proceedings and to defend his circumstantial details—even to the point of recording bowel movements: "I hope the gentle reader will excuse me for dwelling on these and the like particulars, which, however insignificant they may appear to grovelling vulgar minds, yet will certainly help a philosopher to enlarge his thoughts and imagination, and apply them to the benefit of public as well as private life, which was my sole design in presenting this and other accounts of my travels to the world; wherein I have been chiefly studious of truth." It was Swift's later account of Yahoos as vicious and savage beasts (in human figure) who discharge their excrements from trees upon passers-by that earned him the enmity of so many immaculate Victorian minds. Alexander Pope's *Dunciad*, wherein Edmund Curll fishes Cloacina's "nether realms for Wit," is similarly remarkable for the urination contest. Curll sends upward the highest stream, winning a hero's victory.[13]

Nor are the novelists in the least immune from what might be appropriately termed "chamberpottery." Fielding and Smollett represent innumerable instances of flying jordans and overturning piss pots in *Joseph Andrews* and *Roderick Random*. And in *Humphry Clinker*, a novel in which backsides are exposed as frequently as possible in reason, when people at Hot Well complained of the mud and slime beneath the pump room caused by the river at low ebb, Dr. Deitrich Linden steps forth, conducting "a learned [and tasteful] investigation of the nature of stink." Ultimately, the sage doctor concludes by praising stench: "Stercoraceous flavour, condemned by prejudice as a stink, was, in fact, most agreeable to the organs of smelling; for, that every person who pretended to nauseate the smell of another's excretions, snuffed up his own with particular complacency; for the truth of which he appealed to all the ladies and gentlemen then present." He himself, "when he happened to be low-spirited, or fatigued with business, found immediate relief and uncommon satisfaction from hanging over the stale contents of a close-stool, while his servant stirred it about under his nose."[14]

James Joyce is likewise interested in the secrets of pungent effluvia. In addition to his *Chamber Music*, verses obviously intended to be heard with a decided tinkle, he provides one of the more memorable outhouse scenes in literature when his Leopold Bloom spends a chapter meditating in the privy. As a matter of fact, Joyce had the annoying habit in pubs of leaping up and dashing into the lavatory himself—to record "epiphanies" that his friends' conversation randomly provided: "He recorded under 'Epiphany' any showing forth of the mind by which he considered one gave oneself away."[15]

If the bathroom and the outhouse have borne a portion of vital satiric tradition over the centuries, does it survive into the twentieth? Despite some prognostications that ours is an age too vicious or effete to produce satire, we are bound to discover that it is not so.[16] In 1957 Kingsley Amis predicted that "we are in for a golden age of satire."[17] But our century has ever been a fine one for satire, and I suspect that it will be considered in future as having been a great satiric era. A brief survey of selected instances of modern satirists' uses of the toilet might help to make this more clear.

With a kind of placid, humorous inevitability, indecorum infiltrates most modern satires. Evelyn Waugh's Mrs. Algernon Stitch, in her black minicar, suavely observes a man she believes she knows who ducks into a London building. With her car she promptly follows, bounding tidily down a flight of stairs until she comes to rest in a gentlemen's public lavatory. Quite a crowd begins to gather. " 'I can't think what you're all making such a fuss about,' she said. 'It's simply a case of mistaken identity.' " Accidents will happen, especially in satire. In Ionesco's *Bald Soprano*, in the same accidental fashion, chamber pots commence appearing. Mary, the maid, returns to the Smith home after an afternoon off. Casual and slightly rude upon any occasion, she announces to her employers, for no reason, "I bought me a new chamberpot."[18]

Humbert Humbert in Nabokov's *Lolita* is tortured by the same fortuitous infringements of the unexpected. Having, he had hoped, effectually drugged his Lolita at the Enchanted Hunters Hotel, he now awaits his chance to fondle and make free with her insensitive body. She appears not drugged in the least, however, and Humbert must toss all night, a vampire without a prize. During his vigil, the noises of gracious American living become markedly noticeable. Elevators clap and rattle; cheerful partners in the corridors chatter. "When that stopped, a toilet immediately north of my cerebellum took over. It was a manly, energetic, deep-throated toilet, and it was used many times. Its gurgle and gush and long afterflow shook the wall behind me. Then someone in a southern direction was extravagantly sick, almost coughing out his life with his liquor, and his toilet descended like a veritable Niagara, immediately beyond our bathroom."[19] Here, at the long-awaited climax of his sexual intriguing, the sensitive-souled rapist is appalled by the teeming machinery of vulgar, materialist America. We, the taut readers, are coerced into quivering and flushing with him, all the way.

Most blatant and overt, of course, as might be expected, is Samuel Beckett. Bound not at all by the Jamesian ethic that Huxley rebuked, Beckett pointedly interrupts his famous *Waiting for Godot*, assaulting dramatic continuity after the manner of Aristophanes, by having Vladimir suddenly bolt from the stage to relieve himself.[20] Toiletries in modern literature, in short, are everywhere. In Golding's *Lord of the Flies*, the young intellectual, Piggie, is beset by weakness: he is fat, wears glasses, and has asthma—and diarrhea. But in this last, he is not unique; in the tropical climate, all the boys, subsisting upon fruits, are diarrhetic. And the sure sign that "things are breaking up" and "going rotten" in their pitiful demicivilization is evidenced by the collapse of toilet training. Ralph tries to warn them.

"We chose those rocks right along beyond the bathing-pool as a lavatory. That was sensible too. The tide cleans the place up. You littluns know about that. . . . Now people seem to use anywhere. Even near the shelters and the platform. . . . That's dirty."

Laughter rose again.[21]

Shortly, the whole fabric of this tenuous pseudosociety will come toppling down. Cleanliness may not be next to godliness, but its reverse, in *Lord of the Flies*, is virtually infernal.

Indeed, the pressing requirements of the bowel and the bowl, the satirist is quick to note, emerge as a lowest common denominator. In George Stewart's *Doctor's Oral*, Joe Grantland, after a grueling hour in his English Ph.D. examination, finds himself given a five-minute recess. Joe dashes to the john. All the professors, despite their hauteur and even malice, follow galvanically after. As they all stand like cattle in a row before the urinary trough, Joe suddenly reflects: "In spite of everything, these professors weren't so different from him after all. In fact at one moment Joe and four of them were standing up side by side, separated only by inch-and-a-half slabs of marble. Here was democracy for you! 'Each in his separate stall.' "[22] Here is a particularly complacent kind of urinalysis that envisions the stool as the great leveler of mankind. Lenny Bruce, for one, was tired of the pretense that it wasn't.

I know intellectually there's nothing wrong with going to the toilet, but I can't go to the toilet in front of you. The worst sound in the world is when the toilet-flush noise finishes before I do.

If I'm at your house, I can never say to you, "Excuse me, where's the toilet?" I have to get hung up with that corrupt facade of "Excuse me, where's the little boys' room?"

"Oh, you mean the tinkle-dinkle ha-ha room, where they have sachets and cough drops and pastels?"

"That's right, I wanna shit in the cough-drop box."[23]

Of course, much twentieth-century literature continues earlier chamberpottery—comedy and games and spilt milk in the bathroom. Such is the case with Portnoy's poor father, Jack. Like Smollett's Matt Bramble before him, Jack is comedy's costive man: he's constipated, but good. He has not moved his bowels in a week. Incessantly he sits forlornly, upon the can, while Mamma shouts encouragement in to him from the sidelines. " 'Look, I'm trying to move my bowels,' he replies. 'Don't I have enough trouble as it is without people screaming at me when I'm trying to move my bowels?' "[24] As he repeatedly emerges from his duty, Sophie ever inquires:

"You, did you move your bowels?"
"Of course I didn't move my bowels."
"Jack, what is it going to be with you, with those bowels?"
"They're turning into concrete, that's what it's going to be."[25]

Withholding man is ever the same, this constricted father—ever sleeping nights, while sitting (and waiting) on the can.

The chamberpottery is more overflowing in Donleavy's *The Ginger Man*, in which the comedy resides in discharging fecal matter upon others. Sebastian Dangerfield's second-floor toilet pipe collapses as he is contributing his morning oblation. Alas, his wife Marion is on the first floor, directly beneath. She screams, and he hastens to descend.

"You idiot, Sebastian, look at me, look at the baby's things."

Marion trembling in the middle of the kitchen floor covered with strands of wet toilet paper and fecal matter. From a gaping patch in the ceiling poured water, plaster and excrement.

"God's miserable teeth."[26]

Similar mishaps befall Ebenezer Cooke in Barth's *The Sot-Weed Factor*, which is about a naïf who illustrates the comical man who befouls himself. In Plymouth, Eben, the innocent would-be poet, is beset by two coarse, gruff men, Captain Scurry and Captain Slye. Threatened with destruction, with no one at hand to save him, Eben's "legs and sphincters both betrayed him; unble to say on, he sank with wondrous odor to his knees and buried his face in the seat of his chair." In a trice, the noble laureate of Maryland besmirches himself and becomes a "stinkard." Later in the novel, cowardice and malaise serve Captain John Cook ill in his "Secret History." His men having drunk foul water, all, aboard ship in the Nanticoke River, "grewe wondrous grip'd of there bowells, and loose of there bladders, & took a weakness of there reins," so that they are soon all beshat. They toss their pants overboard and expose "there bummes" over the gunwales, that they might discharge themselves into the sea.[27] Their disorder lasts for days. Only the stupendous and corpulent Sir Henry Burlingame restrains himself. Then, as they are about to step ashore one day, with the men farting and Burlingame trembling with his need for relief, they are attacked by Indians. Burlingame was first upon the bow-sprit, ready to step ashore, but the sight of the natives attacking terminates his days of resolve and constraint.

The Salvages giving out with terrible whoops & hollowings, did so smite with fear this Burlingame, that at last he forewent entire the hold of his reins, and standing yet in our prowe like unto an uglie figure-head, he did let flie the treasure he had been those severall daies a-hoarding. It was my ill fortune to be hard behind him, and moreover, crowch'd down beneath his mightie bumme. . . . I was in a trice beshitt, so much so, that I cd by no meanes see out of my eyes, or speake out of my mouth.[28]

Poor Smith, in the aftermath, slipping in the sewage, topples ashore, and the Indians successfully capture the entire crew. No better debunking of "true history" is more grossly portrayed, beset, and bemired than that perpetrated here.

And lastly, satire of the chamber pot is equally well employed to interrupt the determined lover. In Hawkes's *The Cannibal*, Ernst Snow, the deformed, half-crazed duelist and coward, falls frenetically in love with Stella, the general's daughter. Although she is riding home with another gentleman on the first evening Ernst meets her, he is puffed up with ideals of Germanic heroism, love-lust, and the state and commences to race madly after her carriage. The romantic quest is wonderfully undercut, for Ernst must pause to piss. "He felt that his belt would burst, and so, just before reaching the line of Heroes, he stopped in the park. He thought that his mother would see, would stand looking at him in the dark, so he pushed behind the foliage, behind a bush that scratched at his fumbling hands. The rain became stronger and stronger and still he was rooted behind the bush."[29] Never was romantic lover so cruelly retarded and disrupted.

Not merely ancient heroes and romantic suitors are driven to seek necessary relief. The same fate befalls modern Wall Street bankers and investors. In Tom Wolfe's *The Bonfire of the Vanities*, the ace bond trader Sherman McCoy is expected to be so busy on the trading floor that he barely can find the time to excrete. And indeed, when McCoy (a self-styled master of the universe) wishes to glance at the newspaper (containing news of a growing scandal about himself), his only recourse is repeatedly to smuggle the paper (folded inside a manilla business envelope) covertly into one of the bathroom stalls: the only place in modern industry and business where one can be alone, to take a—peek.[30]

Yet the satirist utilizes bathhouse and scatological humor to serve purposes that go beyond chamberpottery, beyond the merely comic, debunking, and anticlimactic. Toilet humor at this higher level becomes more bizarre, more far-fetched, more fantastic. An element of the grotesque is added, and the bathroom parodies and exposes many facets of human folly and vice, well beyond simple constipation, cowardice, mischance, and melodramatic passion. Here bodily function, the daily necessities of nature, and the toilet itself become symbols and analogs, like the Roman *cena* or massive dining room feast, for the broader concerns and larger failings of men.[31] It is almost suitable, in this more comprehensive context, that the bathroom becomes colored and distorted by features of lunacy and nightmare.

Alan Sillitoe perfectly illustrates the commencement of the bathroom scene's transformation to the comic unknown. Michael Callen is a nondescript Nottingham bastard, now in London and utterly devoted to the British concept of "getting on." At length, he is recruited by a smuggling ring, and his job, in an overcoat superhumanly overladen with gold bricks, is to stroll past the inspectors at the airport and to fly gold out of the country.

My legs and shoulders were aching from too much weight . . . and . . . I had to go to the lavatory. . . . all was not well, because when I had finished, I couldn't get up. The coat hung around me like a cloak of rock. In one way I didn't want to get up, but to sit there and muse in my own stink till someone found me, or [until I got caught].

I stayed a minute on my knees, hands resting on the rim of the toilet. It was had to move from this position, but at least I was mobile, because even if I got no more upright than this I'd be able to shuffle across the departure hall and up the plane steps on my knees, giving out that I was on a pilgrimage to my favourite saint's shrine. . . . No, that wouldn't do, so I crawled around the wall and back again. This hadn't been part of the training. . . . I was on top of the toilet now, and by a quick but risky flip backwards my feet hit the ground in the right place, and I was shaken but standing, just as the number of my plane was announced as departing from Gate Number Thirteen. I fastened my trousers, then the coat, picked up my briefcase, and was on my way to the pressurized unknown.[32]

Beyond such such criminal comedy lies the pathological. Nathanael West's Miss Lonelyhearts discovers homosexuality in the toilet. He is perfectly capable of an eerie ambivalence, suffering (Christ-like) for the sorrows of the world and yet vituperative (Shrike-like) with violence and revenge. He has been drinking whiskey at a speakeasy with Ned Gates. Together in the late snowy winter night, they stagger through a park and into its lonely "comfort station."

An old man was sitting on one of the toilets. The door of this booth was propped open and he was sitting on the turned-down toilet cover.
Gates hailed him. "Well, well, smug as a bug in a rug, eh?"
The old man jumped with fright, but finally managed to speak. "What do you want? Please let me alone." His voice was like a flute; it did not vibrate.
"If you can't get a woman, get a clean old man," Gates sang.
The old man looked as if he were going to cry, but suddenly laughed instead. A terrible cough started under his laugh, and catching at the bottom of his lungs, it ripped into his throat. He turned away to wipe his mouth.[33]

Ruthlessly, Gates and Miss Lonelyhearts pull the old man out of his stall and drag him, giggling with terror, to an Italian bar. Increasingly they bully him, professing to be noted psychiatrists determined to expose his "homosexualistic tendencies." Ultimately, the old man, stiff with effeminate propriety, rebukes them, and they become violent: in a rage, the men determine to beat their aged victim.

Monomaniacal, too, is Alexander Portnoy. From the age of thirteen onward, he uses the bathroom, not futilely as his father had, but as the setting for orgies of masturbation. "Then came adolescence—half my waking life spent locked behind the bathroom door, firing my wad down the toilet bowl, or into the soiled clothes in the laundry hamper, or *splat*, up against the medicine-chest mirror, before which I stood in my dropped drawers so I could see how it looked coming out."[34] He abuses himself with sock, brassiere, apple, milk bottle.

If only I could cut down to one hand-job a day, or hold the line at two, or even three! But . . . I actually began to set new records for myself. Before meals. After meals. *During* meals. Jumping up from the dinner table, I tragically clutch at my belly—diarrhea! I cry, I have been stricken with diarrhea!—and once behind the locked bathroom door, slip [out] a pair of underpants that I have stolen from my sister's dresser. . . . So galvanic is the effect of cotton panties . . . that the trajectory of my ejaculation reaches startling new heights: leaving my joint like a rocket it makes right for the light bulb overhead, where to my wonderment and horror, it hits and it hangs. Wildly in the first moment I cover my head, expecting an explosion of glass, a burst of flames—disaster, you see, is never far from my mind. . . . I am the Raskolnikov of jerking off— the sticky evidence is everywhere![35]

Yet newer, dizzying heights are still to be attained.

Well, [one] afternoon I came home from school to find my mother out of the house, and our refrigerator stocked with a big purplish piece of raw liver. . . . I believe that I have already confessed to the piece of liver that I bought in a butcher shop and banged behind a billboard on the way to a bar mitzvah lesson. Well, I wish to make a clean breast of it, Your Holiness. That—she— it—wasn't my first piece. My first piece I had in the privacy of my own home, rolled round my cock in the bathroom at three-thirty—and then had again on the end of a fork, at five-thirty, along with the other members of that poor innocent family of mine.

So. Now you know the worst thing I have ever done. I fucked my own family's dinner.[36]

The roué Piet Hanema, in Updike's *Couples*, who has slept with nearly every eligible woman in Tarbox, advances to newer goals at one of the group parties. He steals into the bathroom behind the newly delivered mother Foxy Whitman, with whom he has been having an affair. She finishes using the toilet, and then he pees. They have been wanting to see one another for weeks. "You're mad to be in here." she exclaims, but Piet is heedless, resolute.

"Wait. Please. Let me see your breasts.
"They're all milky."
"I know. Just for a moment. Please. I do need it." They listened for steps on the stairs; there were none. . . . Her mouth opened and her tongue, red as sturgeon, touched her upper lip as she reached behind her to undo snaps. Her gown and bra peeled down in a piece. Fruit.

"Oh. God."
She blushed. . . . "I feel so gross."
"So veiny and full. So hard at the tops, here."
"Don't get them started. I must go home in an hour."
"And nurse . . . nurse me."
"Oh darling. No."
"Nurse me."[37]

Although Foxy hesitates, Piet drops suddenly to his knees on the toilet tile and, clasping her behind, commences to suck upon a breast whose milk is "sickeningly sweet." Closing his eyes in a delirium of heedless feasting, he wildly, blindly, strokingly sucks. Then, suddenly, the spell is broken: "Knocks struck rocklike at the unlocked door inches behind them. Harsh light flooded him. He saw Foxy's free hand, ringed, grope and cup the sympathetic lactation of the breast jutting unmouthed. She called out, as musically as before. 'One moment, please.' "[38] It is none other than Angela, Piet's wife. Awkwardly, while Foxy flushes the toilet to cover his retreat, he clambers out of the tiny bathroom window and drops one story onto the hard winter ground. Several party people out on the lawn curiously observe his rather handsome but furtive plummet, but he is successful in his narrow escape. Another pleasant little bathroom caper rushes to a close.

Doubtless the most flamboyant and insane comic scene in the toilet occurs in Terry Southern's *Candy*. While having a casual drink in Greenwich Village's Riviera Bar, the naive Candy encounters a stranger who claims to be a gynecologist and insists that she needs a "periodic checkup"—now. He dashes out and returns to the bar with his bag, eager to commence the "inspection."

Candy was amazed. "Here? In the Riviera? Good grief, I don't. . . . "

"Oh yes," said Dr. Johns. "Just here . . . this will do nicely." He had led the girl to the door of the men's toilet, and quickly inside. It was extremely small, a simple cabinet with a stool, nothing more. He locked the door.

"Good Grief," said Candy, "I really don't think. . . . "

"Oh yes," Dr. Johns assured her. "Perfectly all right." He put his little bag down and started taking off her skirt. "Now we'll just slip out of these things," he said.

"Well, are you sure that . . ." Candy was quite confused.

"Now, the little panties," he said, pulling them down. "Lovely things you wear," he added and lifted her up onto the stool.

"Now you just stand with one foot on each side of the stool, limbs spread, that's right and . . . oh yes, you can brace yourself with your hands against the walls . . . yes, just so . . . Fine!

He bent quickly to his kit and took out a small clamp and inserted it between the girl's darling little labias, so that they were held apart.

128   Themes

"*Good!*" he said. "Now I just want to test these clitorial reflexes—often enough, that's where the trouble strikes first." And he began to gently massage her sweet pink clit. "Can you feel that?"

"Good Grief yes!" said Candy, squirming about, "are you sure that this. . . ."

"Hmmm," said Dr. Johns. "Normal response there all right. Now I just want to test these clitorial reflexes to tactile surfaces." And he began sucking it wildly, clutching the precious girl to him with such sudden force and abandon that her feet slipped off the stool and into the well of it. During the tumult the flushing mechanism was set in motion and water now surged out over the two of them, flooding the tiny cabinet and sweeping out of it and into the bar.

There was a violent pounding at the door.

"What in God's name is going on in there?" demanded the manager, who had just arrived. He and the bartender were throwing their weight against the door of the cabinet which by now was two feet deep in water as the doctor and Candy thrashed about inside.

"Good Grief!" she kept saying. They had both fallen to the floor. The doctor was snorting and spouting water, trying desperately to keep sucking and yet not to drown.

Finally with a great lunge the two men outside broke open the door. They were appalled by the scene. "Good God! Good God!" they shouted. "What in the name of God is going on here!"

A police officer arrived at that moment and was beside himself with rage at the spectacle.[39]

Such lunacy and speed are reminiscent of Voltaire, and both *Candide* and *Candy* (titles deliberately alike) are lunatic parodies—*Candide* of the philosophical adventure story, *Candy* of the pornographic novel. Here, the harried pace and bizarre events lead us toward incredible mayhem and, what is more, to distinct sexual anticlimax.

Günter Grass carries us one step further, toward the religious, the visionary. The German narrator, Pilenz, is in "quest" of his childhood hero, "The Great Mahlke," after World War II. Of course, Mahlke is gone entirely, and the novel traces the memories Pilenz reviews of Mahlke, which amount to an almost religious adoration (satirically complicated by the fact that Mahlke, like Hitler, is virtually without adorable qualities). At one point during the war, Pilenz is called up into the military labor service. Mahlke had passed through the training camp the previous year, leaving behind his name—carved in the barracks latrine.

My only justification for telling you even this much is that a year before me . . . the Great Mahlke had worn denims and clodhoppers in the same compound, and literally left his name behind him: in the latrine, a roofless wooden box planked down amid the broom and the overhead murmuring of the scrub pines. Here the two syllables—no first name—were carved, or rather chipped, into a pine board across from the throne, and below the name, in flawless Latin, but in an unrounded, runic sort of script, the beginning of his favorite sequence: *Stabat Mater dolorosa*. . . . The Franciscan monk Jacopone da Todi would have been ever so pleased, but all it meant to me was that even in the Labor Service I couldn't get rid of Mahlke. For while I relieved myself, while the maggot-ridden dross of my age group accumulated behind me and under me, you gave me and my eyes no peace: loudly and in breathless repetition, a painstakingly incised text called attention to Mahlke, whatever I might decide to whistle in opposition . . . everything he did, touched, or said became solemn, significant, monumental; so also his runic inscription in the pine wood of a Reich Labor Service latrine named Tachel-North, between Osche and Reetz. Digestive aphorism, lines from lewd songs, crude or stylized anatomy—nothing helped. Mahlke's text drowned out all the more or less wittily formulated obscenities which, carved or scribbled from top to bottom of the latrine wall, gave tongues to wooden boards.

What with the accuracy of the quotation and the awesome secrecy of the place, I might almost have got religion in the course of time.[40]

Grass's irony is effective because it is subdued. Pilenz's "devotions" in the outhouse are utterly ludicrous, but his tone remains solemn, sacral, portentous. Still, a bathroom is a bathroom and refuses quite stubbornly to become a church.

A similar technique is employed in Eliot's "Sweeney among the Nightingales"; the juxtaposing of the commonplace-sounding "Sweeney" with nightingales is ironic and absurd. So it proves to be in the poem as well: we meet there the modern "apeneck Sweeney," carousing with prostitutes at an inn. His modern life is, despite all the ceremonious and threatening imagery of foreboding, utterly tasteless and uneventful. Then, suddenly, Eliot abandons the account of these boorish people and turns to images of nightingales (suggesting, of course, the legend of King Tereus), of the Sacred Heart (suggesting Christ), and of Agamemnon dead (with suggestions as well of Oedipus at Colonus). All these later figures connote lives tragically lost and yet purveying significant values and meaning, whereas, in contrst, Sweeney and his rabblement connote valuelessness. Irony is fostered by the bringing of two such groups together, as if there were some analogy, some correlation. And the final touch is given to the irony in the concluding lines, as even the stately Agamemnon is meanly befouled. For the nightingales

    sang within the bloody wood
When Agamemnon cried aloud,
And let their liquid siftings fall
To stain the stiff dishonoured shroud.[41]

Nothing and no one are safe from the satirist's excrement and frequently subtle execration. Here, the high diction and the religious imagery carry us far from the ordinary jakes.

A final step toward unreality would be for the satirist to cultivate insanity and nightmare. This is precisely what Slawomir Mrozek, the Polish satirist, does in his short story "From the Darkness." Supposedly a "report" to city comrades from a fellow Communist in a remote village, the story increasingly becomes a hive of lunacy and dementia. Reporting upon other people's being in "the grip of terrible ignorance and superstition," the putative author of the "report" turns out to be the most ignorant and superstitious of them all. It is night, and he dares not go outside "to relieve himself" because of ghosts, skeletons, murderers, and unknown forces. And yet, as his "need" to relieve himself enlarges (together with the pace and fury of his imaginings and his fears), all socialist order and planning tumble down, and the narrator is plunged into a mystical and feverish world of paranoia and nightmare. Outside his door, bats are ominously, comically, flitting.

How those bats flap their wings. Christ! how they fly and squeak "pee pee" and again "pee pee." There is nothing like those big houses where everything must be inside and there is no need to go into the bushes.

But there are even worse things than that. As I am writing this, the door has opened and a pig's snout has appeared. It is looking at me very queerly, it is staring at me. . . .

Have I not told you that things are different here?[42]

With this last Kafkaesque touch—bats brazenly squeaking out a joyful urinary hymn, we come to the close of our survey of scatological rites, satiric fun, and grotesque games in the toilet. The unmentionable is still being spoken out—loudly—and the traditions of satiric singing are very much alive.

12
Cannibals

If bowels and toilets are considered unmentionable by so-called polite society, then cannibalism is much worse: a topic that normally can be expected to generate in its audience horror and revulsion. For that reason, cannibalism is understandably favored by our satirists. In *Inferno* 32, Dante, having descended to the lowest and vilest circle of hell, encounters Count Ugolino eternally gnawing upon the neck and brain of his betrayer, Ruggieri, the archibishop of Pisa. We know that we are in the pit of hell, for cannibalism remains for mankind—even for our own jaded century—a dreadful and all but unspeakable crime. One modern critic, Robert J. Lifton, suggests that death has become "unmanagable" for us in our era, has become a topic wholly repressed: "We hide from ourselves the very fact of death." Exactly the same may be said of cannibalism. With offhanded wit, Hans Zinsser takes a casual view of recurrent spates of cannibalism among the various species; he observes that "in the imperfect development of cohabitation on a crowded planet, the habit of eating one another—dead and alive—has become a general custom, instinctively and dispassionately indulged in." But it is not so; civilized society has insisted upon passionately denying such "indulgence" in any form whatsoever; any aboriginal interest in anthropophagy has been vigorously refuted and repressed. Even psychiatry is certain in its condemnation: "Coprophagia," Frederic Wertham flatly asserts, "is always an indication of mental disease, and cannibalism in our time, with the exception of extreme catastrophic hunger situations with impending death, is unthinkable for any person in his right mind."[1] It is a highly charged topic, commonly taboo.

For precisely this reason the vestiges of tales of man-eating hold for us a grim fascination. We are awestruck before the child-eating feasts of primitive mythology—the gruesome dinners of Thyestes in Seneca's drama, of Tereus in Ovid's *Metamorphoses*, of Tantalus in Pindar's *Olympian Odes*. Indeed, the classically mythic theme of Saturn's eating of his own children has captured the imagination of innumerable later generations; Goya's original wall painting, *Saturno devorando a un hijo*, is one of the most powerful and frightening in the annals of art, just as *Titus Andronicus* remains one of Shakespeare's (and the Renaissance's) most macabre plays.[2] As a matter of fact, one of the Enlightenment's "justifications" for the slave trade out of Africa remained the proliferating tales of cannibalism and cruelty among the tribes; benign Europeans were, it was claimed, "rescuing" natives and transporting them to the new world of Christianity and civilized captivity where they would be forced to adhere to more sanitary diets.[3] Doubtless the high point of so-called Christian tolerance assuredly occurs in the course of Defoe's *Robinson Crusoe* (1719), when the irate and self-righteous protagonist slowly comes to terms with his spontaneously eager desire to slaughter all the South American cannibals he happens to encounter.

To this day such a subject arouses in us a sense of shock, together with an uneasy attraction. Therefore, it is no accident that an all-time best-seller, since its appearance in 1897, had been Bram Stoker's *Dracula*. The theme of the malevolent vampire sucking a maiden's blood has continuously horrified and titillated—throughout innumerable editions, as well as upon stage and screen. More recently, the story of the Donner party, trapped in the Sierra Nevada in the winter of 1846, and of its members' survival by the consuming of the dead, has again received attention in book-length recapitulation by Richard Rhodes. The Uruguayan plane crash in the Andes in 1972, that similarly led to the eating of the dead, has now appeared as a novel and as a motion picture, *Alive!*[4]

The problem of our taboo and our dis-ease results from, of course, our unconscious sense of our own roots, our own origins. A mere three or four thousand years ago our ancestors were savages, lurking in the bush. Scholarship into the origins of primitive rites has pretty well established that the ancient burnt offering was at one time a human sacrifice, that the communal feast of old consisted of decoctions of human flesh and blood.[5] We were there. Now we see through a glass, darkly; yet what we shall perceive is apt to be our own contorted and malignant face.

Precisely because of his terror and decorum, then, man is peculiarly subject to the assaults of satirists, who will not let him disavow or disremember his past, the skeletons, as it were, in his pantry closet. Because of its perennial power to startle, therefore, cannibalism has been throughout history the subject of satire; the satirist repetitiously rubs the spectator's nose in a topic the observer would ardently prefer to leave alone. Ronald Paulson proposes that the regular theme of cannibalism serves as "a metaphor for aggression," suggesting "the corruption of an ideal."⁶ The forthright portrayal of a voracious cannibalism is aggressive, all right, but it is too blatantly distasteful to most of us merely to indicate a deviation from a norm. Here would be an instance of overkill; the subject is too horrible to contemplate. Rather, satire belabors the reader with the dreadful exactly because it does shock; the topic repeatedly serves as a time-honored attention-getting device—capable of breaking down our papier-mâché walls of dignity, aloofness, and high seriousness. Satire insists upon the descent into the bestial, like Circe converting men into swine. Let's face it: for the cultured and fastidious, cannibalism leaves a bad taste in the mouth.

Diogenes and other early Cynics antagonize and startle audiences by advocating, among other things, free love; even "incest and cannibalism may be justifiable in certain circumstances," A.A. Long observes. Juvenal mockingly reports of the Egyptians that their dainty preferences banish goat meat and mutton from their tables, but not the carcasses of men. He proceeds to recount how the citizens of Ombi enjoy tearing their enemies apart and eating them raw. Petronius has the apparently opulent Eumolpus insert in his will the mandate that his heirs, clients, and obsequious parasites must literally swallow his body before they can devour his wealth. Montaigne whimsically defends such barbarous savages, suggesting that they are perhaps more respectable than the denizens of Europe.⁷ In *Candide*, Voltaire amusingly recounts how the Princess of Palestrina came to lose one buttock to furnish a banquet in Russia, and Byron's *Don Juan* sweetly records how a shipwrecked crew, cast for many days in a lifeboat upon the sea, drew lots and then dined upon Pedrillo, Don Juan's own beloved "pastor" and "master." Even the staid H.G. Wells in *The Time Machine* (1895) takes a dim view of man's future. He introduces into the grim later history of the planet a society of ruined, classically dressed aristocrats preyed upon and consumed by the vestiges of the factory laborers long since gone underground and now evolved into a weak-eyed species of molelike Morlocks, or cannibals, who, turning the tables of history, now feed upon their superiors. Doubtless the most famous instance in literature of purposeful, reasonable cannibalism remains Jonathan Swift's sardonic masterpiece "A Modest Proposal."

One might well expect, with such a recurrence over the centuries of this theme in satire, the subsequent tapering-off and diminution in the modern era. Yet such is distinctly not the case. If anything, our age witnesses a sharp increase in the treatment of cannibalism. Mark Twain introduces a mad, cannibalistic parliamentarian in one of his tales. Ambrose Bierce "proves," in an essay, that our ancestors were anthropophagous and hopes to induce readers to return to past tried-and-true traditions. Lord Dunsany, with an O. Henry twist, solves the mysterious case of a girl's vanishing, when it is discovered that her boyfriend, at the time of her disappearance, purchased appetizing meat sauce, in "The Two Bottles of Relish." Evelyn Waugh's *Black Mischief* recounts how Basil Seal, at a festival among the headhunters in the bush, unknowingly (and imprudently) dines upon his girlfriend Prudence. T.S. Eliot creates a revue-and-ragtime little ditty about Sweeney the Cannibal eating the missionary Doris. Even two scientists, Stanley Garn and Walter Block, can aloofly analyze the nutritional value of man-eating, only to conclude (perhaps a little wistfully) that people-as-food hardly supply us with enough calories and protein; we would therefore, they explain with tongue-in-cheek and mock solemnity, require with human flesh a dietary supplement. Similarly, Norman Mailer, in *Cannibals and Christians* (the title richly suggests former New World tribal cuisine), concludes that man's "modern condition," "psychically so bleak," implies acts of destruction, even of cannibalism, lying just below the surface within us all.[8]

In fact, increasingly in our century cannibalistic satire becomes more prevalent, more ferocious, more grim. We have witnessed mass slaughter—culminating in the bomb and the gas chamber—what has been designated the Holocaust.[9] Given such an atmosphere, artists are hard put to exceed reality—or even to capture its terrible dimensions. In seven novels, Kurt Vonnegut, Jr. has never been able, as he explains, to approach the fire bombing of Dresden, which he lived through during World War II. Nevertheless, he skirts about the issue in *Slaughterhouse-Five* with images of "corpse mines" and of schoolgirls "boiled alive in a water tower by my own countrymen."[10] In short, the horrors of the twentieth century have incited satirists to refurbish, to reanimate, older treatments of cannibalism in order to cope with the extravagance of the present scene. In such a manner are old myths vitalized and reestablished.

For in our era of massive technology and mass communications, we are simply inundated by a plethora of revolutionary ideas and weapons. In such a dangerous world, all things are possible—and indeed positively in evidence. The anarchist in a Chesterton novel is perfectly willing, on principle, in fact, to violate any principle or order.

"I say we are merciful," [claims one anarchist], "as the early Christians were merciful. Yet this did not prevent their being accused of eating human flesh. We do not eat human flesh—"
"Shame!" [cries another]. "Why not?"[11]

On the other hand, absolute service to the "people's" totalitarian state is comically portrayed in Slawomir Mrozek's drama *Out at Sea*. Among three "comrades" cast out on a raft, the two hefty survivors brainwash the frail thin one into "electing freedom" and nobly sacrificing himself for the state, allowing the others to apportion him as food. It is all a matter of patriotic Communist rhetoric.[12]

Similarly, the dispassionate scientist is capable of investigative laboratory murder; in Čapek's *War with the Newts*, for example, the humanlike salamanders, who have been taught all man's qualities and abilities, are nonetheless subject to "experimentation" in the laboratory and as "inferiors" are offered cheerfully up to destruction. Newt fat is found to be good industrial lubricant, but newt flesh persists in being unpalatable. The scientist, however, devoted to his vocation, perserveres:

Dr. Pinkel ascertained after many experiments performed on himself that these harmful effects disappear if the chopped meat is scalded with hot water . . . and after washing thoroughly it is pickled for twenty-four hours in a weak solution of permanganate of potash. Then it can be cooked or stewed, and tastes like inferior beef. In this way we ate a Newt called Hans; he was an able and intelligent animal with a special bent for scientific work; he was employed in Dr. Pinkel's department as his assistant, and even refined chemical analysis could be entrusted to him. We used to have long conversations with him in the evenings, amusing ourselves with his insatiable thirst for knowledge. With deep regret we had to put Hans to death, because my experiments on trepanning him made him blind. His meat was dark and spongy, but did not cause any unpleasant effects. It is clear that in case of war Newt flesh could form a welcome and cheap substitute for beef.[13]

Furthermore, our advanced machines threaten to consume us. Thus, in John Barth's *Giles Goat-Boy*, the gigantic WESCAC computer, that controls society's motives and methods, continuously, ominously threatens to EAT (by "Electroencephalic Amplification and Transmission") the citizenry.[14] Even our utopias (or, more properly, dystopias) dramatize the descent of man, as in William Golding's *Lord of the Flies*, to the point at which boys ferret one another out, as one would hunt wild boars in the jungle bush. Utopias otherwise frequently characterize a dull and overpopulated future, as in Barry Hannah's "Eating Wife and Friends," in which in a future American Depression citizens declare open season for stalking and dining upon relatives and intimates. In Anthony Burgess's *The Wanting Seed*, with the breakdown of social order, cheerful mobs increasingly engage in overt cannibalism—forming "dining clubs," then slaughtering, spitting, baking, and basting their savory fellow men. In Aylesbury, where man is more "refined," corpses were canned, and the inhabitants are considered "civilized cannibals." "It makes all the difference," one of the inhabitants placidly and contentedly explains, "if you get it out of a tin."[15]

Doubtless the height of "gentility" and "propriety" is achieved in J.P. Donleavy's manual of etiquette and good manners for all occasions, when he describes how to consume one's neighbors like a gentleman. Saul Bellow ironically has his conservative writer-protagonist, Charles Citrine, make something of a fortune when an old script of his work "Caldofreddo," concerned with cannibalism and forgiveness, becomes a smash film hit across two continents.[16] Satire vehemently and savagely responds to the nineteenth century's talk of "progress" and an idealism that prescribed the inevitable emergence of idyllic supermen and socialistic superstates. Decline, degeneracy, and descent are the central themes of our reactionary literature.

If possible, it is with a kind of escalation, in the latter portion of this century, that the literary picture becomes still more nightmarish, hallucinatory, and grisly. Burgess's reference to "tinned" delicacies is echoed by the surrealistic savagery of George P. Elliott's story "The NRACP," in which America's entire black population is systematically rounded up, shipped to a massive concentration camp in Nevada, butchered, cooked, and efficiently distributed in cans for everyday human consumption. By a horrible conjunction, methodical social planners have at one stroke resolved both the "Negro Problem" and the "Food Problem" with wonderful simplicity. In a similar vein, dramatist Fernando Arrabal contributes his share to the trend that presents the sickening in the open, for in his play *The Architect and the Emperor of Assyria*, he dramatizes the architect's slaying and eating of the emperor onstage. In one scene the diner genteelly cuts off a foot for consumption and nicely taps the corpse's brain behind the ear so that he might suck off the nutritious nucleic acids. In the next scene, the victim's bones are patently strewn about the set.[17] We have been forced to partake of it all.

Novelist Gabriel García Márquez tells of the enormously aged and depraved Caribbean tyrant who grows mad from fear and pain until he imagines one further conspiracy against him that involves his minister of defense, the one man who had been his friend and "soul comrade," General Rodrigo de Aguilar. At midnight during an annual banquet held for the suspect presidential guard, all anticipate the arrival of the great minister of defense. The tyrant gives a sign,

and then the curtains parted and the distinguished Major General Rodrigo de Aguilar entered on a silver tray stretched out full length on a garnish of cauliflower and laurel leaves, steeped with spices, oven brown, embellished with the uniform of five golden almonds for solemn occasions and the limitless loops for valor on the sleeve of his right arm, fourteen pounds of medals on his chest and a sprig of parsley in his mouth, ready to be served at a banquet of comrades by the official carvers to the petrified horror of the guests as without breathing we witness the exquisite ceremony of carving and serving, and when every plate held an equal portion of minister of defense stuffed with pine nuts and aromatic herbs, he gave the order to begin, eat hearty gentlemen.[18]

We can be absolutely certain that under the surveillance of such a tyrant, everyone dined with stupor and alacrity.

Possibly the most haunting and ghoulish of such recent grotesqueries is John Hawkes's novel *The Cannibal*. The entire book portrays modern Germany's interminable repetitive cycle—brutish boastfulness and militant jingoism that leads to disastrous warfare, defeat, and nationwide misery, desolation, and waste. Then the cycle stupidly commences again. Seen in such a light, all Germany is an actual madhouse, ever on the verge of opening its doors and unleashing a ravening insanity upon the Western world.[19] At the center of this mythic spiral and whorl is portrayed the aged duke at his "fox-hunt," symbol of a decadent and mirthless martial artistocracy and its "games." But the "fox" that he stalks relentlessly throughout the novel is in fact Jutta's little son. In a spine-tingling climax, the boy is captured by the aristocrat, mutilated and murdered, then methodically hacked, sliced, and cut into pieces.

He hacked and missed the joints, he made incisions and they were wrong as the point of the blade struck a button. The fox kicked back. . . . It took all his ingenuity to find, in the mess, the ears to take as a trophy, to decide which were the parts with dietician's names and which to throw away. . . . It was necessary to struggle, first holding the pieces on his lap, then crouching above the pile, he had to pull, to poke, and he resented the dullness of the blade. . . . Every time a bone broke his prize became mangled, every piece that was lost in the mud made the whole thing defective.[20]

Subsequently, this rumpled, amputated mass is boiled in a broth and served with Prussian ceremony and poise as a welcome repast to the boy's aunt. The point is made brutally clear: the modern world is at heart a wretched inversion of Rousseauistic innocence; in the place of romantic simplicity, optimism, and perfectability is set a barbarous killer instinct in a cursed race. Instead of spiritual progress, there is demonic regression and reversion. Man moves downward and backward.

Thereafter, it is but a short step from the Kafkesque lunacy of John Hawkes to the epical presentation of John Gardner's *Grendel*. Here is *Beowulf* retold from the monster's, the cannibal's, point of

138 Themes

view. With his musings, his hesitations, his hang-ups, and his acute self-consciousness, Grendel slowly transforms into a wayward, neurotic twentieth-century man. Or, to put it the other way, contemporary man is revealed as a monster. "All order, I've come to understand," muses the ratiocinating monster, "is theoretical, unreal—a harmless, sensible, smiling mask men slide between the two great, dark realities, the self and the world—two snake-pits. The watchful mind lies, cunning and swift, about the dark blood's lust, lies and lies and lies until, weary of talk, the watchman sleeps. Then sudden and swift the enemy strikes from nowhere, the cavernous heart. Violence is truth."[21] Grendel is such a potentially dangerous and violent man—but without the mask. On the contrary, in much of recent literature, the disguise has been doffed, the false face lifted, only to reveal (and to expose) the bloodthirsty fangs of your commonplace joe, your everyday guy. The beast in the jungle is the man in the street. That is our current mythology. Like any other myth in its flower, it is vigorous and flourishing; it is credible, appalling, and—gustatorily or disgustingly—alive.

13

Dystopias and Machines

Most people in the twentieth century are no enemies to technology and machines; the concept of progress has come to mean for them sudden improvements in our gadgets. Inevitably, they virtually idolize the latest battery-run screwdrivers and self-cleaning ovens, CD players and VCRs, computers and golf carts, security systems and automated tellers. In short, technology is not in the least unsavory, as were topics like cannibalism and excrement.

Yet, we are just a bit uncomfortable about our robots, motors, and utensils. Every one of us has at times fantasized about (and paranoically dreaded) some incredible instrument panel of an awful contrivance going awry, possibly flooding us with radiation, blackouts, dioxin, synthetic chromosomes, and artificial disease. What can we do if all our engines run amok? What happens when our equipment becomes smarter than we are? Such thoughts are not untenable: we do at times indulge in such technophobian fancies. The satirist, as usual, steps forward blythely to agitate us and upset our balance. James Thurber informs us of one such victim of the machine. He tells

about a housewife who bought a combination ironing board and card table.... The husband, coming home to find the devilish contraption in the parlor, was appalled.

"What's that thing?" he demanded. His wife explained that it was a card table, but that if you pressed a button underneath, it would become an ironing board. Whereupon she pushed the button and the table leaped a foot into the air, extended itself and became an ironing board.... the thing finally became so finely sensitized that it would change back and forth if you merely touched it—you didn't have to push the button. The husband stuck it in the attic (after it had leaped up and struck him a couple of times while he was playing euchre), and on windy nights it could be heard flopping and banging around, changing from a card table to an ironing board and back.[1]

Nonetheless, yet another viewpoint exists on this subject as well: many of us are apt to be smug or complacent about industrialization.

We are inclined to think too grandly of ourselves and of our material achievements. Once again, the satirist will step in to humble us; he will create mock science fictions and ruptured utopias, showing us how, in the future, mechanisms will have fully dehumanized us and letting us know that subsequent generations will become the slaves and victims of metallic and mathematical monsters. However the satirist might treat mechanization, you may rest assured that he will be disquieting.

By the close of the nineteenth century, the realities of industrialization had been fully developed and accepted (however much the romantics resisted it). Nonetheless, with the advent of our present century, a new phase in the struggle fully emerged: the fictive concept that not only had the machine triumphed but it had also "taken over," become victorious, vanquished mankind, fully prevailed. Utopias turned "sour," and fictions like *We, 1984,* and *Brave New World* suggested that the antiutopia or dystopia was the true vision of our immediate future.[2]

Much of this dis-ease about machinery and technology, what Stanislaw Lem calls the "techno-revolution," has remained, in the popular arts, benign.[3] Amusingly, on television the computer panel in "Star Trek" and the robot in "Lost in Space" stand out as the most sane and intelligent figures on these programs; and the interest in the Bionic Man and the Bionic Woman, in Robocop, indicates that the public is still very willing indeed to take its superheroes with a substantial dose of automated mechanization and replacement parts. Yet the prognosis does not remain wholly optimistic.

Arthur Asa Berger conjectures that "high" culture is far more suspicious of monstrosity and industrialized invention than are the propagators of popular arts: "The dominant thrust of high literature has been a revulsion against science and the machine. Novelists and poets generally see science and technology as a threat to humanity and recoil against it almost in panic. Thus most contemporary utopian novels are *dystopies* which see societies of the future as totalitarian and antihuman." On the other hand, Berger argues, comic book writers look toward "nature" and repeatedly represent the hero's conquest of technological monsters.[4]

Berger is not entirely correct. Two of the most noticeable developments among comic book heroes of late are their genesis and appearance. In the past, major heroes were normal human beings (Batman), or given added vigor by human means (Captain America) or by Merlin-type gods (Captain Marvel), or else they brought their supernatural powers with them to planet earth (Superman). More recently new heroes have been created by accident, by exposure to gamma rays, by unholy laboratory experiments. These beginnings imply that heroes are made rather than born. In addition, the most striking feature about recent "heroes" is their rank unsavoriness, their sheer ugliness. No longer does one encounter the handsome swain swathed in colored silks, tights, and scarfs, but rather the raw, hideous mechanisms of a debauched and polluted society—Iron Man (with his plug-in battery-recharged heart), distorted Plastic Man and Mr. Fantastic, the volatile Human Torch, unnatural Spider Man, and the chief grotesque crime fighters (who appear little better than monsters themselves) the Hulk and the rock-creature the Thing. In two decades, we have come a long way from neatness and sobriety, cleanliness and decorum in the comics. Manufactured gallants are distinctly threatening to get out of hand.

Motion pictures, too, present a mixed reaction. One of the first short reels by Lumiere played humorously with mechanization. *The Sausage-Machine* (1897) depicted dogs being fed on a conveyer belt into a contraption that issued continuous links of sausage at its nether end. Since that time, much of cinema has merely continued to toy with the theme of the rampant machine. Chaplin's *Modern Times* (1936), Guinness's *Man in the White Suit* (1951), and Tati's *Mon Oncle* (1956-57) merely suggest the absurdities of industrial living—white-line arrows and flashing-light directives, cannibalistic cogwheels, belching and burping engines that seek to consume everyday civilized life. Of darker aspect are pictures like Otto Rippert's *Homunculus* (1916), Fritz Lang's *Metropolis* (1926), René Clair's *A Nous la Liberté* (1932), Wilcox's *Forbidden Plant* (1956), or Truffaut's *Fahrenheit 451* (1966), which represent a hypermechanized era interchangeable with the criminal, or worse. Recent science fiction features (not to mention Kubrick's *2001: A Space Odyssey* [1968]) often favor the outright apocalyptic, in which man brings his world rushing and tumbling to an end.[5]

Despite the powerful portrayal of mechanized dehumanization in some of these films, much in the cinema is sober and tame, too many directors "preferring to approach scientific subjects with a mixture of straight-faced solemnity and plodding worthiness," demonstrating "the characteristic American ambiguity about technology."[6] "The cinema, a machine itself, enabled the machine to acquire tremendous powers and to develop its possibilities in advance of scientific fact. On the screen, the machine loses its impersonal, inhuman, and mathematical nature and becomes a poetic object.[7] Nevertheless, the powerful films by men like Lang, Clair, Chaplin, and Kubrick do constitute forceful indictment of automated and mechanical society and dramatize a reaction against technology that is increasingly prevalent in our century's literature.

To be sure, a large cause of this reaction against science and its instruments results from the growing sense, at the outset of the present century, that the idea of progress, Newtonian classical mechanics, Hegelian idealism, Comtean positivism, all had wavered, toppled, or fallen. Furthermore, romanticism's suspicion of any mechanism that impeded or inhibited the pastoral, individualist, unique, and spontaneous overflow of powerful feelings accorded all too few accolades to the newly developing sciences. Finally, science and technology were undermined by modernism itself. For in the seventeenth century the bifurcations of self and other, of God's words and God's works, have led to modernity's schizophrenia and the "divided self."

This "modern" spirit is quite well described by Matthew Arnold. Modern man, Arnold reports, lacks all the virtues of ancient Greece; he has lost calm, cheer, steady objectivity. In their stead is nervous mental insecurity: "the Dialogue of the mind with itself has commenced; modern problems have presented themselves; we hear already the doubts, we witness the discouragement, of Hamlet or of Faust." Arnold appears, prophetically, to have been right. Wylie Sypher speaks of "the loss of self" in the modern period, when man becomes virtually a faceless "functionary," and Lionel Trilling discusses "the radical, subversive energy of the modern period."[8] Hans Meyerhoff also addresses modernism's bald "pessimism":

Pessimism is not only the title of one of Spengler's essays but a general attitude or orientation pervading the twentieth century.

It is much easier for us to appreciate the negative reaction to this faith in progress which, pricked by Voltaire's Mephistophelian ridicule of Leibniz' faith in the best of all possible worlds, and assaulted by various forms of pessimism in the nineteenth century (Schopenhauer, Tennyson, Hardy, etc.), has steadily declined ever since, until the prevailing intellectual attitude of our own age makes such a faith appear, at best, naive; at worst, a dangerous illusion.[9]

Beyond pessimism, Tony Tanner detects, in recent American novels, a strain of paranoia: "Narrative lines are full of hidden persuaders, hidden dimensions, plots, secret organizations, evil systems, all kinds of conspiracies against spontaneity of consciousness, even cosmic take-over. The possible nightmare of being totally controlled by unseen agencies and powers is never far away in contemporary American fiction."[10]

In such a literary climate, it is small wonder that scientific inventions have been all but universally greeted in literature with uneasiness, distrust, even terrific chagrin. Arnold's words of 1853 are almost repeated in William Barrett's analysis of 1972: "Contrary to the confidence in our powers of technology and information, the prevailing image of man we find in modern art is one of impotence, uncertainty, and self-doubt."[11]

Before we survey the immediate scene of intimidating science in modern fiction, however, let us briefly examine one early romantic exemplar of the modern theme. The concept of "forbidden knowledge" has been with us for several thousand years, and of course, Adam and Eve are the primal instances of such fatal "curiosity."[12] Moreover, such a concept is normally conjoined with the idea of an unearthly or godlike hubris or aspiration: we associate the stories of Prometheus, the Tower of Babel, medieval alchemy, and, to be sure, Dr. Faustus with this recurrent tragic pattern. But only in modern times do we encounter such a "Prometheus" inventing a machine—a human machine that willfully causes the inventor's own destruction. Such a story is Mary Shelley's *Frankenstein*, a gothic tale that has been of perennial interest since its publication in 1818.

Dr. Frankenstein virtually embodies Arnold's "modern": lacking utterly in classic calm, cheerfulness, and objectivity and beset by discouragement and doubt. He disavows the monster from the moment of its inception, and he can never bring himself to accept it, to mollify it, or to destroy it. Instead, he tumbles in an incessant fever of vacillation and uncertainty. Inevitably, of course, his creation—increasingly assuming the characteristics of Milton's Satan—tortures him, pursues him, does him to death.

This romantic fiction becomes the paradigm of all subsequent literature concerning the machine. For since the Industrial Revolution we have had a stormy and ambivalent affair with technology. We rely upon it, we are devoted to it; it becomes the backbone of our leisure and our modern state. Yet we falter before this creation; we doubt, and ultimately we despair. Thus we surround the machine with demonic fictions. Just as God created a man who falls and subsequently produces a philosophy of the death of God, so, in modern fiction, has man created the machine. And the machine ultimately engenders the death of man. Ironically, it is a fitting "tragedy," and a romantic one; for it is performed in an atmosphere of apocalypse, nightmare, and cataclysm, a new Wagnerian *Gotterdammerung*, the crashing and falling of worlds.

Our own century naturally continues the exposé and the assault of the machine. Our writers are primarily distrustful of the Victorian mindset that all too readily honored railroads, textile mills, child labor, expositions, coal towns, mass production, soot, smog, and smoke. In *Decline and Fall*, Evelyn Waugh presents a lunatic mechanic, Professor

Silenus, who is "remodeling" what had once been an elegant English country house.

"The problem of architecture as I see it," he told a journalist who had come to report on the progress of his surprising creation of furro concrete and aluminum, "is the problem of all art—the elimination of the human element from the consideration of form. The only perfect building must be the factory, because that is built to house machines, not men. I do not think it is possible for domestic architecture to be beautiful, but I am doing my best. All ill comes from man," . . . he said gloomily. . . . "Man is never happy except when he becomes a channel for the distribution of mechanical forces."[13]

It is precisely the possibility that man might well become mechanized, dehumanized—an automaton—that causes so many modern writers to manhandle our machines.

E.M. Forster's story "The Machine Stops" (1916) dramatizes a society living in isolation and dependent upon the universal machine to feed, clothe and bed it down; the machine's exhaustion and demise signal the collapse of this future civilization. Karel Čapek's important play R.U.R. (1921) introduces the "robot" and indicates that machinery will overtake and eventually destroy present civilization altogether. Likewise highly influential is Kafka's symbolic story "In the Penal Colony" ("In der Strafkolonie," 1919), in which an electronic torture device of the utmost sophistication punishes and destroys human life at agonizing leisure. Of similar symbolic intent is Elmer Rice's *The Adding Machine* (1923), in which the dead in limbo practice upon the business machines that have replaced them, and Eugene O'Neill's *Dynamo* (1928), in which men become the fanatic worshipers of electricity and its automated, thunder-making machines.

In the thirties and forties, a brief period of comic interlude appears (before the bomb). E.B. White introduces his computer that needs a drink in "The Hour of Letdown," James Thurber creates Walter Mitty with his inevitable visions of machines going "pocketa-pocketa-pocketa," and Donald Barthelme imagines an inflation of a gaseous balloon that almost totally covers the sky above New York City.[14] Similarly, Harold Pinter conceives "Trouble in the Works" (1955), wherein workers "take a turn against" their machines' products; they have come to mistrust "hemi unival spherical rod ends," "speed taper shank spiral flute reamers," "nippled connectors," "male elbow adapters," and similar suggestive (and aggressive) products. Recent mechanized employees, in sum, have become hostile to manufactured (and humanized) bawdy equipment. In the manner of Robbe-Grillet, Robert Coover, as in "The Elevator," contrives variable scenarios of constantly alternating, rising and falling fictions.[15] Reality here becomes the primordial dancer—and inflamer—of mechanistic potentialities.

Yet increasingly in the latter portion of this century, the picture becomes more grim. For we encounter death on a grand scale—orchestrated by deportations, chemical and atomic warfare, concentration camps, and carefully engineered genocide. Hence the image of the machine's primal governance of human life becomes still more serious, more prevalent, more ferocious in recent letters. One need only think of George P. Elliott's "The NRACP" (1966). Vonnegut's *Player Piano* (1952) rehearses once again the machine-oriented society that might not work but that is nonetheless irreplaceable. Two major recent novels—Barth's *Giles Goat-Boy* (1966) and Pynchon's *Gravity Rainbow* (1973)—possess symbolic visions of mechanistic accomplishment and success (one portraying a world governed by a WESCAC computer, the other by the mechanic determinism of the V-2 rocket's mysterious trajectories). Recent ratiocinative science fictions by the Polish author Stanislaw Lem, however, go one step further. *Memoirs Found in a Bathtub* (1971) ultimately shows American spies as the victims and slaves of an incredibly mysterious and treacherous Pentagon computer and spy center buried beneath the Rocky Mountains.

Perhaps most insidious have been the flurry of fictions hastening to pronounce the destruction of the entire world. Such creations are *apocalyptic* in the older, extirpatory sense of the word.[16] They fully expose a "power of blackness" that witnesses a cataclysm: simple extinction without the slightest opportunity for rebirth or regeneration. Such a fiction is Nevil Shute's *On the Beach* (1957), that observes the death of the entire planet from cobalt-bomb radiation. Such is Stanley Kubrick's film *Dr. Strangelove* (1963), that almost gleefully posits the onset of the first—and last—nuclear war. And such is Kurt Vonnegut Jr.'s *Cat's Cradle* (1963), wherein the latest scientific invention, like Medusa's head, deep-freezes the planet's population into statuary.

If anything can be more forbidding than the demolition of the world, it might well be the development of an upside-down Darwinism. Arthur Clarke's *2001: A Space Odyssey* (1968), for example, suggests that a superior civilization of the future created such advanced computers that the inventors no longer found any need for their own bodies, allowing their spirit and intellect to pass into the machines. At this point, one supposes, we have returned to Mary Shelley's *Frankenstein*—for the machine becomes the superior intellect that must infallibly prevail. Increasingly and more insidiously in our century, then, writers represent the machine as taking over our lives. That which interferes with our lives becomes more and more the symbol of the exacerbated, the encroaching, and the celebrated.[17]

Nevertheless, I do not wish to give the impression that the machine is to be despised. After all, much of the material I have been tracing here is satiric, and satire succeeds by shocking us—precisely because it "speaks for the Devil." Reverting to Arnold's concept of modern man's self-doubts, William Barrett praises our era's scientific productivity and invention:

This doubt has even shaken our confidence in progress, which was once an unquestionable article of faith. A few decades ago the distrust of technology was an avant-garde position. Today that distrust has become so widespread that it has become banal. One hesitates to add to it, and in fact one feels pushed toward defending technology. It is, after all, the most adventurous, creative, and original part of our culture. There can hardly be any more striking symptom of loss of heart than when a civilization begins to doubt what it does best.[18]

What Barrett urges is largely true—and yet I am not at all fully convinced that mankind merely "doubts" or debunks what it creates, "what it does best." For modern man is convinced—and I would even say proud—of the vast scientific revolutions and technological innovations of recent times. He is doubtful, rather, about his own mind and heart.

In *Cannibals and Christians*, Norman Mailer reprints his little "treatment" of the end of the world. Ecologically, this future earth is in trouble. Our great American president talks the world into believing—and into democratically voting for—the detonation of the entire planet, so that the president (with ninety-nine other great and creative men of foresight) might, in a solitary rocket ship, be propelled out of the solar system to find a "new world" to build, to populate, to aspire in, and to expand upon. And yet, it is never clear (the caustic Mailer would never have it so) whether this wondrous leader is really such a gullible Mosaic galactic colonist or whether he is the maniacal solipsist and fanatic dupe of the most fantastic ego-trip of them all. The question, although distinctly put, is never properly answered in Norman Mailer's tale. Modern man, then, is not so entirely fearful of his apparatus and his equipment as might at first appear, but he is positively livid with fear and trembling about the ambiguities, perplexities, and delusions of the all-too-human inventors of machines. To underscore my point, let us listen to Mailer describe the finale of his story—and of the world.

"Forgive me, all of you," says the President.
"May I be an honest man and not first deluded physician to the Devil." Then he presses the button.

The earth detonates into the dark spaces. A flame leaps across the solar system. A scream of anguish, jubilation, desperation, terror, ecstasy, vaults across the heavens. The tortured heart of the earth has finally found its voice. We have a glimpse of the spaceship, a silver minnow of light, streaming into the oceans of mystery, and the darkness beyond.[19]

14

Entropy and Armageddon

The satirist effectively irks and disquiets his readers by teasing them with tedium, shocking them with scatology, nauseating them with cannibalism, and rattling them with a melee of machines. But doubtless the most unpleasant subject the satirist can broach entails the death of the universe. There is enough wallop in that scenario to catch anybody's attention.

In his rather sensational Rede Lecture at Cambridge in 1959, C.P. Snow described a divided world, "the two cultures," made up of isolated and hostile groups, scientists and humanists. In reproaching the smug liberal arts types, Sir Charles observed that he had often asked members of an ignorant audience "how many of them could describe the Second Law of Thermodynamics. The response was . . . negative. Yet I was asking something which is about the scientific equivalent of *Have you read a work of Shakespeare's?*" John Hollander once commented that Snow indeed made an unfortunate lapse in choosing as an example of ignorance the principle of entropy or the concept of the universal dissipation of energy in irreversible time that is the second law of thermodynamics, since "it is the one bit of 'science' which every American schoolboy knows."[1]

The concept of entropy has been around for some time and has had every opportunity of filtering into the general public consciousness—and settling there. Originally deriving from Sadi Carnot's studies of the behavior of gases and the efficiency of steam engines, the idea of the inability to obtain maximum work from a given fuel and the tendency in time for the dissipation of energy was articulated by Clausius in 1850 and generalized as the second law of thermodynamics by William Thomson (later to become Lord Kelvin) in 1852. Thomson applied the law to the universe as a closed system and foretold its "heat death" as forces finally reached equilibrium at a low temperature. Hermann von Helmholtz elaborated Thomson's principle in 1854, and much stress was placed upon the randomness of mounting disorder. Clausius introduced the term *entropy* (analogous to *energy*) to describe such dissipation in 1865.[2] These ideas were articulated and repeated in the late nineteenth and early twentieth centuries by such men as Ludwig Boltzmann, J.W. Gibbs, Max Planck, Sir Arthur Eddington, and Sir James Jeans.[3] Similarly, entropy has since that time become a primal concept in communications theory, that postulates in a system increased static and disorder until communications break down.[4] With a vengeance, then, do Hamlet's words assume new ominous meaning: "The rest is silence." Such a concept has become a primal metaphor in modern literature, in which, in T.S. Eliot's phrase, the world is conceived as ending lamely with ridiculous and lumpish inertness—not with a "bang," but a "whimper." "The basic point needs no arguing. In art, in literature, in science, in our culture as a whole we are a void-haunted, void-fascinated age."[5]

Actually, of course, the renown of the law of entropy was early overshadowed by the Darwinian theory of evolution, which it predated. For some time, evolution appeared to reinforce ideas of progress that had been rife in the Enlightenment and the nineteenth century, but almost as a kind of deliberate reaction against progressivist attitudes, the later nineteenth century and subsequently the twentieth have increasingly favored pessimistic readings of human and galactic history. In such a climate entropy was destined to come strongly into its own.

In fact, so fully have entropic ideas been embraced among painters and writers that it has become too well known indeed. Since the dada movement following World War I, there have been recurrent movements that are overtly antiart, and a number of works in music, painting, and literature are deliberately (and even hopelessly) random and chaotic. Monroe Beardsley laments that too many specious artists appeal to the "indeterminacy" principle of Heisenberg to justify such creations; or else they fatuously argue that "because the second law of thermodynamics promises an inexorable downhill march to a statistical heat-death, what else can a conscientious artist do but play along with nature by maximizing the entropy of his works?" R.P. Blackmur argues that the serious artist resists "disorder" and "torpor," but he is in our century in a fateful atmosphere in which society favors "uniform motion" and a lumpish proletariat, what Ortega y Gasset discerned as the result of the ascendancy of a new minimally cultured, minimally motivated mass man.[6]

Society takes on the aspect of uniform motion. The artist is the hero who struggles against uniform motion, a struggle in marmalade.

For the artist regards uniform motion as the last torpor in life. Torpor . . . we prefer to believe . . . is the running down of things. For three generations we have heroized the second law of thermodynamics, which is the law of the dissipation or gradual unavailability of energy within any system—which is the law of entropy or the incapacity for fresh idiom, time and perception going backwards. Entropy, from the point of view of the rational imagination, is disorder.[7]

Tony Tanner is particularly struck by "the frequency with which 'entropy' occurs, as a word or a tendency, in recent American fiction." He believes it points to "a disposition of the imagination" in contemporary America. He notes that writers who use the word include Norman Mailer, Saul Bellow, John Updike, John Barth, Walker Percy, Stanley Elkin, Donald Barthelme and Thomas Pynchon.[8] To such a group we can add George P. Elliott's David Knudsen, a hopeless, drifting, selfless man suffering radiation sickness from fallout in a hydrogen bomb explosion in the Pacific. His physicist father early "dispirited" him to talk of entropy and theories, maintaining that "something or other was likely to fail or prove itself to be no good." David's whole life consists of slowly discovering "what the void is like," an icy equilibrium where "$a = b = c = d = e$."[9]

Again, Susan Sontag's Diddy (or Dalton Harron) is a man without spirit or drive, "not having . . . job or identity, not having a cause . . . lacking a . . . goal." He wanders into a dream world of corpses multiplying, a world of what he had almost always inhabited—death. Such a Diddy is entropy personified: "Diddy . . . not really alive . . . Diddy making everything unpredictable. . . . Everything running down: suffusing the whole of Diddy's well-tended life. Like a house powered by one large generator in the basement. Diddy has an almost palpable sense of the decline of the generator's energy . . . sending forth a torrent of refuse that climbs up into Diddy's life."[10]

Similarly, William Burroughs's fiction is chock-full of chaos—excessive speed and collage and yet frustrating overall inertia—what in *Nova Express* he calls "terminal stasis." In *Naked Lunch* he portrays this chaos by his imagery of the whole of American society suffering from cancerous "un-D.T., Undifferentiated Tissue," a "degenerate . . . lifeform," "fallen to the borderline between living and dead matter." Elsewhere in *Naked Lunch*, in a limply appended "Atrophied Preface," the human race is considered over: "Thermodynamics has won at a crawl. . . . Time ran out." Other novelists go further. In a sudden burst of speed in *Cat's Cradle* (1963), Kurt Vonnegut, Jr., hastens the deep-freezing of planet earth, destroying everything. And Alvin Greenberg's novel of wounded, aimless wandering, *Going Nowhere* (1971), suggests even in its title the primary tendencies of entropic literature.[11]

Tony Tanner's argument appears to imply that "paranoid" views of onrushing and inevitable entropy are particularly contemporary visions of the last several decades, especially confined to a host of American writers. But this is not so; for the visions of a world-devouring running-down have been dominant as a theme for the last hundred and more years. Wyndham Lewis in his old age conceived of the entire modern movement as having gotten lost in violent extremes and avant-garde run amok, bringing heterogeneity and superficiality to all our creations: "We seem to be running down, everywhere in life, to a final end to all good things." This decline to "triviality" in the fine arts is almost ludicrously portrayed by Lewis as he lamely laments modern manufactured products: "paper is not what it was, in our newspapers, our books, our writing materials and so on, steel products, such as scissors, etc., become less and less reliable; the gut used in surgical dressing is no longer graded; but it is not necessary to enumerate this decline in detail."[12]

Surely the most remarkable visionary artist of the entropic is Samuel Beckett, whose fictions abound in lame, static, and maimed creatures fastened in cells and trash barrels. Murphy is forever deposited in his rocking chair; Malone is perennially torpid and immobile. We also recollect the endless posture of "waiting" of Beckett's exhausted inhabitants of *Waiting for Godot* (1952). In like manner, the predominant motif of Nathanael West's *Miss Lonelyhearts* (1933) is the lethal randomness of events and the irrevocable decline of human affairs toward chaos and exhaustion; Miss Lonelyhearts displays "an almost insane sensitiveness to order," an order always being deranged. "He sat in the window thinking. Man has a tropism for order. Keys in one pocket, change in another. Mandolins are tuned G D A E. The physical world has a tropism for disorder, entropy. Man against Nature. . . . Keys yearn to mix with change. Mandolins strive to get out of tune. Every order has within it the germ of destruction. All order is doomed."[13]

Moreover, the central image of Céline's influential work *Voyage au bout de la nuit* (1932) is a crazy journey toward death and silence. A key image, for instance, is Broadway in a "sickly twilight": "Like running sore this unending street, with all of us at the bottom of it, filling it from side to side, from one sorrow to the next, moving towards an end no one has ever seen, the end of all the streets in all the world." In like manner, as if taking his ideas from Trotsky, Yevgeny Zamyatin conceives of revolution as a perpetual "revolving." Any fixity in the state, he demonstrates in his dystopian *We* (1921), tends to produce totalitarian entropy—against which his revolutionary characters oppose rebellion and energy.[14]

One should also reflect that the idea of a profligate dissipation had captured the entire sensibilities of the fin de siècle French decadents and the late Victorians.[15] H.G. Wells, in *The Time Machine* (1895), and Camille Flammarion, in *La Fin du monde* (1894), suggested the death of our planet and dramatized the dying out in the future of our sun. Even in the 1870s Flaubert in his notes for the completion of his *Bouvard and Pecuchet* (1881) indicates that "Pecuchet sees the future of humanity in dark colours. The modern man is lessened, and has become a machine." But, most of all, Pecuchet predicts the "final anarchy of the human race."[16]

The promulgation of ideas of falling-off, decay, and inertia have particularly proliferated in literature, then, during the past century and a half. Moralists have complained that our major authors contributed to creating what Henry Miller called "the Universe of Death." George P. Elliott, with some distaste, perceives most of modern literature, despite its celebration of energy, as suffering from decline and entropy. Saul Bellow likewise objects to "antipersonalists" writers who reduce man to an "anonymous force," and he laments the recent acceptance in letters of ideas of indeterminacy and entropy. But one must wonder whether simple "affirmation" or happy world views would prove satisfying in our era. The great and penetrating visions of our world—devised by Dostoyevsky, Proust, Mann, Joyce, Gide, Musil, Faulkner, Grass—are significantly pessimistic and grimly lacking in riotous good cheer. In fact, Leslie Fiedler has argued, our literature—if it is to be honest—"*must be negative* . . . for the irony of art in the human situation lies in this . . . works of art are *about* love, family relations, politics, etc.; and to the degree that these radically imperfect human activities are represented in a perfectly articulated form, they are revealed in all their intolerable inadequacy. The image of man in art . . . is the image of a failure."[17]

Perhaps most important, outside the confines of literature, such ideas of decline helped to fashion entire views of history, as in Oswald Spengler's *Decline of the West* (1918–22). Similar ideas are represented, say, by Erich Auerbach, who perceives ours as the period of "crisis" in which "European civilization is approaching the term of its existence."[18] Doubtless the most pervasive influence upon a philosophy of history induced by the second law of thermodynamics can be found in *The Education of Henry Adams* (1906). In those great passages of terrible recognition, the "educations" of Henry Adams come to a climax: Adams finally witnesses the defeat of two thousand years of Christianity, represented by the archaic power of the Virgin, and the emergence of raw modern energy and force, represented at the Paris Exposition of 1900 by the dynamo. Furthermore, not only is this newer "dynamic" force machine-made, more aloof, more brutal, but it also provides "no unity," but rather "Multiplicity"—a "Chaos" that defies any "synthesis."[19] If the nineteenth century witnessed an incredible acceleration in knowledge, Adams nonetheless conjectures that it will peak, "like meteoroids," and "pass beyond, into new equilibrium," "or suffer dissipation altogether."[20] Here, fully dressed, according to Adams, is the vision of "a dynamic theory of history" based upon the concept of entropy in its irreversible process.

Furthermore, Adams elaborates his discussion of the effects of entropy upon America in *The Degradation of the Democratic Dogma* (1919). For him, entropy implied the slow failure of the American political experiment; in addition, "it meant only that the ash-heap was constantly increasing in size. . . . every reader of the French or German papers knows that not a day passes without producing some uneasy discussion of supposed social decrepitude;—falling off of the birth rate;—decline of rural population;—lowering of army standards;—multiplication of suicides;—increase of insanity or idiocy,—of cancer,—of tuberculosis;—signs of nervous exhaustion,—of enfeebled vitality,—'habits' of alcoholism and drugs,—failure of eye-sight in the young,—and so on, without end."[21] Adam's allusion to a constantly accumulating "ash-heap" brings to light another figurative image that Susan Sontag also employed, with Diddy's picturing of his life as a large generator running haywire, "sending forth a torrent of refuse." Here is a kindred image, of the increased proliferation of "junk" and detritus that accompanies many entropic visions in literature and art.

Characters in Donald Barthelme's *Snow White* (1967), we recall, busily manufactured "plastic buffalo humps," adding necessary "stuffing" and "sludge" to a society committed to the steady promulgation of ever-rising quantities of trash and detritus—until such productivity in the future attains to "100 percent."[22] And indeed, the proliferation of garbage is an ominous theme: one thinks of the Cleveland Wrecking Yard in Richard Brautigan's book *Trout Fishing in America* (1967), or of Ezra Pound's "Portrait d'une Femme" (1913), that describes a Victorian matron who is a listless ocean awash with facts, opinions, and gewgaws—the dead letter office of a dying civilization. We recall also the insidious piles of ashes and dust mounting up in London and surrounding the home of the wealthy Harmons in Dickens's *Our Mutual Friend* (1865).

All these instances image forth, to be sure, alarmist signs and symbols of a decaying society. Modern literature is full of such figures, and of "underground men" and outsiders (as in Dostoyevsky and Ralph Ellison and Camus) who take refuge in hiding from such a culture. Archibald Geikie, for example, delivered a paper in 1868 that conjectured that soil erosion was so severe that eventually there would be no land masses left upon the planet.[23] Since that time, we have had more and more theses predicting the demise of trees, air, natural resources, and food supply, together with gloomy prognostications about the multiplication of refuse, radioactivity, toxins, cosmic rays, and the like.

All these depressive and downward-oriented philosophies hardly result solely from the second law of thermodynamics. For most of two thousand years in the West, Greek ideas of a decline from a golden age in the pristine past and then a Christian eschatology based upon the book of Revelation that anticipated the imminent destruction of the universe were predominant world views.[24] It was all that Francis Bacon and other scientific hopefuls in the seventeenth century could do to stanch the prevalent moods of pessimism. Only briefly, during the Enlightenment and into the nineteenth century, did a new benevolence, meliorism, and attendant ideas of progress prevail. Then, as suddenly, by the middle of the nineteenth century the reaction to this new optimism vehemently set in. Ideas of human "degeneration" (built into the genes) began to proliferate by midcentury.[25] These were accompanied by a pessimistic naturalism and determinism and were aided and abetted by dark satanic visions of a corrupt or infected romanticism. The movement of French decadence in the arts and subsequent schools of nihilism have similarly prospered. Such trends helped to foster new interest in every extremity of response to crisis: mental illness, ennui, paranoia, suicide, absurdity, inertia, and silence.[26] Ever since, we have had to live with an essentially decline-structured conception of our world.

Faced with all these movements heralding decline and decay, one thing is certain. C.P. Snow was certainly wrong about the humanist's ignorance of the second law of thermodynamics. For, in a climate of ideas that has been for some 150 years morbid, cynical, and despondent, ideas of entropy have played a powerful role. They have provided traditional structural and metahistorical readings of human history with the glamor of mathematical principle and scientific law.[27]

Late in his life, the great poet William Butler Yeats took to dabbling furiously in the occult and even married a woman gifted in automatic writing; she took dictation from spirits of the supernatural world. For a time Yeats was so entranced and beguiled by this influx of otherworldly commerce that he even offered to the spirits to give up writing poetry entirely. "No," was their written reply to him, "we have come to give you metaphors for poetry."[28] In a striking and similar way, science—so long mistrusted by the humanists—has brought to literature and the arts the latest myth, and entropy has indeed bestowed upon us in the modern world vital metaphors for our poetry.

In our own era, no greater or more ingenious species of metaphor can be found than that within our satire. Satire has ever dealt with depravity and decline as its central message and motif, tracing vigorously, dismayingly, and flamboyantly the downturn from good news to bad. Alvin Kernan notes that in formal verse satire, authors such as Juvenal, Horace, and Pope string together upon a thread a number of works that illustrate "the general corruption of society." That is precisely the general pattern to be found everywhere in literary satire, in which, as in Murphy's Law, things go wrong.[29] Here, with Murphy's and similar pronouncements, modern pseudoscience has merely codified what in satire had always been omnipresent: the concept of perpetual corrosion, senility, and degradation. Thus, Juvenal affirms that all vice nowadays is at the apex. Alexander Pope concurs: "Nothing is Sacred now but Villany." Senecan dramas rehearsed the same lesson: *fata se vertunt retro*, "fate inverts itself," gets twisted up, turned upside down. In every case, the traditional satirist insistently cries that poetic justice has been banished, happy endings dispelled, and stupidity and evil triumphant.[30]

For that reason, it is curious that a number of critics in the twentieth century have repeated the opinion that satire itself has declined and possibly died out. Matthew Hodgart suspects, for instance, that satire is "a somewhat archaic survival which is being abandoned by the avant-garde of literature."[31] On the contrary, it could well be argued that such gloomy notions of satire's demise are the gossip and gleeful prognoses spread abroad by the satirist himself, lovingly depicting the evolution of misery and the progress of decline. Evelyn Waugh for one—a satirist if there ever was one—flatly denies that he is satiric at all. Satire, he testily explains, thrives in centuries with standards and morals, in ages presuming that the guilty can be made to feel shame. "All this has no place in the Century of the Common Man where vice no longer pays lip service to virtue." What Waugh perceives "today" is "the disintegrated society"; tomorrow brings "the dark age opening."[32] Here the satirist outrageously denies his occupation as part and parcel of his strategy of heralding doom and inducing discomfort in the reader. Yet Waugh notwithstanding, complacent assertions that ours is no noteworthy age of satire cannot be farther from the truth.

Indeed, the sure sign that satire is alive and well can readily be established by observing the sheer numbers of satiric authors who embrace decline and retail the advancement of entropy. It is no accident that the major authors referred to in these pages—Dickens and

Flaubert; Mann, Musil, and Grass; Zamyatin, West, and Céline, Vonnegut, Barth, Barthelme, and Pynchon—are themselves the major satirists of our century. If their voices are uniformly raised in angelic celebration of debauchery and inertia, then it is precisely because they are our most impressive satiric singers. And it ought to go without saying that entropy has provided them with but one additional and wonderful metaphor for their continuous haunting, and mellifluous song.

Part IV. Conclusion

The preceding chapters of this book illustrate two major points: that the subjects and strategies of the satiric grotesque belong to an age-old tradition, and that such satiric grotesquerie is wonderfully on the upswing, richly creative and alive in the twentieth century. Of course, as always, there was bound to be a chorus of naysayers and complainers, critics who argue that our literature is too negative, repellent, ugly, and depressing. But notwithstanding all this noisome foofaraw, we can point rather contentedly to a literature of the grotesque that has in our era been dynamic and inventive.

15

The Death of the Humanities

"There is no health anywhere," Anthony Burgess recently intoned, musing upon current American fiction. He finds characters reduced to "thinghood," protagonists without "the values out of which the novel-form was begotten." For Burgess, such nonnovels merely present "porn, corruption, death"; he finally laments that "we need humanity [even] to observe the death of humanity." These observations are moot: any reader knows about the decline of SAT scores, the decline of interest in humanities and foreign languages, or even the decline of capacity to overcome substandard English. One professor has even grandly labeled all reading and writing "elitist," and he predicts that the electronics communications revolution will liberate the next generation from literacy entirely.[1] Ours is the century of total war: it has witnessed, in Henry Adams's words, the triumph of the dynamo over the Virgin; it has beheld the flourishing of the dystopia that predicates not merely Toffler's future shock but future wretchedness; and much of its science fiction and black humor has utilized the theme of entropy and the unwinding of the universe.

Nearer home, a host of cultural observers detect "the death of tragedy," "the death of satire," "the death of the past," and the "fall of American Humor."[2] John Barth doubtless sums up these gloomy anticipations when he speaks of "the literature of exhaustion."[3] Moreover, a rising froglike chorus of analysts lament almost all of literature, with its indecency, "sickness," and "deviations."[4] The latest critic caught up in this most furious, slavering dither is John Gardner who finds that something dreadful "has gone wrong in recent years with the various arts." For him, contemporary art is "bad," "mediocre," "dull," "heretical," and "wrong," for it is the work of "nihilists, cynics, and merdistes," "supports death and slavery," and "must be driven out."[5]

Our militant sense of modern "horrors," if permitted to get out of hand, approaches hysteria—and the absurd. For assuredly, some of our plaintive contemporary observers seem quavering, stentorian, and unstrung. We have traveled a flight-shot beyond mere pessimism, the

Spenglerian foreboding of a Decline of the West, to a romantic espousal of anticipated universal holocaust. We have been impelled beyond the two cultures, the tripartite high-, mid-, and mass-cult, and the schizophrenic divided self into fragmentation, shrapnel, and shards. From the point of view of an Othello, "Chaos is come again."

But we must remember that this doomsaying is an attitude, a posture, a single (and therefore constricting) point of view. All civilizations have adopted at various times the dark perspective. The hero of the Gilgamesh epic, no less than Euripides, Tacitus, the *Beowulf* author, Breughel, or the saturnine and atrabilious melancholiacs of the late Renaissance, has perceived quite clearly the panic and perplexities of human existence as well as we have. Innumerable societies have embraced a reading of history as decline, history as march of the barbarians, over the centuries, both before and after Hesiod and Lucretius.[6] And furthermore, the idealized pastoral world has always been juxtaposed with the supposedly corrupt city; indeed, each generation conceives of an ideal that existed in the recent past.[7] Therefore it is interesting to note that man has always placed nirvana in the past or the future, never in a present that is so rigorously actualized and in transit.

Horace's "laudator temporis acti se puero" in the *Ars Poetica*, the aged grumbler who praises the world of his boyhood, is a commonplace figure. One eternally laments the passing of his own pristine springtime, and of course the elderly in Joyce's "The Dead" rue the passing of earlier operatic stars and are convinced that we shall never hear their likes again. "Mais où son les neiges d'antan?" Nostalgically, man ever grasps for the flown and benighted past that nevermore can return.

In such a broad sense, no time in history is "happy" and "affirmative"; such terms are part of the jargon of language arts programs, political Hegelians, HEW, and the Madison Avenue contrivers of slogans for social and moral uplift—so many spiritual athletic supporters and ethical brassieres. But the fact remains that most of man's history is not endearing, most of his comedy not painlessly funny, most of his tragedy hardly cathartic, pedagogically instructive, or exalting.

Tragedy, for its part, invites us to find in it some pedagogic purpose, but the invitation cannot really be thought to be made in good faith. We cannot convince ourselves that the two Oedipus tragedies teach us anything, or show the hero as learning anything. . . . We [might] find ourselves in the unhappy situation [of arguing] . . . that Lear and Gloucester suffered to good purpose because their pain "educated" them before they died. When . . . a great tragedy is made to yield such conclusions as that fate is inscrutable and that it is a wise child who knows his own father, or . . . that the universe is uncomfortable and its governance morally incomprehensible, we decide that tragedy has indeed nothing to do with the practical conduct of life except as it transcends and negates it, that it celebrates a mystery debarred to reason, prudence, and morality.[8]

Ultimately, are not the incessantly lucid pictures of inscrutability, of apocalypse, of decline and fall themselves mere topoi, recurrent and significant conventions of Western literature and the humanities? Must satire, stoicism, and professional historical projections of cycles and of gloom require special apologetics or justification at so late a date? Seen from a particular point of view, the "divided self" is precisely what is called for in the complex, the urbane, and the ironic consciousness that tolerates (and even requires) a Timon, a Socrates, an Aristophanes, and a Sophocles at the forefront of its population.

MURPHY'S LAW: If anything can go wrong, it will.
Corollary 5. Left to themselves, things tend to go from bad to worse.[9]

The Murphy pronouncements merely happen to be the latest comic and mock scientific codifications, like Parkinson's Laws, the Chilholm Effect, and the Peter Principle, that continue to thrive in our society. Yet things cannot be all wrong when there is a Mark Twain, an H.L. Mencken, a W.C. Fields, a James Thurber, a Lenny Bruce, or a Woody Allen in our midst. The ideal of humanism, after all, is the bold-faced insistence upon the careful scrutiny of humanity in all its aspects and especially in all its multifarious (even contradictory and devious) forms.

"Homo sum: humani nil a me alienum puto": Since we are human, nothing human should be alien to us.[10] Such a concept remains true, even after we concede that today there are more humans upon the planet than ever before, even after we admit that a worldwide network of communications conveys to us human behavior with a speed and in a quantity never before conceived, and even after we confess that recently Darwin, Dostoevsky, Freud, Kafka, Einstein, Cassirer, Sartre, Stravinsky, and García Márquez have coerced us into peering into the heart of darkness of this selfsame mankind. Nowhere has there been such a viewing as in our black comedy of the grotesque. In sum, the picture we have been getting is sharper than ever before, delivered in technicolor, in 3-D, in stereo—and yet it is still not entirely dusk and melancholy.

The historian J.H. Plumb acknowledges that our present age appears baffled, seemingly meaningless, and unpleasant, yet he reminds us that there are more historians alive today than perhaps the sum total of all historians who have ever lived before. This plentitude applies equally well to scientists, artists, nurses, and metaphysicians. Today, he argues, we must admit that "ordinary" humans can secure "a richer life than their ancestors": "There is more food in the world, more opportunity of advancement, greater areas of liberty in ideas and in living than the world has ever known: art, music, literature can be enjoyed by tens of millions, not tens of thousands. This has been achieved . . . by the application of human ingenuity [and] . . . rationalism."[11]

If an honest and inclusive world view were projected upon an enormous screen, we would expect that a considerable representation of wretchedness would be included in that portrayal. And so it should, if we were to pay the least homage to honesty and reality. The same holds true in the arts. Whitman was grandly inclusive in his verse: "I am not the poet of goodness only, I do not decline to be the poet of wickedness also." William Carlos Williams provides a suitable exposition of this Whitman text, explaining the gesture that seeks to incorporate wickedness: "The commonplace, the tawdry, the sordid all have their poetic uses if the imagination can lighten them."[12] Yet the imagination can lighten only that which it has been able to confront and depict. The modern era, in its prevalently wry and grotesque manner, has deliberately enabled its imagination to play upon the wicked and the paltry, the sordid and the mundane, in a concerted and even painful quest for comprehension and enlightenment.

A classic instance of such a quest in the modern novel is Manuel Puig's *Kiss of the Spider Woman* (*El Beso de la Mujer Arana* 1976). On the surface, Puig's novel seems totally natural: two prisoners slowly come to admire and appreciate one another through acts of mutual aid and loving kindness. They both seem to grow, learning to renounce exploitation of others. Perhaps it is the rest of society that is unkind. One prisoner relates a number of standard cinema story lines: one about a woman who helplessly and repeatedly turns into a panther, another about a witch doctor's voodoo that converts numerous peons into zombies. Even when films are not overtly grotesque, however, they nonetheless distort and distend reality: a Nazi film glorifies the SS, turning innocent Jews into archfiends; another film depicts frustrated lovers who transform themselves, one into a prostitute, the other into a derelict, dying of alcoholism. Even so, the Nazi film purports to be a patriotic spy thriller, and the other postures as a sentimental musical romance.

Doubtless society, weaned upon such "entertainments," is itself infected and unsound. Supposedly, the two prisoners are poised on the outer fringes of society, the one a violent political revolutionary, the other a perverse homosexual and seducer of minors. Nor is prison an island or haven from the cruel and obfuscating outside world. For the one prisoner wishes to "exploit" the other as a possible "contact" with his guerilla cadre in Buenos Aires, and the other is a "spider woman," seeking to entangle the revolutionary in a shabby homosexual amour. Meanwhile, prison officials and espionage agents attempt throughout the novel to manipulate both prisoners for arcane reasons of state.

Is anyone in such a society free from machination and false representation? No one is. And yet, curiously, the two prisoners (trebly incarcerated in a distorting and repressive society) do change and pulsate and grow, finding moments of distress, sorrow, happiness—even of laughter and release—in the midst of their bondage. Against all probability, they manage (in Dylan Thomas's phrase) to "sing in their chains like the sea."[13] Nevertheless, both men, Valentin and Molina, sustain at a number of levels deliberate intentions to use and abuse other human beings; their motives, in short, are tainted. Is there no redress? Or is man eternally condemned to be mixed—a fusion of pathetic apportionments of animal, vegetable, and human? Alas, such a decoction defines, and with profundity, the essence of the grotesque. "What a piece of work is a man, how noble in reason, how infinite in faculties; in form and moving how express and admirable, in action how like an angel, in apprehension how like a god: the beauty of the world, the paragon of animals! And yet to me what is this quintessence of dust? Man delights not me."[14]

Manuel Puig's (and William Shakespeare's) portrayal of the human condition is anything but affable, romantic, or serene. Yet, despite the complaints and objections of numerous high-flown moralist and desperate cynics, our arts and sciences are hardly on the verge of dying out. Indeed, if this book has attempted anything at all, it has sought to illustrate the vigor of satiric humor, the amplitude of its horrific imagery, the challenges of its startling ideas, and the continuity it sustains within an age-old, ongoing tradition. In this atmosphere of copious creativity, it should be patently obvious that comedy, satire, history, the novel—nay, culture itself—have not yet perished from the earth, but are, rather, quick and various and cunning, and very much alive.

Notes

Introduction

1. Preface to the 1st ed. of *Poems* (1853), in *The Poems of Matthew Arnold*, ed. Kenneth Allott (London, 1965), 591. Arnold is referring to fifth-century Athens, but these modern insecurities well describe Arnold's own era.

2. In *Die protestantische Ethik und der Geist des Kapitalismus* (Tübingen, 1904-5), Max Weber perceives that the nineteenth century became an industrial iron age, filled with mechanic conformity; he rejected idealistic theories of progress. Quotation from Thomas R. McDaniel, "Thoughts on a Dissertation," *Humanities in the South* 44 (Fall 1976): 8.

3. The quoted terms have been employed as titles in book-length studies by a number of critical observers: Ortega y Gasset, Julien Benda, Harold Lubin, Harry Levin, Wylie Sypher, Leslie Fiedler, Robert Martin Adams, Mark Hillegas, Ihab Hassan, and George Steiner.

4. See, for instance, George Knox, "Apocalypse and Sour Utopias," *Western Humanities Review* 16 (Winter 1962): 11-22; Irving Howe, "The Fiction of Anti-Utopia," in *Decline of the New* (New York, 1970), 66-74; and W.K. Thomas, "The Underside of Utopias," *College English* 38 (1976): 356-72.

5. Henry James, "The Art of Fiction" (1885), in *The Future of the Novel*, ed. Leon Edel (New York, 1956), 10, 17.

6. Ihab Hassan, *Radical Innocence: The Contemporary American Novel* (New York, 1966), 334.

7. Tony Tanner, *Saul Bellow* (London, 1965), 115.

8. Louis I. Bredvold, "The Gloom of the Tory Satirists," in *Pope and His Contemporaries*, ed. James L. Clifford and Louis A. Landa (New York, 1949), 16. George Bernard Shaw's Lucifer makes a similar point: "I will now go further, and confess to you that men get tired of everything, of heaven no less than of hell; and that all history is nothing but a record of the oscillations of the world between these two extremes." Shaw, *Man and Superman* (Baltimore, 1952), 170.

9. Lionel Trilling, "The Fate of Pleasure: Wordsworth to Dostoevsky," in *Romanticism Reconsidered: Selected Papers from the English Institute*, ed. Northrop Frye (New York, 1963), 90.

10. Fyodor Dostoevsky, *Notes from Underground*, trans. Mirra Ginsburg (New York, 1974), 37, 38.

11. Irving Deer and Harriet Deer, "The Power of Negative Thinking," in *Person to Person: Rhetoric, Reality, and Change*, ed. Irving Deer, H.A. Deer, and

J.A. Gould (New York, 1973), 243-62. See also Leslie Fiedler, *No! in Thunder* (Boston, 1960).

12. Terence, *Heauton Timorumenos*, l. 77: "I'm a man: nothing human is alien to me."

1. Deadly Laughter

1. I borrow the phrase from Saul Bellow's novel concerning a listless, unstable man suspended between civilian life and the military; he awaits imminently being inducted into the army during World War II. See Bellow, *Dangling Man* (New York, 1944).

2. For almost two thousand years the Judaeo-Christian concept of a sacred, linear, unfolding history predominated, only to become secularized in the seventeenth and eighteenth centuries. See C.A. Patrides, *The Grand Design of God: The Literary Form of the Christian View of History* (London, 1972), a revised version of his 1964 volume, *The Phoenix and the Ladder: The Rise and Decline of the Christian View of History*. This constitutes, in effect, a major revolution in the realm of Western consciousness; see J.B. Bury, *The Idea of Progress* (New York, 1932), Charles Van Doren, *The Idea of Progress* (New York, 1967), and W.W. Wagar, ed., *The Idea of Progress since the Renaissance* (New York, 1969). Science and rationalism matured this secular concept of progress into a burning faith. But from the mid–nineteenth century onward, we have been witnessing a still more drastic intellectual revolution, which denies progress entirely. A coherent early attack was mounted by the near-anarchist Georges Sorel, in his *Les Illusions du progrès* (Paris, 1908), and most thinkers in our era substantiate the repudiation of earlier "faith"—not merely the faith in Christianity but in humanism as well. See, for instance, chap. 9, "Progress at Bay," in Robert Nisbet, *History of the Idea of Progress* (New York, 1980), 317-51.

3. Jonathan Swift, *A Tale of a Tub to Which Is Added the Battle of the Books and the Mechanical Operation of the Spirit*, ed. A.C. Guthkelch and D. Nichol Smith, 2d ed. (Oxford, 1958), 129, 146.

4. Olga is speaking at the close of "The Three Sisters," in *Chekhov: The Major Plays*, trans. Ann Dunnigan (New York, 1964), 312.

5. I borrow the phrase *performing self* from an essay of that title that examines a number of twentieth-century authors who are "notorious self-advertisers." Richard Poirier, *The Performing Self: Compositions and Decompositions in the Languages of Contemporary Life* (New York, 1971), 86-111. And in using the term *cult of the ego*, I am thinking of a major study of destructive modern solipsism, Eugene Goodheart, *The Cult of the Ego: The Self in Modern Literature* (Chicago, 1968). The great romantic creator of a posturing self—as dashing, ardent, obsessive, accursed—was Byron; see Peter L. Thorslev, Jr., *The Byronic Hero: Types and Prototypes* (Minneapolis, 1962). A number of recent studies examine the emergence since the Renaissance of particularly self-conscious, role-playing individual "selves" in modern society; consult, for example, John O. Lyons, *The Invention of the Self: The Hinge of Consciousness in the Eighteenth Century* (Carbondale, Ill., 1978).

6. The best relevant studies are Renato Poggioli, *The Theory of the Avant-Garde*, trans. Gerald Fitzgerald (Cambridge, Mass., 1968), and Roger Shattuck, *The Banquet Years: The Origins of the Avant-Garde in France, 1885 to World War I*, rev. ed. (New York, 1968).

7. D.H. Lawrence, "Study of Thomas Hardy," in *Phoenix: The Posthumous Papers of D.H. Lawrence*, ed. Edward D. McDonald (London, 1961), 409.
8. "Pitié pour nous qui combattons toujours aux frontières / De l'illimité et de l'avenir." "La Jolie Rousse," ll. 28-29, from *Calligrames* (1918), in Guillaume Apollinaire, *Oeuvres Poétique*, ed. Marcel Adéma and Michel Décaudin (Paris, 1956), 314.
9. From Marinetti's Foundation Manifesto, in Jane Rye, *Futurism* (New York, 1972), 9.
10. Jean Anouilh, "Antigone" (1944), adapted and trans. Lewis Galantière, in *Contemporary Drama: Eleven Plays*, ed. E.B. Watson and B. Pressey (New York, 1956), 131.
11. Wylie Sypher, *Loss of the Self in Modern Literature and Art* (New York, 1962). An acute study of the causes, both internal and external, of the fragmentation and "disintegration" of the individual in the twentieth century is Erich Kahler, *The Tower and the Abyss: An Inquiry into the Transformation of the Individual* (New York, 1957).
12. Earlier Christian ideas of apocalypse are offset by secular ideas of progress in the seventeenth and eighteenth centuries (see Ernest Lee Tuveson, *Millennium and Utopia* [Berkeley, 1949]), but pessimism was one significant vein of thought in the Renaissance. Consult Victor Harris, *All Coherence Gone* (Chicago, 1949), and Henry Vyverberg, *Historical Pessimism in the French Enlightenment* (Cambridge, Mass., 1958). Despite romantic exuberance, there was a dark Byronic strain, and by the mid–nineteenth century, second-generation romantics in France openly espoused "decadence"; consult G.L. Van Roosbroeck, *The Legend of the Decadents* (New York, 1927), Noël Richard, *Le Mouvement décadent: Dandys, esthètes et quintessents* (Paris, 1968), and George Ross Ridge, *The Hero in French Decadent Literature* (Athens, Ga., 1961). Such ideas of cultural decay spread; see Jerome Hamilton Buckley, "The Idea of Decadence," in *The Triumph of Time: A Study of the Victorian Concepts of Time, History, Progress, and Decadence* (Cambridge, Mass., 1966), 66-93, and Matei Calinescu, *Faces of Modernity: Avant-Garde, Decadence, Kitsch* (Bloomington, 1977). By the 1890s an influential book in Europe was Max Nordau, *Entartung*, or *Degeneration* (Berlin, 1892–93; English trans., 1895), which stressed the artist's mental deterioration and society's degeneration owing to social ills. Such ideas were carried further by Henry Adams, *The Degradation of the Democratic Dogma* (1919; rpt. New York, 1958), by his younger brother's work (Brooks Adams, *The Law of Civilization and Decay* [New York, 1893]), and of course by Oswald Spengler.
13. "For a thousand years or so, roughly from the time of Charlemagne to 1914, the wars of Christendom . . . [had derived from] a single, continuous tradition. . . . within that tradition [it was] assumed without question that [most] battles . . . were not only justifiable but holy. . . . Full of internal contradictions . . . the Christian heroic tradition proved viable for centuries." Suddenly in our century, with the world wars, that tradition of heroism died. "We inhabit for the first time a world in which men begin wars knowing that their avowed ends will not be accomplished." Some leaders, to be sure, still do not know that "they were merely dupes of history.., unaware that history had rendered them comic" and absurd, but it is a dominant topic of our literature. Leslie Fiedler, *Waiting for the End* (New York, 1964), 28-29, 31. For the lasting and devastating impact of World War I, consult Paul Fussell, *The Great War and Modern Memory* (New York, 1975). *(continued on page 168)*

Notes to Pages 12-16

Frederick J. Hoffman, in *The Mortal No: Death and the Modern Imagination* (Princeton, 1964), carefully studies the great increase in the incidence and impact of violence and violent death in modern literature and life. The decline of religions and their sanctions have ensured the proliferation of "naturalistic" death—in which society is deprived of "moral, confessional, and willed" explanations for dying. The great shock in this century was World War I in which the depersonalization, enormity, and unreality of death were encountered on a grand, unprecedented scale (13, 15). On modern warfare and its terrible ingenuities, see Liddell Hart, *The Revolution in Warfare* (London, 1946).

14. George Santayana, "The Poetry of Barbarism," in *Essays in Literary Criticism*, ed. Irving Singer (New York, 1956), 149.

15. "The Eighteenth Brumaire of Louis Bonaparte," in Karl Marx and Friedrich Engels, *Basic Writings on Politics and Philosophy*, ed. Louis S. Feuer (Garden City, N.Y., 1959), 320.

16. T.S. Eliot, "The Love Song of J. Alfred Prufrock" (1917), ll. 48-51, in *The Complete Poems and Plays* (New York, 1952).

17. Thomas Mann, "Conrad's 'Secret Agent,' " in *Past Masters and Other Papers*, trans. H.T. Lowe-Porter (Freeport, N.Y., 1968), 240-41.

18. Eugène Ionesco, "Experience of the Theatre," in *Notes and Counter Notes*, trans. Donald Watson (New York, 1964), 26.

19. See Maurice Valency, *The End of the World: An Introduction to Contemporary Drama* (New York, 1980), esp. 419-37.

20. George Steiner, "After the Book?" in *On Difficulty and Other Essays* (Oxford, 1980), 186. This "disintegrative process," Erich Kahler argues, concerning the arts, owes to increasing dominance in recent centuries of the irrational and the unconscious over consciousness; see Kahler, *The Disintegration of Form in the Arts* (New York, 1968), esp. 28.

21. I borrow the term employed by J.L. Styan to describe modern tragicomedy, particularly that kind of drama whose unpleasant setting and Brechtian "alienation-effects" in some sense contribute to the audience's discomfort; see Styan, *The Dark Comedy: The Development of Modern Comic Tragedy*, 2d ed. (Cambridge, Eng., 1968).

22. Flannery O'Connor, "The Displaced Person," in *The Complete Short Stories of Flannery O'Connor* (New York, 1971), 200. O'Connor's grotesquerie has attracted considerable critical attention. See, for example, Gilbert H. Muller, *Nightmares and Visions: Flannery O'Connor and the Catholic Grotesque* (Athens, Ga., 1972); Carol Shloss, "Extensions of the Grotesque," in *Flannery O'Connor's Dark Comedies* (Baton Rouge, 1980), 38-57; Marshall Bruce Gentry, *Flannery O'Connor's Religion of the Grotesque* (Jackson, Miss., 1986); and Zhong Ming, "Designed Shock and Grotesquerie: The Form of Flannery O'Connor's Fiction," *The Flannery O'Connor Bulletin* 17 (1988): 51-61. O'Connor herself did see and appreciate peacocks; in fact, she raised them. See her own memoir, "The King of the Birds," in Flannery O'Connor, *Mystery and Manners: Occasional Prose*, ed. Sally Fitzgerald and Robert Fitzgerald (New York, 1969), 3-21.

23. George Gordon, Lord Byron, *Don Juan*, ed. Leslie A. Marchand (Boston, 1958), 4.4.1-4, p. 136.

24. *King Lear* 4.1.2-6. All quotations of Shakespeare's plays are taken from *The Complete Works of William Shakespeare*, with a preface by Christopher Morley (Garden City, N.Y., 1936).

2. Satiric Gothic, Satiric Grotesque

1. Maximillian E. Novak, "Gothic Fiction and the Grotesque," *Novel* 13 (Fall 1979): 50n. Consult the trenchant analysis of the later eighteenth century's mood and art in England by Northrop Frye, "Towards Defining an Age of Sensibility," *Journal of English Literary History* 13 (June 1956): 144-52, frequently reprinted. Much recent American literature has been attracted to revitalizing the gothic and the horrible; see the works of such novelists as Flannery O'Connor, John Hawkes, Truman Capote, Carson McCullers, James Purdy, and J.D. Salinger. Consult Irving Malin, *New American Gothic* (Carbondale, Ill., 1962).

2. See James William Johnson, *The Formation of English Neo-Classical Thought* (Princeton, 1967), esp. chap. 2, "The Role of Historiography" (55-68), on the decline of history; see p. 61 on Temple, pp. 63ff. on Swift. Henry James, as in "The Pupil," frequently perceived vulgar moderns and vulgar modern Americans as trooping through the once-sacred precincts of Europe like barbarian invaders: see his "Preface to 'What Maisie Knew,' " in *The Art of the Novel: Critical Prefaces*, with an introduction by Richard P. Blackmur (New York, 1934), 152. And the imminent return of an invading barbarian horde was a central tenet in the satiric mythos of Evelyn Waugh; see Alvin B. Kernan, "The Wall and the Jungle: The Early Novels of Evelyn Waugh," *Yale Review* 53 (Dec. 1963): 199-220.

Richard Gilman, in *Decadence: The Strange Life of an Epithet* (New York, 1979), has argued that the term *decadence* itself is essentially meaningless. I would suggest, however, that the term obtains force because a great many writers associate the internal moral decline of a society (archetypally Rome) with its assault and destruction from without. This is the case, as we have noted, with Swift, James, and Waugh; the reader might also consider disparate examples such as poems by Verlaine ("Langueur"), C.P. Cavafy ("Waiting for the Barbarians"), and Auden ("The Fall of Rome")—all of which make this same assumption and utilize this general myth. Such a mythos is vitally alive in the twentieth century, a mythos that cultivates genres describing decline and general collapse—dystopias, negative science fictions, and apocalyptic tales of the end of the world.

3. Especially on the dark visions of Twain, Dickens, and Flaubert, see John R. Clark and William E. Morris, "Humor in the Nineteenth Century: Decline and Fuel," *Mosaic* 9 (Summer 1976): 219-26. Concerning the blending of the gothic with the grotesque, Alan Spiegel in a curious article contends that in America modern southern writers tend to employ the grotesque (i.e., to create grotesque characters), whereas northern writers utilize the gothic. Consult Spiegel, "A Theory of the Grotesque in Southern Fiction," *Georgia Review* 26 (1972): 426-37.

4. Seminal studies of the grotesque are Thomas Wright, *A History of Caricature and Grotesque in Literature and Art* (1865), rpt. with an introduction by Frances K. Barasch (New York, 1968); and Wolfgang Kayser, *Das Groteske, Seine Gestaltung in Malerei und Dichtung* (Oldenburg, 1957), and its English ed., *The Grotesque in Art and Literature*, trans. Ulrich Weisstein (Bloomington, 1963). The observations of John Ruskin, *Stones of Venice* 3.3, and *Modern Painters* 4.8, are still extremely relevant. For a full description, with excellent photographs of Nero's palace, consult Michael Grant, "The Golden House: Art and Luxury,"

in *Nero: Emperor in Revolt* (New York, 1970), 162-95. For my study of Seneca and the grotesque, consult Anna Lydia Motto and John R. Clark, " 'There's Something Wrong with the Sun': Seneca's *Oedipus* and the Modern Grotesque," *Classical Bulletin* 54 (Jan. 1978): 41-44. One recent critic examines the grotesque effect generated when ancient myth confronts modern realities; his study explores several nineteenth- and twentieth-century texts. Consult Geoffrey Galt Harpham, *On the Grotesque* (Princeton, 1982).

Of lesser importance, but still of some interest, are M.B. van Buren, "The Grotesque in Visual Art and Literature," *Dutch Quarterly Review of Anglo-American Letters* 12 (1982): 42-53, and Arthur Clayborough, *The Grotesque in English Literature* (Oxford, 1965).

5. See Bakhtin's introduction, esp. 1-34, in Mikhail Bakhtin, *Rabelais and His World*, trans. Héléne Iswolsky (Cambridge, Mass., 1968). Consult also William R. Magretta and Joan Magretta, "Lina Wertmuller and the Tradition of Italian Carnivalesque Comedy," *Genre* 12 (Spring 1979): 25-43. The broad use of the "comic grotesque"—in plays and in pamphlets—is also stressed in Neil Rhodes, *Elizabethan Grotesque* (Boston, 1980). Rhodes also notes that the grotesque traditionally calls for "two kinds of response which are mutually incompatible"; hence the audience is confronted with "frivolity and the macabre, or, more generally, [with] laughter and revulsion" (10).

6. Vitruvius Pollio *De Architectura* 7.5.3-4, in *On Architecture*, ed. and trans. Frank Granger (Cambridge, Mass., 1970), 2: 105.

7. Horace *Ars Poetica* 1-8 (my translation). See Homer *Odyssey* 12.39-46; and Virgil *Aeneid* 5.864-65; 6.273-91, 574-607, for treatment of monsters. Seneca is notorious for presenting supernatural elements in his plays; consider *Agamemnon* 766-68, the host of omens in the *Oedipus*, and supernatural figures and phenomena in the *Thyestes*.

8. Consult G. Wilson Knight's famous essay "*King Lear* and the Comedy of the Grotesque" in *The Wheel of Fire* (New York, 1957), 160-76. Works that stress the "tension" of mirth and horror in the grotesque include Frances K. Barasch, *The Grotesque: A Study in Meanings* (The Hague, 1971); Philip Thomson, *The Grotesque* (London, 1972); and Michael Steig, "Defining the Grotesque: An Attempt at Synthesis," *Journal of Aesthetics and Art Criticism* 29 (Winter 1970): 253-60. Satiric and demonic features and the grotesque's relationship to the picaresque are stressed in Barbara C. Millard, "Thomas Nashe and the Functional Grotesque in Elizabethan Prose Fiction," *Studies in Short Fiction* 15 (Winter 1978): 39-48.

David Hayman claims, in fact, that Mikhail Bakhtin has overstressed the grotesque's playful side; Hayman notes that the romantics invested "pathos and dread" into the concept of the grotesque. Hayman, "Toward a Mechanics of Mode: Beyond Bakhtin," *Novel* 16 (1983): 106-7. Similarly, Bernard McElroy argues that too many critics have taken the grotesque lightly, dealing with its relationship to play. Concurring with Ruskin, McElroy emphasizes the terrible and the fearful in the grotesque, especially considering features that suggest the primitive, the uncanny, the magical, and the irrational—features that focus upon "corporeal degradation." See McElroy, *Fiction of the Modern Grotesque* (New York, 1989), esp. 1-29.

9. Although the other arts have "the workes of Nature" for their "principall object," "Onely the Poet, disdayning to be tied to any such subiection, lifted vp with the vigor of his owne inuention, dooth growe in effect another nature, in making things either better than Nature bringeth forth, or, quite a

newe, formes such as neuer were in Nature, as the *Heroes, Demigods, Cyclops, Chimeras, Furies,* and such like: so as hee goeth hand in hand with Nature, not inclosed within the narrow warrant of her guifts, but freely ranging onely within the Zodiack of his own wit." Sir Philip Sidney, *Sidney's Apologie for Poetrie,* ed. J. Churton Collins (Oxford, 1907), 7, 8.

10. See John O. Lyons, *The Invention of the Self: The Hinge of Consciousness in the Eighteenth Century* (Carbondale, Ill., 1978); Arnold Weinstein, *Fictions of the Self: 1550–1800* (Princeton, 1981); and Stephen D. Cox, *"The Stranger within Thee": Concepts of the Self in Late Eighteenth-Century Literature* (Pittsburgh, 1981).

11. See Monroe C. Beardsley, "Dostoyevsky's Metaphor of the 'Underground,' " *Journal of the History of Ideas* 3 (1942): 265-90; Harry Levin, *The Power of Blackness: Hawthorne, Poe, Melville* (New York, 1958); and Darlene Unrue, "Henry James and the Grotesque," *Arizona Quarterly* 32 (1976): 293-300.

12. See Renate Matthaei, *Luigi Pirandello,* trans. Simon Young and Erika Young (New York, 1973), 21ff., and Roger W. Oliver, *Dreams of Passion: The Theater of Luigi Pirandello* (New York, 1979), 7. Brecht similarly jolts and perplexes his audience by sudden disruptions and reversals, his well-known *Verfremdungseffekt.*

13. Thomas Mann, "Conrad's 'Secret Agent,' " in *Past Masters and Other Papers,* trans. H.T. Lowe-Porter (Freeport, N.Y., 1968), 240-41. This passage is quoted in William Van O'Connor's essay on recent grotesquerie in American fiction, "The Grotesque: An American Genre," in *The Grotesque: An American Genre and Other Essays* (Carbondale, Ill., 1962), 5. Concerning the grotesque in twentieth-century art, Bernard McElroy verifies Mann's prediction: "There seems to be an affinity which makes the grotesque not only typical of our art, but perhaps its most characteristic expression, indeed at times even its obsession" (*Fiction of the Modern Grotesque,* 16-17).

14. Tennessee Williams, "This Book," introduction to Carson McCullers, *Reflections in a Golden Eye* (New York, 1950), xii, xviii, xvi.

15. "Of Friendship," in *The Essayes of Montaigne,* trans. John Florio (New York, n.d.), 1.27, p. 144.

16. *Alexander Pope: Selected Poetry and Prose,* with an introduction by William K. Wimsatt, Jr., 2d ed. (New York, 1972), 381. On the *Dunciad,* consult Tony Tanner, "Reason and the Grotesque: Pope's *Dunciad,*" *Critical Quarterly* 7 (1965): 145-60.

17. Geoffrey Galt Harpham cites "The Metamorphosis" as a perfect example of a work that alienates the audience, suddenly shocking it and instilling what Kayser termed a "fear of life"—the awful growing suddenly out of the quotidian. Harpham goes further, noting that, although ideas of what is grotesque vary in each generation, he nonetheless hopes to "fix" some constants in audiences' reactions: he suggests that the viewer must respond in a threefold way—with astonishment, with disgust or horror, and with laughter. Harpham, "The Grotesque: First Principles," *Journal of Aesthetics and Art Criticism* 34 (Summer 1976): 461-68.

18. Consult Richard M. Cook, "Popeye, Flem, and Sutpen: The Faulknerian Villain as Grotesque," *Studies in American Fiction* 3 (Spring 1975): 3-14.

19. W. Gordon Cunliffe, *Günter Grass* (New York, 1969), 66. See also Leslie A. Willson, "The Grotesque Everyman in Günter Grass's *Die Blechtrommel,*" *Monatshefte* 58 (1966): 131-38.

20. On mutilated figures as archetypal, see Peter L. Hays, *The Limping Hero: Grotesques in Literature* (New York, 1971). On wit and satiric strategies, see William York Tindall, *Samuel Beckett* (New York, 1964), 35f.

3. Degrading the Hero

1. In addition to Sigmund Freud's *Civilization and Its Discontents* (1930), trans. Joan Rivière (Garden City, N.Y., 1958), and *Jokes and Their Relation to the Unconscious* (1916), trans. James Strachey (New York, 1963), the reader should also consult *Totem and Taboo: Resemblances Between the Psychic Lives of Savages and Neurotics* (1918), trans. A.A. Brill (New York, n.d.).

2. See esp. A.V. Judges, ed., *The Elizabethan Underworld* (London, 1930); Frank W. Chandler, *The Literature of Roguery* (Boston, 1907); and idem, *Romances of Roguery* (New York, 1899). Recent studies include Robert Alter, *Rogue's Progress: Studies in the Picaresque Novel* (Cambridge, Mass., 1964); Alexander A. Parker, *Literature and the Delinquent* (Edinburgh, 1967); and Richard Bjornson, *The Picaresque Hero in European Fiction* (Madison, Wis., 1977).

3. See Steven Marcus, *The Other Victorians: A Study of Sexuality and Pornography in Mid-Nineteenth Century England* (New York, 1975).

4. Lionel Trilling, "The Two Environments: Reflections on the Study of English," in *Beyond Culture: Essays on Literature and Learning* (New York, 1965), 219.

5. Velma Bourgeois Richmond, "The Humanist Rejection of Romance," *South Atlantic Quarterly* 77 (1978): 296. Richmond refers to McLuhan's *The Mechanical Bride*, which mentions a correspondence between the contemporary appeal of Superman in the popular culture and the similar appeal of angels in the Middle Ages.

6. Similarly, it can be suggested that, in Old Testament Hebrew society, the lonely rural prophets (such as Isaiah, Jeremiah) stand in sharp critical contrast with the organized religious bureaucracy of the city-dwellers, typified by the Sadducees.

7. Oswald Spengler, *The Decline of the West*, trans. Charles F. Atkinson (London, 1932), 1: 32.

8. Quoted in Robert Douglas Mead, *Hellas and Rome* (New York, 1972), 59.

9. C.W. Mendell, "Satire as Popular Philosophy," *Classical Philology* 15 (1920): 140-41. Mendell's article cogently urges the continuity between the practical and popular diatribe traditions initiated by early Cynics—Diogenes, Menippus, Bion—and the later development of the genre of Roman verse satire.

10. On Antisthenes, see Eduard Zeller, *Outlines of the History of Greek Philosophy*, trans. L.R. Palmer (London, 1955), 108; see also 109-12, 227-29, 272-74. All the Cynics in some sense emulated Diogenes' waggery and doggishness. Lucian terms Menippus "the secret dog who bites as he laughs"; *Bis Accusatus* 33. That Diogenes was normally referred to as Dog was commonplace; see Aristotle *Rhetoric* 3.10.1411a24, who refers to Diogenes as "The Dog" without even mentioning his name. Consult the discussion in Farrand Sayre, *Diogenes of Sinope: A Study of Greek Cynicism* (Baltimore, 1938), esp. 87.

11. Diogenes Laertius *Lives of Eminent Philosophers* 6.46; Donald R. Dudley, *A History of Cynicism from Diogenes to the Sixth Century* A.D. (London, 1937), 21, 28.

12. Dudley, *History of Cynicism*, 37. Needless to say, most of our information about Diogenes is legendary. The original man may well have been a conflation of several eccentrics, together with similarly named characters in later fictions and romances; see Farrand Sayre, *The Greek Cynics* (Baltimore, 1948), esp. 50. But this should not prevent us from questioning Sayre and positing a powerful influential Cynic founder, Diogenes, some part of whose life and teaching are indeed preserved in the works of Diogenes Laertius and later authors. See H. von Arnim, *Leben und Werke des Dio von Prusa* (Berlin, 1898), 37ff.

13. A.A. Long, *Hellenistic Philosophy: Stoics, Epicureans, Sceptics* (New York, 1974), 111. Consult *Stoicorum Veterum Fragmenta*, vol. 2, ed. J. von Arnim (Stuttgart, 1964), 743-56. The early Stoics (much to the embarrassment of the later Stoa) even adopted some of these claims; see *SVF* 1: 249ff.

14. On "soapbox lectures," see Lionel Casson, introduction to *Selected Satires of Lucian*, ed. Lionel Casson (Garden City, N.Y., 1962), xii. Eratosthenes compared Bion's garish, motley style with the gaudy robes of the *hetaera*, or prostitute; Diogenes Laertius *Lives* 4.52. On the evolution of later prose, see André Oltramare, *Les Origines de la diatribe romaine* (Geneva, 1926), and Richard M. Gummere, "The English Essay and Some of Its Ancient Prototypes," *Classical Weekly* 14 (April 4, 1921): 154-60. What Bjornson says of the picaresque writer applies equally well to Cynic authors: "By breaking down the traditional separation of styles and expanding the range of acceptable subject matter to include the morally serious treatment of non-aristocratic characters, they constituted one of the most important stages in the transition between earlier literary prose and the modern novel" (*Picaresque Hero*, 3).

15. Diogenes Laertius *Lives* 6.41, 6.43; Abraham J. Malherbe, ed. and trans., "The Epistles of Diogenes," in *The Cynic Epistles* (Missoula, Mont., 1977), Epistle 16, p. 109. Such epistles are, of course, spurious, doubtlessly written during the Augustan era.

16. Diogenes Laertius *Lives* 6.63; Harold W. Attridge, ed. and trans., *First-Century Cynicism in the Epistles of Heraclitus* (Missoula, Mont., 1976), 3.

17. Many critics continue to be surprised to find Hercules a standard Cynic and Stoic hero; he appears too brazen and impulsive to them. Hence they frequently find Stoic treatment of this hero "ambiguous" or "ambivalent"; see, for instance, Eugene M. Waith, *The Herculean Hero in Marlowe, Chapman, Shakespeare and Dryden* (New York, 1962), 30-38.

18. G. Karl Galinsky, "The Comic Hero," in *The Herakles Theme* (Totowa, N.J., 1972), 81-100, 107. See Prodicus's parable "The Choice of Hercules," in Xenophon *Memorabilia* 2.1.21-34.

19. Diogenes Laertius *Lives* 6.71. To be sure, as best as we can reconstruct the Cynic view of Heracles, he represents a contrast with the fatalistic hero suffering his πόνοι as in the tragedies, or merely the muscular athlete of comedy and the satyr plays. Instead, he is simplistic and "natural" man, alien to the intellect and to civilization, and distinctly ethical, ascetic, and individualist. The topic of Hercules as the Cynic avatar is treated extensively in Ragnar Hoistad, *Cynic Hero and Cynic King: Studies in the Cynic Conception of Man* (Uppsala, 1948), esp. 22-73.

20. R.D. Laing, *The Divided Self: A Study of Sanity and Madness* (Chicago, 1960); idem, *The Politics of Experience* (New York, 1967); R.D. Laing and A. Esterson, *Sanity, Madness and the Family* (New York, 1971); Herbert Marcuse, *Eros and Civilization* (Boston, 1955); Norman O. Brown, *Love's Body* (New York, 1966).

21. Richard Poirier, *The Performing Self: Compositions and Decompositions in the Languages of Contemporary Life* (New York, 1971); see Leslie Fiedler, *Freaks: Myths and Images of the Secret Self* (New York, 1978).

22. See Yeats, "The Circus Animal's Desertion" 1.40; Robert Martin Adams, *Bad Mouth: Fugitive Papers on the Dark Side* (Berkeley, 1977), 119-20. Renato Poggioli observes that since the 1870s, when avant-garde ideals became popular among cults and coteries, the "posture" of the avant-garde has always been antagonism—toward tradition and toward the popular audience. Paradoxically, its anarchistic individualism has always been based upon upper- as well as lower-class standards. As a member of a sect and caste, the militant *milieu artiste* repeatedly displays "two postures, now plebeian and now aristocratic, now 'dandy' and now 'bohemian.' " Poggioli, *The Theory of the Avant-Garde*, trans. Gerald Fitzgerald (Cambridge, Mass., 1968), 31.

23. Ronald W. Tobin, "A Hero for All Seasons: Hercules in French Classical Drama," *Comparative Drama* 1 (Winter 1967–68): 288.

24. Michael Ayrton, *The Maze Maker* (New York, 1967), 242-44.

25. See, for instance, Sean O'Faolain, *The Vanishing Hero: Studies of the Hero in the Modern Novel* (Boston, 1957); Harold Lubin, ed., *Heroes and Anti-Heroes* (San Francisco, 1968); the special issue of *Studies in the Literary Imagination* 9, no. 1 (Spring 1976), devoted to "The Anti-Hero: His Emergence and Transformations"; and David Galloway, *The Absurd Hero in American Fiction: Updike, Styron, Bellow, Salinger*, 2d ed. (Austin, Tex., 1981).

4. Debunking the Author

1. Jonathan Swift, *A Tale of a Tub to Which Is Added the Battle of the Books and the Mechanical Operation of the Spirit*, ed. A.C. Guthkelch and D. Nichol Smith, 2d ed. (Oxford, 1958), 55.

2. Jonathan Swift, "Verses on the Death of Dr. Swift, D.S.P.D.," ll. 13-20, in *Swift: Poetical Works*, ed. Herbert Davis (London, 1967), 496-97.

3. Evelyn Waugh, *Black Mischief* (Baltimore, 1954), 7.

4. F.N. Robinson, ed., *The Works of Geoffrey Chaucer* (Boston, 1961), 239.

5. Aubrey Williams, ed., *Poetry and Prose of Alexander Pope* (Boston, 1969), 43.

6. Gilbert Highet, *The Anatomy of Satire* (Princeton, 1962), 244.

7. Pope, "An Essay on Man," in *Poetry and Prose of Alexander Pope*, 407.

8. Robinson, ed., *Works of Geoffrey Chaucer*, 242.

9. Shakespeare's Sonnet 18, l. 13.

10. Juvenal, Satire 7, in *Juvenal: Satires*, trans. Jerome Mazzaro (Ann Arbor, 1965), 89; Persius, Satire 1, ll. 41-43, in *Juvenal and Persius with an English Translation*, trans. G.G. Ramsay, rev. ed. (Cambridge, Mass., 1957), 321.

11. Horace *Epistle* 2.1.269-70; Catullus, *Carmina* 95.8; Martial *Epigrams* 3.2.3-4. Martial's favorite image is that of the fish-wrapper, as in 3.50.9, 4.86.8.

12. John Lyly, "Euphues. The Anatomy of Wit" (1578), in *The Complete Works of John Lyly*, ed. R.W. Bond, 3 vols. (Oxford, 1967), 1: 182.

13. Eccles. 1: 2-4, 10, 11.

14. T.S. Eliot, "Fragment of an Agon" (from *Sweeney Agonistes*), in *The Complete Poems and Plays* (New York, 1952), 80.

15. Alexander Pope, *Dunciad* (1743) 3.155 and the note to l. 156, in *The Dunciad*, ed. James Sutherland, 3d ed., vol. 5 of *The Poems of Alexander Pope* (New Haven, 1963), 327.

16. Swift, *Tale of a Tub*, 34-35. Cf. 1 Macc. 12:53, Deut. 32:26.
17. Samuel Putnam, ed. and trans., *The Portable Rabelais* (New York, 1965), 9; Swift, *Tale of a Tub*, 71.
18. Putnam, ed. and trans., *Portable Rabelais*, 225.
19. Homer Wilbur [James Russell Lowell], *The Biglow Papers* (New York, 1969), 127; Pope, *Dunciad* 1.156, p. 282; Swift, *Tale of a Tub*, 36; Pope, *Dunciad* 1.229-30, p. 287.
20. Miguel de Cervantes, *Don Quixote*, trans. Ozell and Motteux, with an introduction by Herschel Brickell (New York, 1930), 51-54.
21. Laurence Sterne, *A Sentimental Journey and Journal to Eliza*, with an afterword by Monroe Engel (New York, 1964), 117. Mackenzie's novel commences with chapter 11; the remainder is presented in an absurdly disjunct sequence, as follows: chaps. 12-14, 19-21, 25-29, a fragment, 33-36, a fragment, 40, a fragment, 45-46, a conclusion. The curate is presumably indiscriminate when extracting his "wadding."
22. John Harold Wilson, ed., *Six Restoration Plays* (Boston, 1959), 342-43.
23. Richard Brinsley Sheridan, *The Rivals* (London, 1968), 34, 39.
24. Horace, Book 1, Satire 4, trans. Hubert Wetmore Wells, in *The Complete Works of Horace*, ed. Casper J. Kraemer, Jr. (New York, 1936), 21-22.
25. Voltaire, *Candide and Zadig*, ed. Lester G. Crocker (New York, 1968), 82.
26. Francisco Gomez Quevedo, *Quevedo: The Choice Humors and Satirical Works*, ed. Charles Duff (New York, 1926), 53.
27. Catullus, *Carmina* 36.20; Pietro Aretino, *Aretino's Dialogues*, trans. Raymond Rosenthal (New York, 1971), 3; Swift, *Tale of a Tub*, 36.
28. John Dryden, "MacFlecknoe," ll. 100, 103, in *The Works of John Dryden*, ed. E.N. Hooker, et al. (Berkeley, 1972), 2: 56-57.
29. Pope, *Dunciad* 4.71, 81-82, 101-102, pp. 348, 349, 351.
30. Ibid., 4.135-36, 191-92, 653, 656, pp. 354, 360, 409.
31. Matthew Hodgart, *Satire* (London 1969), 115.
32. John M. Bullitt, *Jonathan Swift and the Anatomy of Satire* (Cambridge, Mass., 1953), 44ff.
33. Joseph Bentley, "Semantic Gravitation: An Essay on Satiric Reduction," *Modern Language Quarterly* 30 (1969): 3-19.
34. George Orwell, *1984* (New York, 1949), 63; Kurt Vonnegut, Jr., *Breakfast of Champions* (New York, 1973), 131, 133.
35. George Orwell, *Animal Farm* (New York, 1946), 108.
36. Orwell, *1984*, 51.
37. Günter Grass, *The Meeting at Telgte*, trans. Ralph Manheim (New York, 1981), 120.
38. Horace *Satires* 2.7.
39. Mailer's tale appears in *Cannibals and Christians* (New York, 1970), 380-97. This piece concludes the book. Such strategies are merely comical warnings, satirical ways of shocking—a dominant feature of satire, but not necessarily deliberate affirmations of pessimism or despair.
40. In Branko Mikasinovich, ed., *Modern Yugoslav Satire* (Merrick, N.Y., 1979), 68-69.
41. Stanislaw Lem, *Memoirs Found in a Bathtub*, trans. Michael Kandel and Christine Rose (New York, 1973), 2.
42. *Examiner* no. 18, Dec. 7, 1710, in *The Prose Writings of Jonathan Swift*, ed. Herbert Davis (Oxford, 1959), 3: 32. Swift observes in a letter (Jan. 6, 1708-9) to Archbishop King that "the World is divided into two Sects, those that

hope the best, and those that fear the worst; your Grace is of the former, which is the wiser, the nobler, and most pious Principle; and although I endeavour to avoid being of the other, yet upon this Article I have sometimes strange Weaknesses. I compare the Religion to Learning and Civility which have ever been in the World, but very often shifted their Scenes; sometimes leaving whole Countries where they have long flourished." Harold Williams, ed., *The Correspondence of Jonathan Swift* (Oxford, 1963–65), 1: 117.

43. "Ode to the Athenian Society," ll. 296-300, in Davis, ed., *Swift: Poetical Works*, 17. The theme of the imminent invasion of barbarians is a popular one among satirists and is particularly well utilized by Evelyn Waugh; see Alvin B. Kernan, "The Wall and the Jungle: The Early Novels of Evelyn Waugh," *Yale Review* 53 (Dec. 1963): 199-220.

5. Dislocating the Language

1. Consult Philip Pinkus, "Satire and St. George," *Queen's Quarterly* 70 (1963): 30-49; John R. Clark and Anna Motto, eds., *Satire: That Blasted Art* (New York, 1973), esp. 19-22; and John R. Clark, "Anticlimax in Satire," *Seventeenth-Century News* 33 (1975): 22-26. Alvin Kernan notes in *The Plot of Satire* (New Haven, 1965) that most satires unfold erratically: running downhill, wobbling up and down, or going around in circles.

2. Individual Horatian and Juvenalian satires take up so many topics that they almost madden subsequent critics who wish to sort out themes and perceive coherent form. In addition, overcrowding is regularly a topic and a practice of satire as well: see Alvin B. Kernan, "The Mob Tendency in Satire: *The Day of the Locust*," *Satire Newsletter* 1 (1963): 11-20.

3. Consider Frederick J. Stopp's observation: "Traditionally, satire has always borrowed its ground-plan, parasitically and by ironic inversion, from other forms of ordered exposition in art or in life; misericords bear parodies of the liturgy, ironical encomia are laudatory speeches in reverse." Stopp, *Evelyn Waugh: Portrait of an Artist* (London, 1958), 201. The concept of satire as a genre deriving its shape from other genres, functioning as a parasite dependent upon numerous hosts, is developed at length in Leon Guilhamet, *Satire and the Transformation of Genre* (Philadelphia, 1987).

4. Most studies of satire treat it as essentially rhetorical; here I propose that satire is an art form and is essentially mimetic.

5. Robert C. Elliott rightly extols the "brilliant counterfeiting" of Swift that is "dangerously convincing," for "Swift takes on the guise of the enemy in order to do a wrecking job from the inside." Elliott, "Swift's 'I,' " *Yale Review* 62 (Spring 1973): 383.

6. Consult Harold Williams, ed., *The Poems of Jonathan Swift*, 2d ed. (Oxford, 1958), 101-5.

7. Ian Watt argues that this sense of double audience—the refined and the ignorant—led to the proliferation of indirection and *meiosis* in Augustan literature: see Watt, "The Ironic Voice," in *The Augustan Age: Approaches to Its Literature, Life, and Thought*, ed. Ian Watt (Greenwich, Conn., 1968), 101-14.

8. H.R. Swardson, "Sentimentality and the Academic Tradition," *College English* 37 (April 1976): 747-66.

9. Edmund Wilson, " 'Never Apologize, Never Explain': The Art of Evelyn Waugh," in *Classics and Commercials: A Literary Chronicle of the Forties* (New York, 1950), 140-46.

10. Relevant to this study, critic Robert Scholes perceives an increased interest of late in "fabulation" in artists (like Faulkner, Nabokov, Hawkes) who take a particular "delight in formal and verbal dexterity." Scholes, *The Fabulators* (New York, 1967), 67. But we might assert that satirists have been attracted to such verbal playfulness. Nonetheless, there is now an "almost universal . . . acceptance of the element of playfulness in art," one critic proposes; Geoffrey H. Hartman, *The Unmediated Vision: An Interpretation of Wordsworth, Hopkins, Rilke, and Valéry* (New York, 1966), 162. And game theory has played a considerable role in recent literary criticism; see particularly Johan Huizinga, *Homo Ludens*, trans. R.F.C. Hul (London, 1949); Jacques Ehrmann, ed., *Game, Play, Literature* (Boston, 1971); and Richard A. Lanham, *"Tristram Shandy": The Games of Pleasure* (Berkeley, 1973).

11. C.S. Lewis, *A Preface to Paradise Lost* (New York, 1961), 94.

12. Ben Jonson, "Timber, or Discoveries," in *Ben Jonson*, ed. C.H. Herford, Percy Simpson, and Evelyn Simpson (Oxford, 1947), 8: 592-93.

13. Compare ll. 169-72 from "An Epistle from Mr. Pope, to Dr. Arbuthnot":

> Pretty! in Amber to observe forms
> Of hairs, or straws, or dirt, or grubs, or worms;
> The things, we know, are neither rich nor rare,
> But wonder how the Devil they got there?

John Butt, ed., *The Poems of ALexander Pope* (New Haven, 1963), 603.

14. Horace Walpole, "The Peach in Brandy: A Milesian Tale," in *Hieroglyphic Tales* (London, 1926), 53-54. Much the same ambiguity clings to the expression "God forgive him!" Is the prelate in need of forgiveness because he dined upon a fetus, because he swallowed it at a single gulp, or because he neglected the saying of grace?

15. Evelyn Waugh, *Scoop* (Baltimore, 1943), 67.

16. Thomas Pynchon, *Gravity's Rainbow* (New York, 1974), 545.

17. Charles Neider, ed., *The Complete Short Stories of Mark Twain* (Garden City, N.Y., 1957), 436

18. Aldous Huxley, *Antic Hay* (New York, n.d.), 230.

19. I take *ecstasiated* to be an ugly neologism; satirists, serving the cause of distortion, are particularly expert in creating new words. Thus, for example, Ejner J. Jensen remarks the vitality that Thomas Drant, the Elizabethan satirist, obtains by introducing such "free-wheeling" words as *sparple, prools, nipfarthinge, dindle, chubbyshe,* and *wamblynge.* Jensen, "The Wit of Renaissance Satire," *Philological Quarterly* 51 (April 1972): 400.

20. See *Hamlet* 2.2.545ff. "O, what a rogue and peasant slave am I!"

21. Petronius *Satyricon* 99, in *The Satyricon*, trans. William Arrowsmith (New York, 1963), 104.

22. Northrop Frye, *Anatomy of Criticism* (Princeton, 1957), 162, 34, 229-30, 233-34.

23. Frederick C. Crews, *The Pooh Perplex: A Freshman Casebook* (New York, 1963), 88.

24. Jonathan Swift, *A Tale of a Tub to Which Is Added the Battle of the Books and the Mechanical Operation of the Spirit*, ed. A.C. Guthkelch and D. Nichol Smith, 2d ed. (Oxford, 1958), 170. And how, one may wish to know, does a thinker "unravel" a "point" that has somehow metamorphosed into a knitter's "knot"?

25. John Dryden, "MacFlecknoe," l. 148, in *The Works of John Dryden*, ed. E.N. Hooker et al. (Berkeley, 1972), 2: 58; E.M. Forster, *Aspects of the Novel* (New York, 1927), 111-12; Henry James, "Preface to 'What Maisie Knew,' " in *The Art of the Novel: Critical Prefaces*, with an introduction by R.P. Blackmur (New York, 1934), 149.

26. Susanne K. Langer, *Mind: An Essay on Human Feeling* (Baltimore, 1967), 1: 36.

27. See, for instance, William P. Holden, *Anti-Puritan Satire, 1572-1642* (New Haven, 1954); Walter Wagoner, ed., *Bittersweet Grace: A Treasury of Twentieth-Century Religious Satire* (Cleveland, 1967); Eugene Hollander, *Die Karikatur und Satire in Der Medizin* (Stuttgart, 1905); John A. Yunck, "The Venal Tongue: Lawyers and the Medieval Satirists," *American Bar Association Journal* 46 (1960): 267-70; and C.S. Duncan, "The Scientist as a Comic Type," *Modern Philology* 14 (1916): 281-91. Much of this proliferation of "jargon" is understood to apply to any maker of systems; see D.W. Jefferson, "*Tristram Shandy* and the Tradition of Learned Wit," *Essays in Criticism* 1 (1951): 225-48. For a further discussion together with numerous examples, consult "Parody of Learning," in Clark and Motto, eds., *Satire*, 86-123.

28. *The Life of Lazarillo de Tormes* (1554), trans. J. Gerald Markley (New York, 1954), 3.

29. " 'Tis of Aucassin and of Nicolette," in *Aucassin and Nicolette and Other Medieval Romances and Legends*, trans. Eugene Mason (New York, 1958), 13-14. A number of critics still believe that this tale is "serious"; but see Robert Harden, "*Aucassin et Nicolette* as Parody," *Studies in Philology* 63 (Jan. 1966): 1-9.

30. Mikhail Zoshchenko, "Much Ado About Nothing," in *Nervous People and Other Satires*, trans. Maria Gordon and Hugh McLean (Bloomington, 1975), 233.

31. Hugh McLean, introduction to Zoshchenko, *Nervous People*, xi. Fostering a kind of paradox, Kenneth Burke once proposed that "we might even say that the conditions are 'more favorable,' to satire under censorship than under liberalism—for the most inventive satire arises when the artist is seeking simultaneously to take risks and escape punishment for this boldness, and is never quite certain himself whether he will be acclaimed or punished. In proportion as you remove these conditions of danger, by liberalization, satire becomes arbitrary and effete, attracting writers of far less spirit and scantier resources." Burke, *The Philosophy of Literary Form*, rev. ed. (New York, 1957), 199. This is a beguiling hypothesis that probably will not hold up. A major artist is a major artist, regardless of conditions; nor will his work tend to become "effete" under certain circumstances.

32. Ezra Pound, *Personae: Collected Shorter Poems of Ezra Pound* (London, 1952), 73.

33. Letter to Charles Eliot Norton, December 6, 1886, in Percy Lubbock, ed., *The Letters of Henry James* (New York, 1920), 1: 124; Letter to Robert Louis Stevenson, July 31, 1888, Lubbock, ed., *Letters of Henry James* 1: 138.

34. Henry James, *The Sacred Fount*, with an introduction by Leon Edel (New York, 1953), 163-64. Much later, Mrs. Brissenden patiently explains to the narrator that Gilbert Long continues to be filled with "platitudes," and thus he remains "a prize fool" (292).

35. Thomas R. Edwards, *Imagination and Power: A Study of Poetry on Public Themes* (New York, 1971), 85. Because Edwards is dealing with the poet "speaking out" on public issues, he naturally tends to conceive of satire as

being most ably represented by "formal verse satire," rather than as a far broader and more inclusive fictional genre.

36. Vladimir Nabokov, *Lolita* (New York, 1966), 279-80.

6. Gaming with the Plot

1. Geoffrey H. Hartman, *The Unmediated Vision: An Interpretation of Wordsworth, Hopkins, Rilke, and Valéry* (New York, 1966), 162.

2. Kenneth Burke in the 1930s and 1940s was already postulating that literature and life were simultaneously engaged in drama, gesture, and "symbolic action." The interested reader might consult Stephen Potter, *The Theory and Practice of Gamesmanship* (New York, 1948); Roger Callois, *Les Jeux et les hommes: Le Masque et le vertige* (Paris, 1958); Erving Goffman, *The Presentation of Self in Everyday Life* (Garden City, N.Y., 1959); Eric Berne, *Games People Play* (New York, 1964); Richard Poirier, *The Performing Self: Compositions and Decompositions in the Languages of Contemporary Life* (New York, 1971); Jacques Ehrmann, ed., *Game, Play, Literature* (Boston, 1971); Richard A. Lanham, *"Tristram Shandy": The Games of Pleasure* (Berkeley, 1973); and Harriet Deer and Irving Deer, "Satire as Rhetorical Play," *Boundary 2* 5 (Spring 1977): 711-21. Many a critic, of course, is sceptical, believing that a serious falling-off has occurred since the great age of the modernist innovators: "It is perhaps the high seriousness of [the modernists'] devotion to art which finally distinguishes [them] from their successors, who set more store by jokes and language-games." Peter Faulkner, *Modernism* (London, 1977), 75.

3. Virginia Woolf, "American Fiction," in *The Moment and Other Essays* (New York, 1948), 123.

4. Despite critics' elevated taste and their treatment of melodrama with haughty and often scornful disapprobation, literary traditions utilizing melodrama continue to thrive; it is a popular mode that recurrently thrives and prevails. Consult John R. Clark and Anna Lydia Motto, "Gasps, Guffaws, and Tears: A Modest Defense of Sentimentality, Bathos, and Melodrama," *Thalia* 1 (1978): 61-70.

5. For the modern preoccupation with dystopias, consult Roger Elwood, ed., *Dystopian Visions* (Englewood Cliffs, N.J., 1975), and Harold Berger, *Science Fiction and the New Dark Age* (Bowling Green, Ohio, 1976). For H.G. Wells's influence on the dystopian genre, see Mark R. Hillegas, *The Future as Nightmare: H.G. Wells and the Anti-Utopians* (Carbondale, Ill., 1967).

6. See Joseph Frank, "Spatial Form in Modern Literature," *Sewanee Review* 53 (1945): 221-40, 433-56, 643-53; Robert Humphrey, *Stream of Consciousness in the Modern Novel* (Berkeley, 1954); Leon Edel, *The Modern Psychological Novel* (New York, 1959); and Sharon Spencer, *Space, Time and Structure in the Modern Novel* (New York, 1971). Notably relevant, concerning the influence of twentieth-century scientific thought upon literature, is Irving Deer, "Science, Literature, and the New Consciousness," *ADE Bulletin*, no. 34 (Sept. 1972): 37-45; reprinted in Harry Finestone and Michael F. Shugrue, eds., *Prospects for the 70's: English Departments and Multidisciplinary Study* (New York, 1973), 125-33.

7. J.P. Hodin, "The Spirit of Modern Art," *British Journal of Aesthetics* 1 (June 1961): 183, cited in Stephen Spender, "The Modern as Vision of a Whole Situation," *Partisan Review* 29 (Summer 1962): 361. This interesting essay also appears in Stephen Spender, *The Struggle of the Modern* (Berkeley, 1963), 79-97.

8. Harold Rosenberg, *The Tradition of the New* (London, 1962), 11-12.

9. Hans Meyerhoff, *Time in Literature* (Berkeley, 1955), 110-11.

10. Leslie Fiedler suggests that American writers "have to be sure, profited by their exposure to the avant-garde, just as they have by their awareness of the classical past—but their relationship to both has been essentially that of mockery, their chief connection the utterly ambivalent one of parody." Fiedler, "The Dream of the New," in *American Dreams, American Nightmares*, ed. David Madden (Carbondale, Ill., 1970), 24. Yet we might add that not merely the Americans are so inclined; the whole of the twentieth-century world has participated in an enormous resurgence in the employment of parody. See the particularly revealing study by Thomas R. Frosch, "Parody and the Contemporary Imagination," *Soundings* 56 (Winter 1973): 371-92, and also Margaret A. Rose, *Parody: Meta-Fiction* (London, 1979).

11. "Formal realism's" authenticity is inductive, and "the novel's mode of imitating reality may therefore be equally well summarized in terms of the procedures of another group of specialists in epistemology, the jury in a court of law." Ian Watt, *The Rise of the Novel: Studies in Defoe, Richardson and Fielding* (Berkeley, 1964), 31.

12. Consult Sir Edmund Strachey, "Nonsense as a Fine Art," *Quarterly Review* 167 (1888): 335-65, on Edward Lear and his antecedents, and consider the recent interest in earlier writers of "nonsense": Elizabeth Sewell, *The Field of Nonsense* (London, 1952), on Edward Lear and Lewis Carroll; Kathleen Blake, *Play, Games, and Sport: The Literary Works of Lewis Carroll* (Ithaca, N.Y., 1974); Leonard Forster, *Poetry of Significant Nonsense* ((Cambridge, Eng., 1962), on Christian Morgenstern, Hugo Ball, and the Zurich group of dadaists and founders of the Cabaret Voltaire. See also James Rother, "Modernism and the Nonsense Style," *Contemporary Literature* 15 (Spring 1974): 187-202.

Several critics believe that the twentieth century has witnessed the rise and proliferation of fantasy in literature as a special genre (C.S. Lewis, Tolkien, and science fiction): see Tzvetan Todorov, *The Fantastic: A Structural Approach to a Literary Genre*, trans. Richard Howard (Ithaca, N.Y., 1975); Eric S. Rabkin, *The Fantastic in Literature* (Princeton, 1976); and W.R. Irwin, *The Game of the Impossible: A Rhetoric of Fantasy* (Urbana, Ill., 1976).

13. In mentioning antistories, I am thinking of such collections as Philip Stevick, ed., *Anti-Story: An Anthology of Experimental Fiction* (New York, 1971); Richard Kostelanetz, ed., *Breakthrough Fictioneers: An Anthology* (Baiton, Vt., 1973); and Joe David Bellamy, ed., *The New Fiction: Interviews with Innovative American Writers* (Urbana, Ill., 1974). See Robert Alter, *Partial Magic: The Novel as a Self-Conscious Genre* (Berkeley, 1975), and Jerome Klinkowitz, *Literary Disruptions: The Making of a Post-Contemporary American Fiction* (Urbana, Ill., 1975).

14. A similar transformation is suggested in André Gide's *L'Immoraliste* (Paris, 1902), in which, well-nursed by his wife, Michel recovers from illness in North Africa and becomes increasingly sensuous. As he grows in strength and travels northward, his wife Marceline acquires his disease (tuberculosis); they return again southward, where she lingers and dies. Again, in F. Scott Fitzgerald's *Tender is the Night* (New York, 1934), as the mentally ill Nicole recovers from her illness, her psychiatrist husband, Dick Diver, declines and degenerates into alcoholism and professional ruin. With her cure, he is dismissed, a broken man.

15. Paranoia is, of course, a key theme in much of modern literature—and especially in Pynchon; see Robert Murray Davis, "Parody, Paranoia, and the

Dead End of Language in *The Crying of Lot 49*," *Genre* 5 (1972): 367-77. See also the general comments on paranoia in modern American literature in Tony Tanner, *City of Words: American Fiction, 1950-1970* (London, 1971), esp. 15-17. On the other hand, much of the paranoia is clearly justified, for there has been a regular increase of violence—in literature and in life. See, for example, James B. Twitchell, *Preposterous Violence: Fables of Aggression in Modern Culture* (New York, 1989).

16. Martin Amis, *Einstein's Monsters* (New York, 1987), 73-74.

17. André Gide, *The Counterfeiters with Journal of "The Counterfeiters,"* novel trans. Dorothy Bussy, journal trans. Justin O'Brien (New York, 1951). In France, the journal was published separate from the novel by Librairie Gallimard in 1927.

7. Further Intrusion and Obstruction

1. Many speak of "postmodern" innovations and creations; consider a pair of essays by John Barth, "The Literature of Exhaustion," *Atlantic Monthly* 220, (Aug. 1967): 29-34, and "The Literature of Replenishment: Postmodernist Fiction," *Atlantic Monthly* 245 (Jan. 1980): 65-71. See also Philip Stevick, "Scheherazade Runs Out of Plots, Goes on Talking; the King, Puzzled, Listens: An Essay on New Fiction," *TriQuarterly* 26 (1973): 332-62. There are, of course, some who understandably doubt whether there is a "postmodern" era at all: see Gerald Graff, "The Myth of the Post-modernist Breakthrough," *TriQuarterly* 26 (1973): 383-417.

2. Jerome Klinkowitz, *Literary Disruptions: The Making of a Post-Contemporary American Fiction* (Urbana, Ill., 1975).

3. Brecht's term, *Verfremdungseffekt*, usefully describes strategies utilized to jolt the audience, to keep them on their toes, to prevent passivity and a dull crowd's "identifying with" one's literary characters. Regulated disorder may be found in antiquity and the Middle Ages, perhaps, but its incidence markedly increases as we approach the modern era. A related study of importance is Lawrence D. Kritzman, ed., *Fragments: Incompletion and Discontinuity* (New York, 1981). This collection includes particularly relevant studies of fragmentation in the modern period by John Tytell, Roger Shattuck, and Serge Doubrovsky.

4. Jorge Luis Borges, *Ficciones*, ed. Anthony Kerrigan (New York, 1962), 17-35, 151-57, 45-55; Jorge Luis Borges and Adolfo Bioy-Casares, *Chronicles of Bustos Domecq*, trans. Norman Thomas di Giovanni (New York, 1976).

5. Gabriel García Márquez, *One Hundred Years of Solitude*, trans. Gregory Rabassa (New York, 1971), esp. 267-71.

6. Donald Barthelme, *Snow White* (New York, 1967), 82-83.

7. See Ronald Sukenick, *Up* (New York, 1968); idem, *The Death of the Novel and Other Stories* (New York, 1969); idem, *Out* (Chicago, 1973); Raymond Federman, *Take It or Leave It* (New York, 1976); Jonathan Baumbach, *Reruns* (New York, 1974); and idem, *Babble* (New York, 1976). A number of relevant critical studies have sought to examine the rising tendency to utilize self-conscious and self-reflective characters in much recent literature, as well as the author's own penchant for breaking down the fictional illusion. Consult Patricia Waugh, *Metafiction: The Theory and Practice of Self-Conscious Fiction* (London, 1984), and June Schlueter, *Metafictional Characters in Modern Drama* (New York, 1979).

8. Sukenick, *Up*, 325.
9. William H. Gass, *Willie Masters' Lonesome Wife* (New York, 1971), [55].
10. Preface to Kurt Vonnegut, Jr., *Between Time and Timbuktu* (New York, 1972), xv.
11. Klinkowitz, *Literary Disruptions*, ix, 2. For an extended (and unfavorable) review of this volume, consult George Levine, "Literary Good, Literary Evil," *Chronicle of Higher Education*, April 26, 1976, p. 20.
12. Eccles. 1: 9-10.
13. This is quite a common disruptive practice in the plays of Aristophanes, even outside of the parabasis; in *Clouds*, for example, consult ll. 326, 890, and 1094-1100. Similarly, at the close of Petronius's *Satyricon* 132, Encolpius the narrator (or could it be the author himself for a moment?) suddenly interrupts the absurd melodramatic scene concerned with self-castration and launches into a pious tirade against "prudes" and followers of Cato who condemn "simple" and "fresh" works that speak of the natural—of activities in which all men engage. This speech is firmly undercut at its close when the narrator announces baldly that the "declamation" is over, whereupon the narrative calmly resumes. Catherine Belsey, in *Critical Practice* (London, 1980), 92, employs the term *interrogative text* to describe fictive creations that, unlike works of "classic realism," avoid resolution and "disclosure." In short, such works shun "closure," and whereas other writings normally create a fictive world with the illusion of being real, such a text tends "to employ devices to undermine the illusion, [and] to draw attention to its own textuality." We might add that texts that deliberately use such strategies and seek to engage readers (as they usually do) by shocking and disorienting them might well be termed disjunctive or disruptive texts. On the interfering speaker in literature, consult Wayne C. Booth, "The Self-Conscious Narrator in Comic Fiction before *Tristram Shandy*," *PMLA* 67 (1952): 163-85.
14. In Voltaire's *Candide*, chap. 22, the innocent Candide visits the Parisian playhouse and attends a performance of Voltaire's own tragedy, the *Mahomet*. Similarly, the priest Pero Pérez in *Don Quixote*, while collecting books of romances to be burned, discovers the *Galatea* by Miguel de Cervantes and elects to save it from the flames (1.6). In the midst of Molly Bloom's last breathless soliloquy, she suddenly addresses her maker: "O Jamesy let me up out of this," for a moment bursting the fictional context. James Joyce, *Ulysses* (New York, 1934), 754. See "The Tragedy of a Character" (1911), in Luigi Pirandello, *Short Stories*, ed. and trans. Frederick May (London, 1965), 94-102, from which Pirandello subsequently developed his renowned play, *Six Characters in Search of an Author* (1921).
15. The best work on Menippean satire and its long tradition and influence is Eugene P. Kirk, *Menippean Satire: An Annotated Catalogue of Texts and Criticism* (New York, 1980). For an extensive review article of this work, consult John R. Clark and Anna Lydia Motto, "Menippeans and Their Satire: Concerning Monstrous Learned Old Dogs and Hippocentaurs," *Scholia Satyrica* 6, nos. 3-4 (1980): 35-46.
16. See Erich Kahler, *The Inward Turn of Narrative*, trans. R. Winston and C. Winston (Princeton, 1973), and J.H. Matthews, *Surrealism and the Novel* (Ann Arbor, 1966).
17. The revolt against realism is the topic, largely, of Robert Alter's insightful study, *Partial Magic: The Novel as a Self-Conscious Genre* (Berkeley, 1975).

But see also Paul Regnier, "The Convention of 'Realism' in the Novel," *Genre* 10 (1977): 103-13.

8. Discordant Endings

1. This phrase refers to and plays upon Frank Kermode's title, *The Sense of an Ending* (New York, 1967). The book studies man's perennial apocalyptic imagination and the creation of endings in fictions. My point is that a significant number of fictions refuse to utilize or patently oppose satisfactory or satisfying conclusions. Dustin Griffin, "Satiric Closure," *Genre* 18 (1985): 173-89, considers that satirists have encountered problems in finding and creating satisfactory narrative endings. The article does not explore the idea that satirists particularly seek to generate disruptive, unsuitable finales.

2. For an analysis of this drama, see Anna Lydia Motto and John R. Clark, "*Violenta Fata:* The Tenor of Seneca's *Oedipus*," *Classical Bulletin* 50 (1974): 81-87.

3. *Seneca's Oedipus,* adapted by Ted Hughes (Garden City, N.Y., 1972), 90.

4. Tom Prideaux, "Stage, Screen and Opera: Director Peter Brook Is Master of the Daring and Bizarre," *People,* June 16, 1980, pp. 109-10. For reviews of the play when performed in London, see *New York Times,* April 2, 1968, p. 54, and July 26, 1968, p. 29.

5. Consult Anna Lydia Motto and John R. Clark, " 'There's Something Wrong with the Sun': Seneca's *Oedipus* and the Modern Grotesque," *Classical Bulletin* 54 (Jan. 1978): 41-44. See also Rainer Sell, "The Comedy of Hyperbolic Horror: Seneca, Lucan and 20th Century Grotesque," *Neohelicon* 11 (1984): 227-300.

6. Critics frequently assume, however, that classicism avoids the indecorous and the disruptive. Speaking of the "grotesque," E. E. Kellett asserts: "That taste which finds pleasure in incongruity—in violation of the recognized conventions of art—is one of the few tastes of which, so far as I know, little or no trace is to be found among the ancients." Kellett, *Fashion in Literature* (London, 1931), 215. On the contrary, the Cynics and the satirists of antiquity were masters of a chaotic form, which zestfully fostered violent changes of topic, tone, and scene. This is especially true of Menippean satire, and such stratagems were passed along in the essay as well, particularly as it was developed by Montaigne. On the Menippean traditions, consult Eugene P. Kirk, *Menippean Satire: An Annotated Catalogue of Texts and Criticism* (New York, 1980).

7. On Euripidean plays, see Bernard Knox, "Euripidean Comedy," in *Word and Action: Essays on the Ancient Theater* (Baltimore, 1979), 250-74. Consider the ending of Aristophanes' *Clouds,* in which Strepsiades sets fire to Socrates' think-factory, or of the conclusion to the *Ecclesiazusae,* in which two old lascivious hags, in the new female republic, each drag and pull at the limbs of the young protagonist Epigenes, taking him as captive for their lusts and beds. Similarly, *Birds* concludes with the successful demagogue Pisthetaerus celebrating his new autocracy in the aviary by preparing an elaborate "feast" of roasted bird—his citizenry.

8. Consult Leonard P. Kurtz, *The Dance of Death and the Macabre Spirit in European Literature* (New York, 1934); Northrop Frye, "Yorick: The Romantic

Macabre," in *A Study of English Romanticism* (New York, 1968), 51-85; and Mario Praz's classic investigation *The Romantic Agony*, trans. Angus Davidson (London, 1933).

9. Carson McCullers, *The Ballad of the Sad Café*, in *The Novels and Stories of Carson McCullers* (Boston, 1951), 65-66.

10. Tennessee Williams, *The Theatre of Tennessee Williams*, 3 vols. (New York, 1971), 3: 339; Gabriel García Márquez, *No One Writes to the Colonel and Other Stories*, trans. J. S. Bernstein (New York, 1968), 153-70; Donald Barthelme, *City Life* (New York, 1971), 1-17.

11. Slawomir Mrozek, *Tango*, trans. Ralph Manheim and Teresa Dziieduscycka (New York, 1968), esp. 107. Both satiric films have been highly praised by reviewers: on *S.O.B.*, see *Time*, July 13, 1981, p. 58; and on *Being There*, see the cover story, *Time*, March 3, 1980, pp. 64-68, 71, 73. Significantly, at the close of *Being There* during the credits, the director presents reruns of cut scenes in which Sellers breaks down on the set with helpless laughter.

12. Robert Martin Adams, *Strains of Discord: Studies in Literary Openness* (Ithaca, N.Y., 1958), 13; Thomas Mann, "Conrad's 'Secret Agent,' " in *Past Masters and Other Papers*, trans. H.T. Lowe-Porter (Freeport, N.Y., 1933), 240-41. Frances K. Barasch agrees: "In fiction and drama, in the theater and in art, the grotesque has appeared as the single most characteristic expression of our times." Barasch, introduction to the facsimile reprint of Thomas Wright, *A History of Caricature and Grotesque in Literature and Art* (New York, 1968), viii.

13. On the demise of tragedy in our time, see Joseph Wood Krutch, "The Tragic Fallacy," in *The Modern Temper* (New York, 1929); idem, "Modernism" in *Modern Drama* (Ithaca, N. Y., 1953); and George Steiner, *The Death of Tragedy* (New York, 1961). The best study of the prevalence of parody as a dominant literary mode in our century is Thomas R. Frosch, "Parody and the Contemporary Imagination," *Soundings* 56 (Winter 1973): 371-92.

14. William Styron, *The Long March* (New York, 1968), 119-20.

15. Ibid., 126-27.

16. Antonin Artaud, *The Theater and Its Double*, trans. Mary C. Richards (New York, 1958), 84-85; Eugène Ionesco, "Experience of the Theatre," in *Notes and Counter Notes*, trans. Donald Watson (New York, 1964), 26.

17. The topic was introduced in a seminar at the 1975 Modern Language Association Convention. The 1976 seminar's position papers have been published as Kenneth S. White, ed., *Savage Comedy: Structures of Humor* (Amsterdam, 1978).

18. Consult Richard Pearce, *Stages of the Clown: Perspectives on Modern Fiction from Dostoyevsky to Beckett* (Carbondale, Ill., 1970).

9. Infernal Repetition

1. John Milton, *Paradise Lost* 2.932-42, 947-50, in Merritt Y. Hughes, ed., *John Milton: Complete Poems and Major Prose* (New York, 1957), 254.

2. Samuel Richardson, *Clarissa; or, The History of a Young Lady*, ed. and abridged by George Sherburn (Boston, 1962), 191, 202, 172, 146-47, 279, 302.

3. Horace *Ars Poetica* 139.

4. Eccles. 1:9.

5. Dante *Inferno* 10.36.

6. Milton, *Paradise Lost* 2.555-61. For an excellent treatment of the incessant touches of farce, comedy, irony, and absurdity in the portrayal of Satan and the fallen angels, see C.S. Lewis, *A Preface to Paradise Lost* (New York, 1961), chaps. 13, 14.

7. T.S. Eliot, "The Waste Land" 1.62-63, in *The Complete Poems and Plays* (New York, 1952).

8. See especially Benjamin Boyce, "News from Hell," *PMLA* 58 (June 1943): 402-37, and Frederick M. Keener, *English Dialogues of the Dead: A Critical History, an Anthology and a Check List* (New York, 1973).

9. John Dryden, "Absalom and Achitophel," ll. 152-58, in *The Works of John Dryden*, ed. E.N. Hooker, et al. (Berkeley, 1972), 2: 10.

10. William Faulkner, *The Hamlet* (New York, 1957), 371-73.

11. Woody Allen, "Selections from the Allen Notebooks," in *Without Feathers* (New York, 1976), 10.

12. Samuel Johnson, *The History of Rasselas, Prince of Abissinia*, ed. D.J. Enright (New York, 1976), chaps. 21, 22.

13. Gustave Flaubert, *Three Tales*, trans. Walter F. Cobb (New York, 1964), 37.

14. Ibid., 41-42.

15. Ibid.

16. Bruce F. Kawin, *Telling It Again and Again: Repetition in Literature and Film* (Ithaca, N.Y., 1972), 30; "The Eighteenth Brumaire of Louis Bonaparte," in Karl Marx and Friedrich Engels, *Basic Writings on Politics and Philosophy*, ed. Lewis S. Feuer (Garden City, N.Y., 1959), 320. Consult Jean Maloney, "Flyting: Some Aspects of Poetic Invective Debate," Ph.D. diss., Ohio State Univ., 1964. A grand cursing contest or *débat* betwixt an English woman and a French woman is nicely managed in John Barth, *The Sot-Weed Factor* (New York, 1970), 446-72.

17. See, for instance, Mary Tom Osborne, *Advice-to-a-Painter Poems, 1633-1856: An Annotated Finding List* (Austin, Tex., 1949).

18. Alvin B. Kernan, *The Plot of Satire* (New Haven, 1965), esp. 30, 77, 160. The chapter on Waugh is explicitly designated "Running in Circles."

19. William Wordsworth, "Mutability," ll. 1-3, in *Poetical Works*, ed. Ernest de Selincourt (New York, 1950).

20. Gabriel García Márquez, "Big Mama's Funeral" (1962), in *No One Writes to the Colonel And Other Stories*, trans. J.S. Bernstein (New York, 1968), 209.

21. Ibid., 198, 217.

22. Henry James, "Ivan Turgénieff," in *French Poets and Novelists* (1878; Freeport, N.Y., 1972), 318-19.

23. Arthur Bloch, *Murphy's Law and Other Reasons Why Things Go $8uo_{1M}$* ! (Los Angeles, 1977). The latest among the popular "rule" and "law" books include Paul Dickson, *The Official Rules* (New York, 1978), and John Peers, comp., *1,001 Logical Laws, Accurate Axioms, Profound Principles, Trusty Truisms, Homey Homilies, Colorful Corollaries, Quotable Quotes and Rambunctious Ruminations for All Walks of Life* (Garden City, N.Y., 1979).

24. Donald Barthelme, *Snow White* (New York, 1967), 96, 97. An "everted sphere," by the way, is one that has been turned inside out. Critics of satire continue to have trouble with such perverse revolutionary form. Neil Schmitz, for instance, praises Barthelme's scathing representations of a decadent literature and a decadent society, yet he believes that Barthelme, although

"exploding" folly, fails to be constructive, fails to "reconstitute another more ample universe." Schmitz, "Donald Barthelme and the Emergence of Modern Satire," *Minnesota Review* 11 (Fall 1971): 116. Like many others, this critic finds himself dissatisfied with "the negativity of [Barthelme's] satire" (117). Such a critic does not want satire, he wants construction crews, moral uplift, utopia, affirmative action. He isn't going to get them.

10. Ennui

1. Charles Dickens, *Hard Times* (1854), with an introduction by William W. Watt (New York, 1958), 115, 119.

2. Seneca's *De Tranquillitate Animi*, written at the apex of Roman imperial civilization, is entirely devoted to instructing Serenus in the arts of serenity; it seems that he suffers in a civilized, bureaucratic society from a crippling fatigue and restlessness. (See also Seneca's *Epistulae Morales ad Lucilium* 28.) Later, the letters of Pliny the Younger frequently deal with the topic of *taedium*.

Monastic solitude exacerbated the devout Christian's suffering "the dark night of the soul," a mental crisis that alternated states of lassitude, hallucination, and despair. One of the striking figures in Dante's *Purgatorio* is Belacqua (4.97-139), too supine and listless to have worked out his soul's salvation.

3. Lewis Mumford, *Technics and Civilization* (1934; New York, 1963), 271.

4. Seneca *Ep.* 28.1-2; see also 104.7, 20-21. Compare the saying of Crates that Seneca cites in *Ep.* 10.1.

5. In Charles Baudelaire's *Les Fleurs du mal*, this is the title of poem 86 in "Spleen et Idéal." It was originally the Greek title of Terence's Latin play (163 B.C.).

6. See Estelle R. Ramey, "Boredom: The Most Prevalent American Disease," *Harper's*, Nov. 1974, pp. 12-14, 18-20, 22; and John R. Clark, "The Restless Turbulence of Wit: Boredom in the Seventeenth Century," *Seventeenth-Century News* 36 (1978): 7-8. James Sloan Allen argues that nineteenth-century fascination (among romantics, realists, naturalists) with the middle-class values of the commonplace, the trivial, and the banal eventually in our century becomes a despairing and impotent fear and acceptance of the quotidian and the nugatory, contributing to the picayune an aura of terror and menace as it overwhelms our lives. Allen, "Modernity and the Evil of Banality," *The Centennial Review* 23 (1979): 20-39.

7. Hans Meyerhoff, *Time in Literature* (Berkeley, 1955), 114. See all of chap. 3, pp. 85-119, for an acute analysis of fragmented, instantaneous time as it impinges upon all things in twentieth-century thinking.

8. *Rambler*, no. 6, in *The Yale Edition of the Works of Samuel Johnson*, vol. 3, *The Rambler*, ed. W.J. Bate and Albrecht B. Strauss (New Haven, 1969), 35. See also no. 80, on humanity's seeming addiction to "that insatiable demand of new gratifications." Needless to say, Johnson argues, one's anticipated happiness is always shattered by the event (*Idler*, no. 58). All of *Rasselas* is cast within the frame story of men placed in an earthly paradise and infinitely bored. One should also remark in *Rasselas* the gem of a story about the man who renounced the world and retired into the wilderness; after a time, tedium induces him to renege on his vow, and he returns to the world. Observers

conjecture that, like Sisyphus, Tantalus, and other hell-bound creatures, he may be expected to bounce indecisively back and forth between hermitage and metropolis as long as he lives (chaps. 21, 22). Jacques Barzun observes that Faust's magic, like nineteenth-century science, equally promised elixirs only to disappoint: they lead man, through "trial and error" to "a round of desire, disillusion, disgust, and despair." Barzun, "Faust and the Birth of Time," in *The Energies of Art* (New York, 1956), 36.

9. Sonnet 79, ll. 2-7, 12. Lionel Trilling remarks upon Keats's extreme ambivalence about pleasure as if it were strictly a nineteenth-century development: "aching Pleasure . . . Turning to poison as the bee-mouth sips" ("Ode on Melancholy," ll. 23-24). But such ambivalence, such "divided states of feeling," an uneven balancing of joy and sadness, content and discontent, are precisely a feature of the emerging modern self over the last four centuries; see Trilling, "The Fate of Pleasure," in *Beyond Culture: Essays on Literature and Learning* (New York, 1965), esp. 64-69. The classic study of romantic eros somehow helplessly turned to imaginings of grotesquerie, violence, and sadomasochism is Mario Praz, *The Romantic Agony*, trans. Angus Davidson (London, 1933).

10. Curiously, Western man in the latest decades of this century has been singled out as particularly narcissistic, although he might have been considered so over a number of recent centuries. See Christopher Lasch, "The Narcissistic Personality of Our Time," *Partisan Review* 44 (1977): 9-19.

11. John O. Lyons, *The Invention of the Self: The Hinge of Consciousness in the Eighteenth Century* (Carbondale, Ill., 1978), esp. 7, 8. I borrow the useful concept of the performing self from Richard Poirier, *The Performing Self: Compositions and Decompositions in the Languages of Contemporary Life* (New York, 1971). The melodramatic posturer has been especially notable since the era of the Byronic hero. Yet in the modern era the romantic hero—poseur, egoist, guilty rebel, frequent Satanist—has essentially fallen out of fashion. Modern anxiety and intellect deny the isolated self, reject most heroism, and scrutinize the world with a sneering irony and even mockery; see Raney Stanford, "The Romantic Hero and That Fatal Selfhood," *The Centennial Review* 12 (1968): 430-54. A noteworthy study of that romantic tradition is Peter L. Thorslev, Jr., *The Byronic Hero: Types and Prototypes* (Minneapolis, 1962); Thorslev duly notes in chapter 12 the demise of such "heroism" in the modern era, as do Eric Bentley, *A Century of Hero-Worship* (Philadelphia, 1944), Mario Praz, *The Hero in Eclipse in Victorian Fiction*, trans. Angus Davidson (New York, 1956), and Sean O'Faolain, *The Vanishing Hero: Studies of the Hero in the Modern Novel* (Boston, 1957).

12. Montaigne is a good example of this self-conscious type, as is Sir Thomas Browne (on the latter, see the interesting comments concerning his quirky selfhood in Virginia Woolf, "The Elizabethan Lumber Room," in *The Common Reader: First Series* [New York, 1953], 40-48). It might even be proposed that the rise to popularity in the theater of the Jonsonian "humor character" commences, however grotesquely, to delineate such individuals. Blaise Pascal in his *Pensées* (1670) precisely exemplifies the individual reflecting in solitude. He concludes that nothing renders man more weary, unhappy, and wretched than reflection in solitude upon the self's condition. Hence, he argues, men will go to any lengths to generate bustle and stir, to play, make love, go to war. See Pascal, *Pensées: The Provincial Letters*, trans. W.F. Trotter (New York, 1941), pp. 46, 47, 48-52, nos. 127, 130, 131, 139.

13. I am thinking, of course, of Coleridge's "Dejection Ode," and of Wordsworth's "Immortality Ode" in particular. Often the romantic sensibility is even destroyed when it does achieve its heart's desire, as in Keats's enigmatic "La Belle Dame sans merci."

14. William Wordsworth, *Prelude* 3.196-97, in *Poetical Works*, ed. Ernest de Selincourt (New York, 1950).

15. George Steiner, "The Great Ennui," in *In Bluebeard's Castle: Some Notes Towards the Redefinition of Culture* (New Haven, 1971), 1-25. I suspect that no great deed itself undermines a century—for there have been more than a few monstrous deeds—but rather the contemporary populace's imagination of great deeds performed by themselves that causes the letdown, for reality can never live up to fantasy, imaginings, and expectations. Thomas De Quincey remarked in 1823 in his essay "On Knocking at the Gate in *Macbeth*" that the facts of the particularly brutal conduct of the murderer John Williams in 1812 served as a high-water mark that later aspiring criminals could only survey with envy and disappointment: "There has been absolutely nothing *doing* since his time, or nothing that's worth speaking of," an amateur criminal tells the author. This is merely an insight into the frustrated mind of a competitive but peculiar observer. Many doubtless looked to the French Revolution or to Napoleon in much the same way.

16. Barzun, "Byron and the Byronic in History," in *Energies of Art*, 52-53.

17. Villiers de l'Isle-Adam, *Axel, Oeuvres complètes*, (Paris, 1923), 4:261. Verlaine wrote, "I am far from sure that the philosophy of Villiers will not one day become the formula of our century"; cited in Arthur Symons, *The Symbolist Movement in Literature* (London, 1899), 45n.

18. Paul Verlaine, *Oeuvres poétiques complètes*, ed. Y.G. Le Dantec and Jacques Borel (Paris, 1962), 371, 371n, 307.

19. As for the great fashion of artists and intellectuals baiting the bourgeoisie, see the excellent study by César Graña, *Bohemian versus Bourgeois: French Society and the French Man of Letters in the Nineteenth Century* (New York, 1964).

20. André Gide, *Le Journal des Faux-Monnayeurs* (Paris, 1926), 70-71; my translation.

21. The latter two characters appear, respectively, in Sainte-Beuve, *Vie, poésies, et pensées de Joseph Delorme* (1829), and Flaubert, *L'Education sentimentale* (1869). François-René de Chateaubriand's hero appears in *René* (1802) and in *Les Natchez* (1826). On characters like René and Obermann, see the discussion by George Ross Ridge, "Hypersensitivity and the Pathological Hero," in *The Hero in French Romantic Literature* (Athens, Ga., 1959), 53-74.

22. Charles Baudelaire, "Pierre Dupont," in *Oeuvres complètes*, ed. Y.G. Le Dantec and Claude Pinchois, rev. ed. (Paris, 1961), 613.

23. Self-contradiction is one of the key features romantic man detects when he peers inward and studies the self; he confirms the paradox of Heraclitus that into the same river (of time? of life?) a man never steps twice, since the river and the man himself are so rapidly careening and changing. Pascal observes this rapid alteration of the self in *Pensées*, no. 122, and we recollect the almost Jekyll-and-Hyde aspects of Boswell the gentleman and also the rakehell in the *London Journals* (1762-63). Much the same is the essence of Sainte-Beuve's Joseph Delorme: "Defunct Reason was prowling around him like a phantom and accompanied him to the abyss, which it illuminated with a sepulchral glimmer. With frightful vigor, this is what he called 'the headlight

for drowning himself.' In a word, Joseph's soul now no longer offers us more than inconceivable chaos where monstrous imaginations, fresh reminiscences, criminal fantasies, huge aborted thoughts, sage premonitions followed by mad actions, pious transports after blasphemies, all caper and quake confusedly on a bed of despair." Charles Augustine Sainte-Beuve, *Vie, poésies et pensées de Joseph Delorme* (1829), ed. Gérald Antoine (Paris, 1956), 17; my translation. Here the much-touted "alienated" and "divided self" has fully arrived. See also Baudelaire's similar catalog of his own reversals, alterations, and divagations between his intentions and his acts that reminds us of Delorme; in "A Une Heure du matin," among the *Petits Poèms en Prose*, "Le Spleen de Paris" (1869), in *Oeuvres complètes*, 240-41.

24. John Ruskin, *Modern Painters* (1843-1860), vol. 3, part 4, chap. 16, in *Works*, 26 vols. (Boston, 1897), 26: 319.

25. Søren Kierkegaard, *Either/Or*, trans. David F. Swenson and Lillian Marvin Swenson, 2 vols. (Garden City, N.Y., 1959), 1: 19-20. The entire section "Diapsalmata" is relevant for its treatment of dilemma and exhaustion, as in "The Rotation Method."

26. Two salient studies here are Renato Poggioli, "On Goncharov and His Oblomov," in *The Phoenix and the Spider* (Cambridge, Mass., 1957), 33-48; and Geoffrey Clive, "Goncharov and the Spectrum of Boredom," in *The Broken Icon: Intuitive Existentialism in Classical Russian Fiction* (New York, 1972), 63-85.

27. Edmund Wilson, *Axel's Castle: A Study in the Imaginative Literature of 1870-1930* (New York, 1954), 266-67. Reprinted with the permission of Charles Scribner's Sons, an imprint of Macmillan Publishing Company.

28. Ibid., 283, 289.

29. Antonio Machado, *Poesías* (Buenos Aires, 1969), p. 151, ll. 31, 33-36; my translation.

30. Frederick Karl, review of R.M. Adams, *After Joyce* (1977), *English Language Notes* 17 (1979): 75-77. Amid all the slaughter in our era, man's paranoia, his sensing that "someone is out to get him," might not so much be an obsession as a reasonable assessment of the situation: see the interesting remarks in Hendrik Hertzberg and David C.K. McClelland, "Paranoia," *Harper's* 248 (June 1974): 51-54, 59-60. As for preoccupation with degeneration and decay, Richard Gilman has cogently argued that the term *"decadence"* has no ascertainable meaning and should therefore be put away; Gilman, "Reflections on Decadence," *Partisan Review* 46 (1979): 175-87, and idem, *Decadence: The Strange Life of an Epithet* (New York, 1979). But man recurrently (and at no time more than in these last two centuries) is convinced that his society is debauched and in decline, and there is no reason for taking his images, paradigms, and metaphors away from him; consult Lance Morrow, "The Fascination of Decadence," *Time*, Sept. 10, 1979, pp. 85-86.

31. William Barrett, *Irrational Man: A Study in Existential Philosophy* (Garden City, N.Y., 1962), 241.

32. Refer to George Woodcock, "Utopias in Negative," *Sewanee Review* 64 (1956): 81-97; George Knox, "Apocalypse and Sour Utopias," *Western Humanities Review* 16 (Winter 1962): 11-22; Mark R. Hillegas, *The Future as Nightmare: H.G. Wells and the Anti-Utopians* (Carbondale, Ill., 1967); Irving Howe, "The Fiction of Anti-Utopia," in *Decline of the New* (New York, 1970), 66-74; Robert C. Elliott, *The Shape of Utopia: Studies in a Literary Genre* (Chicago, 1970), esp. chaps. 5 and 7; and W.K. Thomas, "The Underside of Utopias," *College English* 38 (1976): 356-72.

33. Most dystopias can be considered a species of science fiction, but much science fiction does not deal with an almost ideal society in collapse, but just with any extraterrestrial society in collapse. See, for instance, Roger Elwood, ed., *Dystopian Visions* (Englewood Cliffs, N.J., 1975); Harold Berger, *Science Fiction and the New Dark Age* (Bowling Green, Ohio, 1976); and Gregory Fitzgerald and John Dillon, eds., *The Late Great Future* (Greenwich, Conn., 1976). The most potent among the recent satiric authors of the science fiction of disaster or exhaustion is Stanislaw Lem.

34. Ideas of the heat-death of the universe have been growing ever more popular since the concept was postulated as an extension of the second law of thermodynamics in 1850 and 1852.

35. William Barrett, *Time of Need: Forms of Imagination in the Twentieth Century* (New York, 1972), 6. The onset of such inertia and self-doubt is well represented by the listlessness of the unrehabilitated former fighting man from World War I in Hemingway's "Soldier's Home"; he has taken to his bed and cannot and will not be reintegrated into society. He cannot function. In 1953 Paddy Chayefsky's television drama *Marty* handsomely presented the whole of youthful society as drenched in boredom, "drugstore cowboys" hanging listlessly around with nothing to do. Recently, Saul Bellow's Charles Citrine has long been collecting data for a projected essay on boredom that, significantly, he is unable to write. For Citrine too leads a life of a dangling man, in suspension—indecisive, nonproductive, uncertain. Bellow, *Humboldt's Gift* (New York, 1975), esp. 108-9, 198-203.

36. E.M. Cioran, *Précis de décomposition* (Paris, 1949), 22, 25; my translation.

37. Samuel Beckett, *Molloy*, trans. Patrick Bowles and Samuel Beckett (1955; New York, 1970), 53.

38. Donald Barthelme, "Games Are the Enemies of Beauty, Truth, and Sleep, Amanda Said," in *Guilty Pleasures* (New York, 1976), 127, 133, 134.

39. See Charles Baudelaire, "Au lecteur," in *Les Fleurs du mal*, ed. Ernest Raynaud, (Paris, 1952), 6. An advertising blurb for Kuhn's *Demon of Noontide* by Princeton Univ. Press reads: "Baudelaire predicted that the 'delicate monster' of boredom would one day swallow up the whole world in an immense yawn"; *PMLA* 91 (1977): 319.

11. Scatology

1. Aldous Huxley, *The Genius and the Goddess* (New York, 1955), 52-53.

2. Alice Hamilton and Kenneth Hamilton, *Elements of John Updike* (Grand Rapids, Mich., 1970), 35; Francis Bacon, "Of Discourse," in *Essays, Advancement of Learning, New Atlantis and Other Pieces*, ed. R.F. Jones (New York, 1937), 96.

3. See Philip Pinkus, "Satire and St. George," *Queen's Quarterly* 70 (1963): 30-49.

4. Adrian Stokes, "Strong Smells and Polite Society," *Encounter* 17 (July-Dec. 1961) 50-56; Captain John G. Bourke, *Scatalogic Rites of All Nations* (Washington, D.C., 1891), 134. Consult Thomas E. Maresca, "Language and Body in Augustan Poetic," *Journal of English Literary History* 37 (1970): 374-88; and Philip Stevick, "The Augustan Nose," *University of Toronto Quarterly* 34 (1965): 110-17.

5. "The Excremental Vision" is the title of chapter 28 of John Middleton Murry, *Jonathan Swift: A Critical Biography* (New York, 1955). See also Milton

Voigt, "Swift and Psychoanalytic Criticism," *Western Humanities Review* 16 (Autumn 1962): 361-67. Occasionally, however, a psychoanalytic critic will take compeers to task, as Norman O. Brown does (concerning attitudes toward Swift) in chapter 13 of *Life against Death: The Psychoanalytic Meaning of History* (Middletown, Conn., 1959). Brown himself considers that "we are nothing but body" and aptly compares the amassing of "filthy lucre" with anal and excremental concerns (292-304). Consult William Makepeace Thackeray's essay "Swift," in *The English Humourists of the Eighteenth Century* (1853); and Aldous Huxley, *Do What You Will* (Garden City, N.Y., 1929), 99-112.

6. Jeremy Sandford and Roger Law, *Synthetic Fun* (Baltimore, 1967), 125. Nor are our ideas of hygienic washing, bathing, and treating food altogether sound; contemporary practices are often as much "ritual," expressing "symbolic systems," as many of the rites and proceedings of primitive tribes. See Mary Douglas, *Purity and Danger: An Analysis of Concepts of Pollution and Taboo* (London, 1966), esp. 34-35. For a fine satiric treatment of American cleanliness as aboriginal ritual, see Horace Miner, "Body Ritual among the Nacirema," *American Anthropologist* 58 (1956): 503-7.

7. Albert Camus, *The Myth of Sisyphus*, trans. Justin O'Brien (New York, 1955), 84; Alexander Pope, "Postscript to the Translation of the *Odyssey*" (1726), in *Eighteenth-Century Critical Essays*, ed. Scott Elledge, 2 vols. (Ithaca, N.Y., 1961), 1: 295.

8. Little work has been done in the field of literary scatology; one might consult what proves to be a slender and hardly thorough study, Jae Num Lee, *Swift and Scatological Satire* (Albuquerque, 1971). Catullus, *Carmina* 36.1.20.

9. Petronius *Satyricon* 27, 47; Martial *Epigrams* 12.61. Elsewhere Bassus is condemned for manuring in a gold chamber pot but drinking only from glass: "Therefore, you shit at a greater cost" than you live (*Epigrams* 1.37).

10. Franceso Berni, "Capitolo dell'orinale," in *Rime*, ed. Giorgio Bàrberi Squarotti (Torino, 1969), 31-33. Concerning the tradition of the paradoxical encomium, consult Henry Knight Miller, "The Paradoxical Encomium, with Special Reference to Its Vogue in England, 1600-1800," *Modern Philology* 53 (1956): 145-78.

11. John Dryden, "MacFlecknoe," ll. 98-103, in Hooker, *Works of John Dryden*, 2:56-57. For studies of the scatological in this poem, see Michael Wilding, "Allusion and Innuendo in *MacFlecknoe*," *Etudes Celtiques* 19 (1968): 355-70; Robert F. Willson, Jr., "The Fecal Vision in *MacFlecknoe*," *Satire Newsletter* 8 (1970): 1-4; and John R. Clark, "Dryden's 'MackFlecknoe,' 46-50," *Explicator* (April 1971): item 56.

12. François Rabelais, *The Histories of Gargantua and Pantagruel*, trans. J.M. Cohen (Baltimore, 1955), 1.13, 17.

13. Jonathan Swift, *Gulliver's Travels and Other Writings*, ed. Louis A. Landa (Boston, 1960), 1.1; 2.1, 101, 157-90.

14. Tobias Smollett, *The Expedition of Humphry Clinker*, ed. André Parreaux (Boston, 1968), 18, 19.

15. James Joyce, *Ulysses* (New York, 1934), 67-69; Oliver St. John Gogarty, *As I Was Going down Sackville Street* (New York, 1937), 294-95.

16. For predictions of the decline of satire and comedy-and-satire respectively, see Herman Scheffauer, "The Death of Satire," *Fortnightly Review* 99 (1913): 1188-99, and Jesse Bier, *The Rise and Fall of American Humor* (New York, 1968). Despite the many virtues of Matthew Hodgart, *Satire* (London, 1969), Hodgart nevertheless feels that satire is "archaic" and inadequate for treating

many topics (77-78, 155). As a matter of fact, what Northrop Frye terms the "low mimetic" mode in literature comes close to describing much modern literature and is quite similar to satire. Consult Frye, *Anatomy of Criticism* (Princeton, 1957), esp. 38-42, and Ihab Hassan, *Radical Innocence: Studies in the Contemporary American Novel* (New York, 1966).

17. "Kingsley Amis, "Laughter's to Be Taken Seriously," *New York Times Book Review*, July 7, 1957, p. 1.

18. Evelyn Waugh, *Scoop* (Baltimore, 1943), 39-40; Eugène Ionesco, *Four Plays*, trans. Donald M. Allen (New York, 1958), 15.

19. Vladimir Nabokov, *Lolita* (New York, 1966), 122.

20. Samuel Beckett, *Waiting for Godot* (New York, 1954), 23-24. Even in his earliest fiction, Beckett was fond of these fecal tricks. In *Murphy*, for instance, the protagonist leaves elaborate instructions in his will that his ashes should be somberly flushed down the toilet at the Abbey Theatre—noisily, and during a performance. Samuel Beckett, *Murphy* (New York, 1970), 269.

21. William Golding, *Lord of the Flies* (New York, 1959), 14, 100.

22. George R. Stewart, *Doctor's Oral* (New York, 1939), 185.

23. Lenny Bruce, *How to Talk Dirty and Influence People* (Chicago, 1965), 192.

24. Philip Roth, *Portnoy's Complaint* (New York, 1968), 22.

25. Ibid., 23, 30-31, 114-15.

26. J. P. Donleavy, *The Ginger Man* (New York, 1959), 45.

27. John Barth, *The Sot-Weed Factor* (New York, 1970), 186, 390-93. From the outset of Barth's career, to be sure, his work contained a distinct savor of the Rabelaisian and the excremental. The legal battle for the vast fortune of the deceased Mack Harrison turns upon his "jibbering idiocy" in his last years, and his penchant for allowing "nothing of his creation—including hair- and nail-clippings, urine, feces, and wills—to be thrown away." Indeed, in addition to his monies, Harrison also bequeathed "several hundred pickle jars" of excrement. Characteristically, much of the remainder of the novel is invested in, and made to "float" upon, these commodious "shares." John Barth, *The Floating Opera* (New York, 1972), 85, 89.

28. Barth, *Sot-Weed Factor*, 390-93.

29. John Hawkes, *The Cannibal* (1949; New York, 1962), 54.

30. Tom Wolfe, *The Bonfire of the Vanities* (New York, 1988), 141-42, 284-86.

31. Consult Lucius R. Shero, "The *Cena* in Roman Satire," *Classical Philology* 18 (1923): 126-43.

32. Alan Sillitoe, *A Start in Life* (New York, 1971), 219-20.

33. Nathanael West, "Miss Lonelyhearts," in *Miss Lonelyhearts and the Day of the Locust* (Norfolk, Conn., 1962), 189-91.

34. Roth, *Portnoy's Complaint*, 17-18.

35. Ibid., 19-20.

36. Ibid., 133-34.

37. John Updike, *Couples* (Greenwich, Conn., 1968), 327-28.

38. Ibid.

39. Terry Southern and Mason Hoffenberg, *Candy* (New York, 1964), 160-61. Southern, indeed, never travels far from these toilet encounters. Guy Grand, the multimillionaire of *The Magic Christian*, loves to corrupt humanity by tempting and tormenting it (in the tradition of Twain's "The Man That Corrupted Hadleyburg" and Dürrenmatt's *The Visit*) with the possibility of "earning" vast sums of money. One of his capers, "making it hot for people," consisted of placing, in summertime in Chicago's crowded Loop, a great

heated vat of blood, urine, and cowshit, into which Grand gleefully stirs ten thousand one-hundred-dollar bills. Then he labels a public sign, "FREE $ HERE," and retreats, waiting patiently to observe the panic and commotion. Terry Southern, *The Magic Christian* (New York, 1964), 16-23.

40. Günter Grass, *Cat and Mouse*, trans. Ralph Manheim (New York, 1964), 98-99.

41. T.S. Eliot, *The Complete Poems and Plays* (New York, 1952), 36.

42. Slawomir Mrozek, "From the Darkness," in *The Elephant*, trans. Konrad Syrop (New York, 1963), 7, 8, 10.

12. Cannibals

1. Robert J. Lifton and Eric Olson, *Living and Dying* (New York, 1974), 3, 19; Hans Zinsser, *Rats, Lice and History* (New York, 1965), 5; Frederic Wertham, *The Show of Violence* (Garden City, N.Y., 1949), 87.

2. For a reproduction of several etchings and paintings, together with a discussion of the meaning of Saturn to Goya in his old age, see Folke Nordtröm, *Goya, Saturn and Melancholy* (Stockholm, 1962), 192-201.

3. See, for instance, J. Robert Constantine, "The Ignoble Savage: An Eighteenth Century Literary Stereotype," *Phylon* 27 (1966): 171-79.

4. Richard Rhodes, *The Ungodly: A Novel of the Donner Party* (New York, 1973); Piers Paul Read, *Alive: The Story of the Andes Survivors* (New York, 1974).

5. See the discussions of Dionysian and similar bacchantic sacrifices and celebrations in Sir James George Frazer, *The Golden Bough* (New York, 1951), 453ff., 339-40, 576ff. For a study of cannibalism and subsequent sublimations, see Eli Sagan, *Cannibalism: Human Aggression and Cultural Form* (New York, 1974). Even though cannibalism is rare in warm-blooded species, especially among mammals, human beings have so indulged. As Konrad Lorenz reports, the earliest traces of human use of fire also uncover the charred bones of roasted people. Lorenz, *On Aggression*, trans. M.K. Wilson (New York, 1967), 115, 251-52, 231.

6. Ronald Paulson, *The Fictions of Satire* (Baltimore, 1967), 9.

7. A.A. Long, *Hellenistic Philosophy: Stoics, Epicureans, Sceptics* (New York, 1974), 111; Juvenal *Satire* 15.11-13, 27-83; Petronius *Satyricon* 141; Montaigne, "Des Cannibales," in *Essais* 1.31. Montaigne in fact argues that savages are closer to nature than we are, more direct and affectionate. Indeed, European society is more cruel, torturing fellows to death, whereas cannibals merely dine upon dead enemies. George Bernard Shaw tends to agree: "The human fact remains that the burning of Joan of Arc was a horror. . . . The final criticism of its physical side is implied in the refusal of the Marquesas islanders to be persuaded that the English did not eat Joan. Why, they ask, should anyone take the trouble to roast a human being except with that object? They cannot conceive its being a pleasure. As we have no answer for them that is not shameful to us, let us blush for our more complicated and pretentious savagery." Shaw, "Preface to *Saint Joan*," in *Bernard Shaw's Saint Joan, Major Barbara, Androcles and the Lion* (New York, 1956), 34.

8. Mark Twain, "Cannibalism in the Cars," in *The Complete Short Stories of Mark Twain*, ed. Charles Neider (Garden City, N.Y., 1957), 9-16; Ambrose Bierce, "Did We Eat One Another?" in *The Sardonic Humor of Ambrose Bierce*,

ed. George Barkin (New York, 1963), 193-94; Lord Dunsany (Edward John Moreton Drax Plunkett), "Two Bottles of Relish," in *21 Great Stories*, ed. A.H. Lass and N.L. Tasman (New York, 1969), 41-55; Evelyn Waugh, *Black Mischief* (Baltimore, 1954), 213-14; T.S. Eliot, "Fragment of an Agon," in *The Complete Poems and Plays* (New York, 1952), 79-80; Stanley M. Garn and Walter D. Block, "The Limited Nutritional Value of Cannibalism," *American Anthropologist* 72 (Feb. 1970): 106; Norman Mailer, "The Metaphysics of the Belly," in *Cannibals and Christians* (New York, 1970), 269-70. An implicit theme throughout Ovid's *Metamorphoses* is "Terras Astraea reliquit" (1.150): In the face of so much crime and evil, Astraea (or pristine justice) has fled our debauched planet entirely and taken up residence in the skies. In like manner, the haunting chagrin and suspense behind much of Herman Melville's *Typee* (1846) is generated by the protagonist's slowly discovering that the happy tribe that holds him captive in the Marquesas Islands is in fact a society of man-eaters. It is patent in such stories that the innocent observer can hardly guess at the depths of depravity lurking within the human heart. With a sardonic twist, Joseph Conrad also explores this cannibalistic theme, but he suggests that love and selfishness can learn to tolerate cannibalism. Conrad, "Falk: A Reminiscence," in *The Nigger of the 'Narcissus,' Typhoon, and Other Stories* (Baltimore, 1963), 258-332.

9. See, for instance, Laurence L. Langer, *The Holocaust and the Literary Imagination* (New Haven, 1975); Robert J. Lifton, *Boundaries: Psychological Man in Revolution* (New York, 1969); and idem, *History and Human Survival* (New York, 1970). But not merely post–World War II traumas have bemused us; Paul Fussell argues that the terrors of World War I's battlefields have permanently cast dark shadows over the entire century's grim and gloomy art. Fussell, *The Great War and Modern Memory* (New York, 1975).

10. "I don't think this book of mine is ever going to be finished. I must have written five thousand pages by now, and thrown them all away." Kurt Vonnegut, Jr., *Slaughterhouse-Five* (New York, 1969), 15, 214, 116.

11. G.K. Chesterton, *The Man Who Was Thursday* (New York, 1960), 31.

12. Consult Slawomir Mrozek, *Six Plays*, trans. Nicholas Bethell (New York, 1967), 81-103.

13. Karel Čapek, *War with the Newts*, trans. M. Weatherall and R. Weatherall (New York, 1967), 137. For a general admiring appraisal of this novel, together with discussion of the ways man is incriminated in it, see John R. Clark and Anna Lydia Motto, "At War with Our Roots: Karel Čapek Revisited," *Studies in Contemporary Satire* 14 (1987): 1-15.

14. John Barth, *Giles Goat-Boy* (Greenwich, Conn., 1968), 129, 299, 414. Men exposed to the computer's rays are destroyed, or their offspring become idiots or maniacs for generations. "That's what it means to be EATen, Billy! The goats, now: they'll eat almost anything you feed them; but only us humans is smart enough to EAT one another!" (90).

15. Anthony Burgess, *The Wanting Seed* (1964; New York, 1976), 172.

16. J.P. Donleavy, "Cannibalism," in *The Un-Expurgated Code: A Complete Manual of Survival and Manners* (New York, 1976), 70-73; Saul Bellow, *Humboldt's Gift* (New York, 1975).

17. George P. Elliott, "The NRACP," in *Among the Dangs* (New York, 1966), 109-42; Fernando Arrabal, *Plays*, vol. 3, trans. Jean Benedetti and John Calder (London, 1970), 87-93.

18. Gabriel García Márquez, *The Autumn of the Patriarch*, trans. Gregory Rabassa (New York, 1977), 119.

19. By an ironic inversion, it is precisely when a new leader is about to commence another destructive war in this novel that the mad lunatics return to the "order" of the insane asylum and spring is in the air. Warfare, in other words, is the only "order" such a society can know; organized madness, its only modus operandi.

20. John Hawkes, *The Cannibal* (1949; New York, 1962), 180-81.

21. John Gardner, *Grendel* (New York, 1972), 138.

13. Dystopias and Machines

1. James Thurber, "Sex Ex Machina," in *The Thurber Carnival* (New York, 1945), 59.

2. See George Knox, "Apocalypse and Sour Utopias," *Western Humanities Review* 16 (Winter 1962): 11-22, and Irving Howe, "The Fiction of Anti-Utopia," in *Decline of the New* (New York, 1970), 66-74. On dystopias as "upside-down or topsy-turvy societies," see J. Max Patrick, introduction to sec. 9, "Utopias and Dystopias, 1500–1750," in *St. Thomas More: A Preliminary Bibliography of His Works and of Moreana to the Year 1750*, comp. Reginald W. Gibson (New Haven, 1961), 294. See also Robert C. Elliott, *The Shape of Utopia: Studies in a Literary Genre* (Chicago, 1970), esp. chaps. 5 and 7, and Glenn Negley and J. Max Patrick, eds., *The Quest for Utopia: An Anthology of Imaginary Societies* (Garden City, N.Y., 1962), 5-6.

3. Stainslaw Lem, "Robots in Science Fiction," trans. Franz Rottensteiner, in *SF, The Other Side of Realism: Essays on Modern Fantasy and Science Fiction*, ed. Thomas D. Clareson (Bowling Green, Ohio, 1971), 317.

4. Arthur Asa Berger, "The Age of Confusion: The Third Generation of Comics," in *The Comic-Stripped American* (New York, 1973), 203.

5. See Denis Gifford, *Science Fiction Film* (New York, 1971), 8-19, 149-51; and John Baxter, *Science Fiction in the Cinema* (New York, 1970), 142-53, 153-66.

6. Baxter, *Science Fiction in the Cinema*, 92, 136.

7. Ado Kyrou, "Science and Fiction," in *Focus on the Science Fiction Film*, ed. William Johnson (Englewood Cliffs, N.J., 1972), 94.

8. Matthew Arnold, "Preface to First Edition of Poems (1853)," in *The Complete Prose Works of Matthew Arnold*, ed. R.H. Super, 11 vols. (Ann Arbor, 1960), 1: 1; Wylie Sypher, *Loss of the Self in Modern Literature and Art* (New York, 1962), 9-14; Lionel Trilling, "Commitment to the Modern," *Teachers College Record* 64 (1963): 407.

9. Hans Meyerhoff, *Time in Literature* (Berkeley, 1955), 103.

10. Tony Tanner, *City of Words: American Fiction, 1950–1970* (London, 1971), 16. Other critics have found a strain of the gothic, the nightmarish, and the apocalyptic running throughout much of American literature; see, for instance, Harry Levin, *The Power of Blackness: Hawthorne, Poe, Melville* (New York, 1958), and Martha Banta, "American Apocalypses: Excrement and Ennui," *Studies in the Literary Imagination* 7 (Spring 1974): 1-30.

11. William Barrett, *Time of Need: Forms of Imagination in the Twentieth Century* (New York, 1972), 6.

12. Consult Howard Schultz, *Milton and Forbidden Knowledge* (New York, 1955), and R. Joly, "Curiositas," *L'Antiquité Classique* 30 (1961): 33-44.

13. Evelyn Waugh, *Decline and Fall* (1928; Boston, 1949), 159.

14. E.B. White, *The Second Tree from the Corner* (New York, 1954), 46-51; James Thurber, "The Secret Life of Walter Mitty," in *Thurber Carnival*, 47-51. On Thurber's continual war with machines and "our machine civilization," see Louis Hasley, "James Thurber: Artist in Humor," *South Atlantic Quarterly* 73 (Autumn 1974): esp. 509. Donald Barthelme, "The Balloon," in *Unspeakable Practices, Unnatural Acts* (New York, 1968), 91-93. This may be taken to be the "early" Barthelme. For a later, darker view, wherein the world is "sagging, snagging, scaling, spalling, pilling, pinging, pitting, warping, checking, fading, chipping, cracking, yellowing, leaking, staling, shrinking, and in dynamic unbalance," the reader should consult "Down the Line with the Annual," in *Guilty Pleasures* (New York, 1976), 3-8. In that story, overwhelmed by defective American products and the positivism of the *Consumer Bulletin*, the protagonist wishes to flee to Australia.

15. Harold Pinter, *A Night Out, Night School, Revue Sketches: Early Plays* (New York, 1968), 91-93; Robert Coover, *Pricksongs and Descants* (New York, 1969), 125-37. Concerning postmodern "playfulness" and a game-oriented "performance" in literature, see, for example, Richard Poirier, *The Performing Self: Compositions and Decompositions in the Languages of Contemporary Life* (New York, 1971); Jacques Ehrmann, ed., *Game, Play, Literature* (Boston, 1971); and the recent new text expanding the concepts of "fiction-making," Alvin B. Kernan, P. Brooks, and J.M. Holquist, eds., *Man and His Fictions: An Introduction to Fiction-Making, Its Forms and Uses* (New York, 1973). Speaking of recent alienated writers, Ihab Hassan suggests that they have turned even against themselves: "From this reflexive energy, this introversion of the alienated will, emerge the arts of silence, of the void, and of death, emerge also the languages of omission, ambiguity, games, and numbers." Hassan, *The Dismemberment of Orpheus: Toward a Postmodern Literature* (New York, 1971), 12.

16. Recently David Ketterer defined the apocalyptic as both destructive and regenerative (as it might be if one refers to the totality of the book of Revelation). See Ketterer, *New Worlds for Old: The Apocalyptic Imagination, Science Fiction, and American Literature* (Garden City, N. Y., 1974), 3-14. Nevertheless, *apocalypse* has been too often used to suggest debacle, havoc, and doom for us to recast its meaning. In addition to works previously cited on apocalypse, see also R.W.B. Lewis, "Days of Wrath and Laughter," in *Trials of the Word: Essays in American Literature and the Humanistic Tradition* (New Haven, 1965), 184-234. A real cataclysm may well be virtually at hand for the inhabitants of earth; see Robert L. Heilbroner, "Ecological Armageddon," in *Peaceable Kingdoms: An Anthology of Utopian Writings*, ed. Robert L. Chianese (New York, 1971), 242-53.

17. The heralding of the twentieth century's unique "alienation" has been encountered often enough; it is caused, as one of the more recent writers phrases it, by "the explosion of the world's technology and populations." Robert Martin Adams, *The Roman Stamp: Frame and Façade in Some Forms of Neo-Classicism* (Berkeley, 1974), 232. Such a literature's themes are entropy and apocalypse; see Robert Alter, *Partial Magic: The Novel as a Self-Conscious Genre* (Berkeley, 1975), chap. 4. Its mode is a frenetic self-consciousness. Among innumerable titles, I will cite but a few: Ihab Hassan, *The Literature of Silence: Henry Miller and Samuel Beckett* (New York, 1967); Jonathan Baumbach, *The Landscape of Nightmare: Studies in the Contemporary American Novel* (New York, 1965); John Vernon, *The Garden and the Map: Schizophrenia in Twentieth-Century*

Literature and Culture (Urbana, Ill., 1973); and Jerome Klinkowitz, *Literary Disruptions: The Making of a Post-Contemporary American Fiction* (Urbana, Ill., 1975).

18. Barrett, *Time of Need*, 364. Wylie Sypher perceptively argues that there has been in fact a correspondence between aesthete and technician since the turn of the century, and he stresses the relationship of both to methodology. Nonetheless, Sypher still perceives technology as Protestant and partially alien—since it stresses parsimony, exactitude, and absolute control. See Sypher, *Literature and Technology: The Alien Vision* (New York, 1968), xv-xxi.

19. Norman Mailer, "The Last Night: A Story," in *Cannibals and Christians* (New York, 1970), 396-97.

14. Entropy and Armageddon

1. C.P. Snow, *The Two Cultures and the Scientific Revolution* (New York, 1959), 16; Tony Tanner, "The American Novelist as Entropologist," *London Magazine*, n.s., 10 (Oct. 1970): 5. Tanner's entire article on the recent literary uses of entropy (5-18) is important; it is incorporated, with changes, into Tanner, *City of Words: American Fiction, 1950–1970* (London, 1971), as chapter 6, "Everything Running Down," 141-52.

2. Stephen G. Brush, "Science and Culture in the Nineteenth Century: Thermodynamics and History," *The Graduate Journal* 7, no. 2 (1967): 493-95; this article, together with its bibliography (477-565), is especially important concerning the origins and proliferation of scientific ideas of entropy and the subsequent impact upon the public, thinkers, and historians. See also Max Jammer, "Entropy," in *Dictionary of the History of Ideas*, ed. Philip P. Wiener, 5 vols. (New York, 1973), 2: 112-20.

3. See Ludwig Boltzmann, "Weitere Studien über das Wärmegleichgewicht unter Gasmolekülen," *Sitzungsberichte der Kaiserlichen Akademie der Wissenschaften in Wein* 66 (1872): 275-370; J.W. Gibbs, "Rudolf Julius Emanuel Clausius," *Proceedings of the American Academy* 16 (1889): 458-65; Max Planck, *Eight Lectures on Theoretical Physics*, trans. A.P. Wills (New York, 1915); Sir Arthur Eddington, *The Nature of the Physical World* (Cambridge, Eng., 1928); and Sir James Jeans, *The Universe around Us* (Cambridge, Eng., 1930).

4. In his influential book *The Human Use of Human Beings: Cybernetics and Society* (Garden City, N.Y., 1954), Norbert Wiener conjectures that in controlled "enclaves" (especially those involving computers) entropy could be resisted and progress made possible, but scepticism concerning progress in the twentieth century largely persists and prevails.

5. *Hamlet* 5.2.352; T.S. Eliot, "The Hollow Men," sec. 5, ll. 28-31; Robert Martin Adams, *Nil: Episodes in the Literary Conquest of Void during the Nineteenth Century* (New York, 1966), 6. Compare William Barrett: "Contrary to the confidence in our powers of technology and information, the prevailing image of man we find in modern art is one of impotence, uncertainty, and self-doubt"; Barrett, *Time of Need: Forms of Imagination in the Twentieth Century* (New York, 1972), 6. Further, John Bayley argues that all truly major artists naturally possess an "unconscious grasp" of forces that disturb the surface of their literary works—regularly providing "tension," "puzzlement," and "contradiction"; Bayley, *The Uses of Division: Unity and Disharmony in Literature* (New York, 1976).

6. Monre C. Beardsley, "Order and Disorder in Art," in *The Concept of Order*, ed. Paul G. Kuntz (Seattle, 1968), 196. This theme is carefully analyzed in Rudolf Arnheim, *Entropy and Art: An Essay on Disorder and Order* (Berkeley, 1971). Consult Jose Ortega y Gasset, *La Rebelión de las Mases* (Madrid, 1929).

7. R.P. Blackmur, *Anni Mirabiles, 1921–1925: Reason in the Madness of Letters* (Washington, D.C., 1956), 6. This theme in the arts is more thoroughly explored in Wylie Sypher, "Existence and Entropy," in *Loss of the Self in Modern Literature and Art* (New York, 1962), 58-86.

8. Tanner, "American Novelist as Entropologist," 5. It is particularly noteworthy that Pynchon's first published story was entitled "Entropy"; consult Joseph W. Slade's discussion of this story in *Thomas Pynchon* (New York, 1974), 32-40.

9. George P. Elliott, *David Knudsen* (New York, 1962), 38, 88.

10. Susan Sontag, *Death Kit* (New York, 1967), 167, 2-3.

11. William Burroughs, *Nova Express*, (New York, 1965), 17; idem, *Naked Lunch* (New York, 1962), 133-34, 224. Consult also Alvin Greenberg's study of entropy in fiction: "The Novel of Disintegration: Paradoxical Impossibility in Contemporary Fiction," *Wisconsin Studies in Contemporary Literature* 7 (1966): 103-24. He refers to, among others, the works of Céline, Henry Miller, Burroughs, Heller, Nelson Algren, and Beckett.

12. Wyndham Lewis, *The Demon of Progress in the Arts* (Chicago, 1955), 96, 97.

13. Samuel Beckett, *Molloy*, trans. Patrick Bowles and Samuel Beckett (1955; New York, 1970), 53; Nathanael West, *Miss Lonelyhearts and the Day of the Locust* (Norfolk, Conn., 1962), 182, 209.

14. Louis-Ferdinand Céline, *Journey to the End of the Night*, trans. John H.P. Marks (Norfolk, Conn., 1960), 192. Céline's imagery is rife with portents of coming destruction and chaos; see Erika Ostrovsky, "The Horseman of the Apocalypse," in *Céline and His Vision* (New York, 1967), 157-82. Consult the twenty-eighth entry, "Entropy and Energy," in Yevgeny Zamyatin, *We*, trans. Mirra Ginsburg (New York, 1972), 140-47. See also Zamyatin's essay "On Literature, Revolution and Entropy (1924)" *Partisan Review* 28 (1961): 372-78. Zamyatin's pathetic plea for incessant revolutions in Russia to prevent loss of energy, vitality, and the encrustations of dogma was as impossible of realization as Ezra Pound's plea that we incessantly "make it new" (1935).

15. Consult G.L. Van Roosbroeck, *The Legend of the Decadents* (New York, 1927); Henry Vyverberg, *Historical Pessimism in the French Enlightenment* (Cambridge, Mass., 1958); Alfred E. Carter, *The Idea of Decadence in French Literature, 1830–1900* (Toronto, 1958); George Ross Ridge, *The Hero in French Decadent Literature* (Athens, Ga., 1961); and Jerome Hamilton Buckley, "The Idea of Decadence," in *The Triumph of Time: A Study of the Victorian Concepts of Time, History, Progress, and Decadence* (Cambridge, Mass, 1966), 66-93. See also Matei Calinescu, *Faces of Modernity: Avant-Garde, Decadence, Kitsch* (Bloomington, 1977), esp. 151-221. Despite Richard Gilman's recent argument in *Decadence: The Strange Life of an Epithet* (New York, 1979), that the term is without precise meaning, we conventionally continue to be attracted by what we take to be a modern "decadence" compared with an earlier, more elevated, and healthy norm; see Lance Morrow, "The Fascination of Decadence," *Time*, Sept. 10, 1979, pp. 85-86.

16. *The Complete Works of Gustave Flaubert*, with an introduction by Ferdinand Brunetiére, 10 vols. (London, 1926), 10: 96.

17. Henry Miller, *The Cosmological Eye* (Norfolk, Conn., 1939), 107-34; George P. Elliott, *Conversions: Literature and the Modernist Deviation* (New York, 1971), 12-13; Saul Bellow, "Literature," in *The Great Ideas Today: 1963*, no. 3 (Chicago, 1963), 170-71, 155; Leslie Fiedler, *No! in Thunder: Essays on Myth and Literature* (Boston, 1960), 4-5.

18. Erich Auerbach, *Literary Language and Its Public in Late Latin Antiquity and in the Middle Ages*, trans. Ralph Manheim (New York, 1965), 6. An undercurrent motif in Auerbach's *Mimesis* is precisely this "moral crisis" and "impending catastrophe" prior to World War I in Europe and reflected in increasing techniques in literature for presenting interiority and multiple points of view, which suggest to him "a symptom of confusion and helplessness " of European culture as well as being "a mirror of the decline of our world." Auerbach, *Mimesis: The Representation of Reality in Western Literature*, trans. Willard Trask (Garden City, N.Y., 1957), 463, 487.

19. Henry Adams, *The Education of Henry Adams*, ed. Ernest Samuels (Boston, 1973), 429, 431, 451. Compare Yeats's apocalyptic vision of the violent onset of a new two-thousand-year cycle of history in "The Second Coming" (1921), ll. 3-8:

Things fall apart; the centre cannot hold;
Mere anarchy is loosed upon the world,
The blood-dimmed tide is loosed, and everywhere
The ceremony of innocence is drowned;
The best lack all conviction, while the worst
Are full of passionate intensity.

20. Adams, *Education*, 496.

21. Henry Adams, *The Degradation of the Democratic Dogma*, with an introduction by Brooks Adams (New York, 1958), 138, 182-83.

22. Donald Barthelme, *Snow White* (New York, 1967), 96, 97. For a further image of trash—the "figures" of consumer's reports on millions of products of products and their vast dangers, ill effects, and capacity to malfunction—see Barthelme's "Down the Line with the Annual": "We are adrift in a tense and joyless world that is falling apart at an accelerated rate. No way to arrest the disintegration that menaces from every side" (in *Guilty Pleasures* [New York, 1976], 4). William H. Gass even argues that virtually all Barthelme produces as a writer—with its fads, multistyles, clichés thrown together—constitutes the imitation of modern trashiness, trashiness recycled; see Gass, "The Leading Edge of the Trash Phenomenon," in *Fiction and the Figures of Life* (New York, 1970), 97-103. That contemporary society does indeed survive (and thrive) in communications by trash and fakery is handily argued in Arthur Herzog, *The B.S. Factor: The Theory and Technique of Faking It in America* (New York, 1974).

23. See Colin Wilson, *The Outsider* (London, 1956), and Melvin Rader, "The Artist as Outsider," *Journal of Aesthetics and Art Criticism* 16 (March 1958): 306-18. Archibald Geikie, "On Modern Denudation," *Transactions of the Geological Society of Glasgow* 3 (1871): 153-90.

24. Hesiod, Lucretius, and others speak of a decline from a golden age through ages of silver, bronze, heroes, and iron; consult Arthur O. Lovejoy, Gilbert Chinard, George Boas, and Ronald S. Crane, eds., *A Documentary History of Primitivism and Related Ideas* (Baltimore, 1935), vol. 1. For Christian views of a coming decline and chaos prior to Judgment Day, consult Victor Harris,

All Coherence Gone (Chicago, 1949); Ernest Lee Tuveson, *Millennium and Utopia* (Berkeley, 1949); and Frank Kermode, *The Sense of an Ending* (New York, 1967).

25. Consult, for instance, Benedict Augustin Morel, *Traité des dégénérescences physiques, intellectuelles et morales de l'espèce humaine* (New York, 1857); Cesare Lombroso, *L'Uomo delinguente*, 4th ed., (Torino, 1889); idem, *Le Crime, causes et remèdes* (Paris, 1899); and especially Max Nordau, *Entartung*, or *Degeneration* (Berlin, 1892–1893; English trans., 1895). Nordau's work attributes most contemporary social ills to the degeneration of the species and particularly singles out artists as decadent in their intellects; Nordau suggests "the intensity of concern." "I believe that no other European book of any kind published during the entire decade aroused so much comment in the American press," one critic observes; John Higham, "The Reorientation of American Culture in the 1890's" in *The Origins of Modern Consciousness*, ed. John Weiss (Detroit, 1965), 38.

26. See Mario Praz, *The Romantic Agony*, trans. Angus Davidson (London, 1933), and Charles I. Glicksberg, *The Literature of Nihilism* (Lewisburg, Pa., 1975). Since the romantic period, an increasing number of writers have been driven toward silence (Rimbaud, Arnold, Valéry, Forster, Salinger), madness (Collins, Cowper, Smart, Artaud, Hölderlin, Lowell), or even suicide (Lautréamont, von Kleist, Nerval, Hart Crane, Hemingway, Plath, Berryman, Sexton). On suicide, see Charles I. Glicksberg, "To Be or Not to Be: The Literature of Suicide," *Queen's Quarterly*, 67 (Autumn 1960): 384-95, and A. Alvarez, *The Savage God: A Study of Suicide* (London, 1971). On the tendency toward silence, see Jacques Barzun, "Romanticism Today," *Encounter* 17 (Sept. 1961): 26-32; George Steiner, *Language and Silence* (New York, 1967); Ihab Hassan, *The Literature of Silence: Henry Miller and Samuel Beckett* (New York, 1967); and Susan Sontag, "The Aesthetic of Silence," in *Styles of Radical Will* (New York, 1969), 3-34.

27. It has long been known that the most obvious "shapes" of history for interpreters would be ones discerning ascent, undulation, or decline; see Lovejoy, Chinard, Boas, and Crane, eds., *Documentary History of Primitivism* 1: 2-3. Recent historians of ideas have become particularly sensitive to the "shaping" impetus on the part of writers of history; consult, for example, Stephen C. Pepper, *World Hypotheses* (Berkeley, 1961), and Hayden White, *Metahistory: The Historical Imagination in Nineteenth-Century Europe* (Baltimore, 1973).

28. Richard Ellmann, *Yeats: The Man and the Masks* (New York, 1958), 222.

29. Alvin B. Kernan, *The Plot of Satire* (New Haven, 1965), 97; Arthur Bloch, *Murphy's Law and Other Reasons Why Things Go ʁuoɹM* ! (Los Angeles, 1977).

30. Juvenal *Satires* 1.147: "omne in praecipiti vitium stetit." This is a complex line: literally, "All vice stands above precipice," that is, highly elevated. Needless to say, the words are deliberately ambivalent; vice is exalted, but set above a pit, surely evoking ideas of poor footing and insecurity. Alexander Pope, "Epilogue to the Satires," *Dialogue* 1.170; Senaca *Agamemnon*, l. 758. Consider also Seneca's comment "prosperum ac felix scelus virtus vocatur; sontibus parent boni ius est in armis, opprimit leges timor": Properous and happy crime is called virtue; the good obey the guilty, right consists in arms, fear besets the law. Seneca, *Hercules Furens*, ll. 251-53. For relevant studies of satire's plotting that runs downhill, consult Philip Pinkus, "Satire and St. George," *Queen's Quarterly* 70 (1963): 30-49, and John R. Clark and Anna Motto, eds., *Satire: That Blasted Art* (New York, 1973), esp. 19-22.

31. Matthew Hodgart, *Satire* (London, 1969), 155; see also 77-78. Robert C.

Elliott, in *The Power of Satire* (Princeton, 1960), remarks that "one could hardly call the twentieth century an age of great satire" (223). And Edward A. Bloom and Lillian D. Bloom, in *Satire's Persuasive Voice* (Ithaca, N.Y., 1979), comment with self-contradiction that "satire by no means withers into moribundity, but we cannot deny that its vital growth now lies well in the past" (27).

32. Evelyn Waugh, "Fan-Fare," *Life*, April 8, 1946, p. 60.

15. The Death of the Humanities

1. Anthony Burgess, "No Health Anywhere," review of Don DeLillo's *Running Dog, Saturday Review*, Sept. 16, 1978, p. 38; Peter H. Wagschal, "Illiterates with Doctorates: The Future of Education in an Electronic Age," *The Futurist* 12 (Aug. 1978): 243-44.

2. See, for instance, Joseph Wood Krutch, "The Tragic Fallacy," in *The Modern Temper* (New York, 1929); idem, "Modernism" in Modern Drama (Ithaca, N.Y. 1953); George Steiner, *The Death of Tragedy* (New York, 1961); Herman Scheffauer, "The Death of Satire," *Fortnightly Review* 99 (1913): 1188-99; Gilbert Seldes, "Satire, Death of," *New Republic*, Jan. 5, 1927, p. 193; Matthew Hodgart, *Satire* (London, 1969), 155; J.H. Plumb, *The Death of the Past* (Boston, 1970); and Jesse Bier, *The Rise and Fall of American Humor* (New York, 1968).

3. John Barth, "The Literature of Exhaustion," *Atlantic Monthly*, 220, (Aug. 1967): 29-34. After exhaustion comes absolute quietus. For nineteenth-century backgrounds of such a tendency, see Robert Martin Adams, *Nil: Episodes in the Literary Conquest of Void during the Nineteenth Century* (New York, 1966).

4. See Robert Martin Adams, *Bad Mouth: Fugitive Papers on the Dark Side* (Berkeley, 1977); Duncan Williams, *Trousered Apes: Sick Literature in a Sick Society* (London, 1971); George P. Elliott, *Conversions: Literature and the Modernist Deviation* (New York, 1971). Similar charges are made about the dirt and foul language currently encountered in the popular arts; see Richard Corliss, "Dirty Words: America's Foul-Mouthed Pop Culture," *Time*, May 7, 1990, pp. 92-95, 97-98, 99-100.

5. John Gardner, *On Moral Fiction* (New York, 1978).

6. Significantly, this view of history as cyclical and inevitable, leading to decline, was popular since the time of Polybius and revitalized in the late Renaissance; consult Hiram Haydn, *The Counter-Renaissance* (New York, 1950), 424-53, 525ff. Jonathan Swift regularly anticipated a civilization's unexpected decline into barbarism. He was most struck, to be sure, by the sudden fall of Rome to savage invaders, and he frequently looked about him in contemporary times for omens of decay and incursions of what he termed "the *Gothick* Strain"; Herbert Davis, ed., *The Prose Writings of Jonathan Swift*, 14 vols. (Oxford, 1939–68), 2: 175. "Some new Invasion of *Goths* and *Vandals* to destroy Law, Property and Religion, alter the very Face of Nature; and turn the World upside down" (9: 50). See James William Johnson, *The Formation of English Neo-Classical Thought* (Princeton, 1967), 63-68. Such a viewpoint is reiterated by Henry James ("Preface to 'What Maisie Knew,' " in *The Art of the Novel: Critical Prefaces*, with an introduction by R.P. Blackmur [New York, 1934], 152) and by Evelyn Waugh (see Alvin B. Kernan, "The Wall and the Jungle: The Early Novels of Evelyn Waugh," *Yale Review* 53 [Dec. 1963]: 199-220). Edward Diller

claims that artists regularly utilize paradox and grotesquerie as a direct response to a world that has lost unity and coherence, a world that has fallen into chaos and muddle. See Diller "Aesthetics and the Grotesque: Friedrich Dürrenmatt," *Contemporary Literature* 7 (1966): 328-35.

7. Consult Raymond Williams, *The Country and the City* (New York, 1973).

8. Lional Trilling, *Sincerity and Authenticity* (Cambridge, Mass., 1972), 83-84.

9. Arthur Bloch, *Murphy's Law and Other Reasons Why Things Go $8uo\iota_M$!* (Los Angeles, 1977), 11.

10. Plautus *Heauton Timorumenos* 77.

11. Plumb, *Death of the Past*, 108, 140. For a similar summation of the contemporary world's hostility toward history and a similar defense, see Frank E. Manuel, *Freedom from History and Other Untimely Essays* (New York, 1971).

12. Walt Whitman, "Song of Myself," l. 463, in *Leaves of Grass and Selected Prose*, ed. Sculley Bradley (New York, 1955), 42; W.R. Benét and H.H. Pearson, eds. *The Oxford Anthology of American Literature*, 2 vols. (New York, 1960), 2: 1313.

13. "Though I sang in my chains like the sea," l. 78 of "Fern Hill," in *The Collected Poems of Dylan Thomas, 1934–1952* (New York, 1971), 180.

14. *Hamlet* 2.2.300-305.

Index

abolitio memoriae, 47
"Absalom and Achitophel" (Dryden), 94, 106
acedia, 106, 107
Adam, Villers de l'Isle, 109
Adams, Henry, 152–53, 159
Adams, Robert Martin, 85
Adding Machine, The (Rice), 144
Adventurous Simplicissimus, The (von Grimmelshausen), 96
Airships (Hannah), 48–49, 135
Aksyonov, Vassily, 70
Albee, Edward, 70
alienation, 30, 196–97 n 17; of audience or reader, 4, 7, 21, 83, 90, 148, 168 n 21, 171 nn 12, 17, 175 n 39, 181 n 3
Allen, Woody, 35, 73, 97, 161
Allestree, Richard, 42
Amis, Kingsley, 120
Amis, Martin, 72–73
angry young men, 1
Animal Farm (Orwell), 46
Anouilh, Jean, 11–12
Antic Hay (Huxley), 55–56
anticlimax, 83–89
Antigone (Anouilh), 11–12
anti-hero, 1, 29–35, 174 n 25
antiheroism, 14, 29–35
Antisthenes, 31–32
antistories, 70, 180 n 13
antiutopia. *See* dystopia
Apocalypse Now (Francis Ford Coppola), 94
apocalyptic, 13, 24, 44–45, 46, 48–49, 95, 113, 145, 148–56, 161, 167 n 12, 196 n 16
Apocolocyntosis (Seneca), 52, 80
Apollinaire, Guillaume, 11
Aragon, Louis, 81
Architect and The Emperor of Assyria, The (Arrabal), 136
A Rebours (Huysmans), 111
Aretino, Pietro, 43–44

Aristophanes, 69, 80, 84, 93, 118, 121, 161
Aristotle, 58, 83
Arnold, Matthew, 1, 84, 142, 143, 146
Arrabal, Fernando, 136
Ars Poetica (Horace), 19, 160
Artaud, Antonin, 83, 88
Ashby, Hal, 85
As I Lay Dying (Faulkner), 81
"Aucassin and Nicolette" (anon.), 60
Auden, W.H., 9
Auerbach, Erich, 152
Austen, Jane, 105
Autumn of the Patriarch, The (García Márquez), 136–37
avant-garde, 10, 81, 166 n 6, 174 n 22, 180 n 10
Axel (Adam), 109
Ayrton, Michael, 34

Babble (Baumbach), 74
Bacon, Francis, 58, 106, 116
Bakhtin, Mikhail, 18
Bald Soprano, The (Ionesco), 120
Ballad of the Sad Café, The (McCullers), 84–85
"Balloon, The" (Barthelme), 144
Barasch, Frances K., 184 n 12
barbarians. *See* Goths
Barrett, William, 113, 143, 146
Barth, John, 2, 35, 70, 74, 78, 79, 113, 123, 135, 145, 150, 156, 159
Barthelme, Donald, 2, 70, 79, 85, 102, 114, 144, 150, 153, 156
"Bartleby the Scrivener" (Melville), 110
Barzun, Jacques, 109
Baudelaire, Charles, 18, 20, 25, 29, 107, 110, 115
Baumbach, Jonathan, 74, 79
Beardsley, Monroe, 149
"Beast in the Jungle, The" (James), 13, 14, 96, 98, 111

Index

beat poets, 69
Beckett, Samuel, 2, 7, 9, 13, 14, 22, 24, 70, 89, 96, 114, 121, 151
Being There (Ashby), 85
Bellow, Saul, 12, 136, 150, 152
Bentley, Joseph, 45
Beowulf, 160
Berger, Arthur Asa, 140
Berni, Francesco, 118
biblical citations, 10, 39, 80, 92, 132
Bier, Jesse, 2–3
Bierce, Ambrose, 2, 99, 133
Biglow Papers, The (Lowell), 40
"Big Mama's Funeral" (García Márquez), 85, 100–101
Bion of Borysthenes, 32
Birthday Party, The (Pinter), 85
"bisinesse," 58, 91, 96, 100
black humor novelists, 1, 12, 159
Black Mischief (Waugh), 134
Blackmur, R.P., 149
blackness, 2
Bloch, Arthur, 99
Block, Walter, 134
Boltzmann, Ludwig, 149
Bonfire of the Vanities, The (Wolfe), 124
boredom, 2, 6, 105–15, 154, 186 n 6, 188 n 15
Borges, Jorge Luis, 48, 70, 74, 78
Bosch, Hieronymus, 18, 95
Bouvard and Pecuchet (Flaubert), 152
Boyd, William, 70
Bradbury, Ray, 49
Brautigan, Richard, 78, 153
Brave New World (Huxley), 95, 140
Breakfast of Champions (Vonnegut), 45–46, 75, 79
Brecht, Bertold, 171 n 12
Bredvold, Louis I., 4
Breton, André, 81
Brook, Peter, 83, 86
Brown, Norman O., 33
Browning, Robert, 18
Bruce, Lenny, 2, 122, 161
Brueghels, the, 18, 95, 160
Büchner, Georg, 20, 25, 83, 96
Buddenbrooks (Mann), 9, 112
Burgess, Anthony, 2, 9, 25, 46, 48, 102, 135, 136, 159
Burke, Kenneth, 178 n 31
Burns, Robert, 66
Burroughs, William, 78, 150
Byron, George Gordon, Lord, 15, 52, 109, 110, 133
Byronic, the, 10

Callot, Jacques, 18
Calvino, Italo, 70, 74, 78
Camus, Albert, 114, 118, 153
Candide (Voltaire), 14, 43, 97, 106, 128, 133
Candy (Southern), 127–28
Cannibal, The (Hawkes), 48, 81, 94–95, 123–24, 137
cannibalism, 2, 6, 13, 32, 48–49, 131–38, 193 nn 5, 7, 193–94 n 8
Cannibals and Christians (Mailer), 134, 146
Canturbury Tales, The (Chaucer), 37, 52, 91
Čapek, Karel, 1, 2, 13, 25, 48, 95, 135, 144
"Captain Carpenter" (Ransom), 14
Cards of Identity (Dennis), 70
Carlyle, Thomas, 29, 81
Carmen (Mérimée), 66
Carmina Burana, 30
carnival grotesque, 18
Carnot, Sadi, 148
Cassirer, Ernst, 161
Cat and Mouse (Grass), 70, 128–29
Catcher in the Rye (Salinger), 70
Catch-22 (Heller), 52, 95, 113
Cat's Cradle (Vonnegut), 48, 95, 145, 150
Catullus, Gaius Valerius, 38, 43, 118
Céline, Louis-Ferdinand, 1, 9, 13, 25, 95, 99, 112, 151, 156
cena, 98, 118, 124
Cervantes, Miguel de, 14, 21, 41, 47, 78, 81
Chamber Music (Joyce), 120
Chaplin, Charlie, 2, 34, 85, 141
Chateaubriand, François-René de, 110
Chaucer, Geoffrey, 37, 52, 58, 69, 80, 91
Chekhov, Anton, 10
Chesterton, G.K., 71, 134
Chimera (Barth), 74, 79
Chisholm, Francis P., 161
Chronicles of Bustos Domecq (Borges), 48
Chronicles of Doodah, The (Walker), 70
cinema, 141
Cioran, E.M., 114
Clarissa (Richardson), 91–92
Clarke, Arthur, 145
Clausius, Rudolf, 148
Clemens, Samuel Langhorne. See Twain, Mark
Clockwork Orange, A (Burgess), 46, 102
Clouds, The (Aristophanes), 118
Coates, Robert M., 71, 81
Collector, The (Fowles), 70
comic-strip characters, 33–34, 35, 140–41
"Common Confusion, A" (Kafka), 22
Comte, Auguste, 142
Congreve, William, 42
Conrad, Joseph, 13, 14, 20, 80
Conversions, The (Mathews), 72
Cool Million, A (West), 14
Coover, Robert, 70, 74, 78, 144–45

Cortazar, Julio, 14, 70
Cosič, Dobrica, 49
Cosmicomics (Calvino), 70, 74, 78
counterculture, 29, 30–31
Couples (Updike), 126–27
Crews, Frederick C., 58
Criers and Kibitzers, Kibitzers and Criers (Elkin), 70
Crying of Lot 49, The (Pynchon), 72
curiosity, 143
Cyberiad, The (Lem), 73–74
Cynics, 31–35

dada, 12, 20, 69
Dali, Salvador, 18
Danaïds, 88
"dangling man," 9
Dante Alighieri, 80, 92–93, 96, 131
dark comedy, 7–25
dark humor, vii
Darkness at Noon (Koestler), 47
Darwin, Charles, 68, 149, 161
David Knudsen (Elliott), 150
Day of the Locust, The (West), 84, 96, 100
"Dead, The" (Joyce), 160
"Death in Venice" (Mann), 13, 14, 48, 96
Death Kit (Sontag), 150, 153
decadence, 3, 4, 12, 13, 154, 167 n 12, 169 n 2, 198 n 15, 201–2 n 6
Decline and Fall (Waugh), 97, 143–44
Decline of the West (Spengler), 152, 159
Dedekind, Friedrich, 52, 99
Deer, Harriet, 4
Deer, Irving, 4
Defoe, Daniel, 132
degeneration, 154, 200 n 25
Degradation of the Democratic Dogma (Adams), 153
DeLillo, Don, 70
"Del passado efimero" (Machado), 112
demonic, 21, 84, 95
Demon of Noontide, The (Kuhn), 107
Dennis, Nigel, 70
Der Mann ohne Eigenschaften (Musil), 1, 15, 96, 112
Descartes, René, 10, 106, 107
destructive repetition, 98
Dialogues (Aretino), 43–44
dialogues of the dead, 93
"Diary of a Madman" (Gogol), 48
diatribe, 32
Dickens, Charles, 2, 18, 20, 51, 71, 89, 105–6, 153, 155
Diogenes of Sinope, 32–33, 133
Directions to Servants (Swift), 99
Discourse on a Stale Subject, Called the Metamorphosis of Ajax, A (Harrington), 118

disenchantment, 1, 2
dismembered antihero, 14
"Displaced Person, The" (O'Connor), 15
Dr. Faustus (Marlowe), 84
Doctor's Oral (Stewart), 121–22
"Dr. Strangelove" (Kubrick), 48, 85, 95, 145
Don Juan (Byron), 99, 133
Donleavy, J. P., 2, 70, 122–23, 136
Donne, John, 27
Don Quixote (Cervantes), 14, 41, 47, 78, 81, 99
Dostoevsky, Fyodor, 4, 13, 14, 20, 48, 81, 96, 111, 152, 153, 161
"Double-Barreled Detective Story, A" (Twain), 54–55
Dracula (Stoker), 132
Dryden, John, 44, 58, 92, 94, 106, 118
Duchamp, Marcel, 2
Dunciad, The (Pope), 22, 39, 44–45, 46, 95, 98, 106, 119
Dunsany, Lord, 133–34
Dürrenmatt, Friedrich, 14
Dynamo (O'Neill), 144
dystopia, 2, 6, 12, 14, 20, 48, 102, 113, 139–47, 151, 159, 179 n 5, 189 n 32, 190 n 33, 195 n 2

Eater of Darkness, The (Coates), 71, 81
Eddington, Sir Arthur, 149
Education of Henry Adams, The (Adams), 152–53
Edwards, Blake, 85
Edwards, T.R., 64
ego, cult of, 10
Einstein, Albert, 161
Einstein's Monsters (M. Amis), 72–73
El Buscón (Quevedo), 43
"Elevator, The" (Coover), 144–45
Eliot, T.S., 2, 9, 12, 34, 39, 48, 50, 56, 68, 76, 96, 111, 115, 129–30, 134, 149
Elkin, Stanley, 70, 150
Elliott, George P., 136, 145, 150, 152
Ellison, Ralph, 13, 96, 153
Emerson, Ralph Waldo, 10
Emma (Austen), 105
Endgame (Beckett), 24, 70
End of the Game and Other Stories (Cortazar), 70
end of the world, 13
End Zone (DeLillo), 70
ennui. *See* boredom
entrapment, 73
entropy, 6, 12, 13, 22, 96, 113, 148–56, 159
Essais (Montaigne), 21, 133
Essay on Criticism, An (Pope), 37
Euripides, 84, 160

Index

Exaggerations of Peter Prince, The (Katz), 75
Examiner, The (Swift), 49
excrement. *See* scatology
expressionism, 12

Fahrenheit 451 (Bradbury), 49
"Famous Prediction of Merlin, A" (Swift), 52
Fan Man, The (Kotzwinkle), 97
fantasy, 73, 180 n 12
Faulkner, William, 7, 13, 22, 23, 35, 81, 96, 152
Faust, 1, 106, 142, 143
Faux-Monnayeurs, Les (Gide), 75, 81
Federman, Raymond, 79
Fiedler, Leslie, 152
Fielding, Henry, 82, 119
Fields, W.C., 161
Fin du monde, La (Flammarion), 152
First Futurist Manifesto (Marinetti), 11
Fitzgerald, F. Scott, 98
Flammarion, Camille, 152
Flashman (Fraser), 99
Flaubert, Gustave, 18, 97–98, 99, 110, 152, 156
Fleurs du mal, Les (Baudelaire), 29
flyting, 98
forbidden knowledge, 143
Ford, Ford Maddox, 35
Forster, E.M., 2, 58, 144
Fowles, John, 70
"Fragment of an Agon" (Eliot), 134
Frankenstein (Mary Shelley), 143, 145
Fraser, G.M., 99
"Freedom" (Cosič), 49
Freud, Sigmund, 12, 18, 29–30, 68, 86, 95, 113, 161
"From the Darkness" (Mrozek), 130
Frye, Northrop, 57, 68

games, 67–76
García Márquez, Gabriel, 7, 13, 14, 22, 23, 24, 35, 48, 78, 85, 100–101, 113, 136–37, 161
Gardner, John, 137–38, 159
Gargantua and Pantagruel (Rabelais), 81, 119
Garn, Stanley, 134
Gass, William H., 79–80
Gay, John, 52
Geikie, Archibald, 153–54
genocide, 49
German expressionism, 20
Ghosts (Ibsen), 84
Gibbs, J.W., 149
Gide, André, 13, 75, 81, 109–10, 152
Giles Goat-Boy (Barth), 35, 74, 79, 135, 145

Gilgamesh (anon.), 160
Ginger Man, The (Donleavy), 70, 122–23
Glass Bead Game, The (Hesse), 70
Goethe, Johann Wolfgang von, 106, 110
Gogol, Nikolai, 48
Going Nowhere (Greenburg), 150
Golden House, 18
Golding, William, 2, 9, 25, 94, 121, 135
Goliards, 30
Goncharov, Ivan, 96, 111
gothic, 7, 17–25, 169 n 1; and grotesque, 169 n 3
Goths, 17, 50, 62, 176 n 43, 201–2 n 6
Goya, Francisco, 18, 95, 132
Grass, Günter, 2, 7, 13, 22, 23, 35, 47, 70, 88–89, 94, 113, 128–29, 152, 156
Gravity's Rainbow (Pynchon), 54, 145
great expectations, 13
Greenburg, Alvin, 150
Grendel (Gardner), 137–38
Grimmelshausen, Johann Jakob von, 21, 96
Grobianus (Dedekind), 52, 99
grotesque, 7, 13, 14, 17–25, 85–86, 169–70 nn 4, 5, 8, 171 nn 11, 13, 17
grottesca, la, 18
Guernica (Picasso), 22
Gulliver's Travels (Swift), 47, 81, 96, 99, 119

Hamilton, Alice, 116
Hamilton, Kenneth, 116
Hamlet, 1, 84, 110, 142, 149
Hamlet (Shakespeare), 56, 84, 163
Hamlet, The (Faulkner), 23, 96
Handful of Dust, A (Waugh), 89
Hannah, Barry, 48–49, 135
Happy Days (Beckett), 24
Hard Times (Dickens), 105–6
Hardy, Thomas, 73
Harrington, Sir John, 118
Hartman, Geoffrey, 67
Hasek, Jaroslav, 35
Hassan, Ihab, 3
Hawkes, John, 2, 48, 81, 94–95, 113, 123–24, 137
Hawthorne, Nathaniel, 16, 18, 20, 84
"Heart of Darkness" (Conrad), 13, 14
Hegel, Georg Wilhelm Friedrich, 142, 160
Heisenberg, Werner, 149
Heller, Joseph, 13, 52, 95, 113
Helmholtz, Hermann von, 148
Hellenistic era, 31
Hemingway, Ernest, 70
Henry, O., 133
Heracles, 33
Hesiod, 160

Hesse, Hermann, 70
Highet, Gilbert, 37
Hodgart, Matthew, 45, 155
Hodin, J.P., 68, 76
Hogarth, William, 18, 95
Hollander, John, 148
Holocaust, 134, 145, 194 n 9
Homer, 10, 19
Homo Ludens (Huizinga), 67
Hopscotch (Cortazar), 70
Horace (Horatius Flaccus), 19, 20, 21, 25, 38, 42, 47, 51, 80, 92, 118, 155, 160
"Hour of Letdown, The" (White), 144
Hughes, Ted, 83, 86
Huizinga, Johan, 67
humanism, 5, 161
Humboldt's Gift (Bellow), 136
Humor (Pirandello), 20
Humphry Clinker (Smollett), 119–20, 122
"Hunger Artist, A" (Kafka), 22, 113
Huxley, Aldous, 1, 55–56, 95, 98, 116, 117, 121, 140
Huysmans, Joris-Karl, 111, 112

Ibsen, Henrik, 84
Ice Cream War, An (Boyd), 70
indeterminacy, 12, 149, 152
infernal, 95
Inferno (Dante), 92–93, 131
insanity, 13, 95–96, 153
In the Labyrinth (Robbe-Grillet), 70
"In the Penal Colony" (Kafka), 144
Invisible Man (Ellison), 96, 153
Ionesco, Eugène, 13, 25, 48, 88, 120
Is Sex Necessary? (Thurber and White), 48
Ixion, 94

Jackson, Shirley, 70
James, Henry, 3, 13, 14, 20, 58, 62–64, 70–71, 80, 96, 102, 111, 116, 121
Jarry, Alfred, 25, 69, 83
Jeans, Sir James, 149
Johnson, Samuel, 52, 97, 108
Jonson, Ben, 21, 53
Joseph Andrews (Fielding), 119
Journey to the End of the Night (Céline), 95, 112, 151
Joyce, James, 1, 2, 15, 68, 80, 112, 113, 120, 152, 160
Juvenal (Decimus Junius Juvenalis), 21, 38, 155

Kafka, Franz, 2, 7, 9, 13, 22, 34, 47, 84, 113, 130, 137, 144, 161
Kahler, Erich, 1
Kant, Immanuel, 63
Karl, Frederick, 113

Katz, Steve, 75, 79
Kawin, Bruce, 98
Keats, John, 59
Kernan, Alvin, 99–100, 155
Kerouac, Jack, 97
Kesey, Ken, 49, 96
Kierkegaard, Søren, 110
King Lear (Shakespeare), 16, 20
King, Queen, Knave (Nabokov), 70
Kiss of the Spider Woman (Puig), 162–63
Klinkowitz, Jerome, 77, 79, 80
Koestler, Arthur, 47
Kotzwinkle, William, 97
Kraus, Karl, 9, 48
Kubrick, Stanley, 48, 85, 95, 141, 145
Kuhn, Reinhard, 107

Labyrinths (Borges), 70
Laforgue, Jules, 20, 110, 113
Laing, R.D., 35
Langer, Susanne, 58–59
"Langueur" (Verlaine), 109
lanx satura, 51
Lardner, Ring, 67
La Rochefoucauld, Duc de, 99
Last Days of Mankind, The (Kraus), 9, 48
"Last Night: A Story, The" (Mailer), 48, 146–47
"Last Year at Marienbad" (Robbe-Grillet), 74
Lawrence, D.H., 10–11
Lazarillo de Tormes (anon.), 59, 81, 97
Lec, Stanislaw, 99
Lee, Charles, 99
Leibnitz, Gottfried Wilhelm von, 63
Lem, Stanislaw, 2, 49, 73–74, 96, 140, 145
Lesson, The (Ionesco), 48
Levi-Strauss, Claude, 13
Lewis, C.S., 53
Lewis, Sinclair, 1, 98
Lewis, Wyndham, 99, 151
Lichtenberg, Georg Christoph, 99
Lifton, Robert J., 131
literary disruptions, 70, 77, 80, 181 n 7, 182 nn 13, 14
litterateur, 37
lobotomies, 49
Lolita (Nabokov), 48, 64–66, 96, 121
Long, A.A., 133
Long March, The (Styron), 86–87
Lord of the Flies (Golding), 94, 121, 135
loss of self, 12, 167 n 11
"Lost in Space" (TV program), 140
Lost in the Funhouse (Barth), 70
"Lottery, The" (Jackson), 70
"Love Song of J. Alfred Prufrock" (Eliot), 12, 48, 96

Index

Lowell, James Russell, 40
Lucian of Samosata, 21, 52, 93
Lucius, or The Ass (Lucian), 21
Lucretius, 160
Lyly, John, 38–39
Lyons, John O., 108

McCarthy, Mary, 98
McCullers, Carson, 84–85
McDaniel, Thomas R., 1, 165 n 2
"MacFlecknoe" (Dryden), 44, 58, 92, 118
Machado, Antonio, 112
machines, triumph of, 2, 6, 135, 139–47
"Machine Stops, The" (Forster), 144
Mackenzie, Henry, 41–42
McLean, Hugh, 61
McLuhan, Marshall, 9, 30
Mailer, Norman, 2, 36, 48, 134, 146–47, 150
Mallarmé, Stéphane, 110
Malone Dies (Beckett), 24, 114, 151
Man and Superman (Shaw), 165 n 8
Manfred (Byron), 110
Mann, Thomas, 1, 9, 13, 14, 20, 48, 68, 85–86, 96, 112, 152, 156
mannerism, 20
Man of Feeling, The (Mackenzie), 41–42
Mansfield, Katherine, 9
"Man That Corrupted Hadleyburg, The" (Twain), 14
Man Who Was Thursday, The (Chesterton), 71, 134
Marcuse, Herbert, 33
Marinetti, Filippo, 11
Marlowe, Christopher, 84
Márquez. *See* García Márquez
Martial (Marcus Valerius Martialis), 38, 118
Marx, Karl, 1, 12
Mathews, Harry, 72, 81
Mayakovsky, Vladimir, 1
Maze-Maker, The (Ayrton), 34
Meeting at Telgte, The (Grass), 47
meiosis, 45, 176 n 7
melodrama, 179 n 4
Melville, Herman, 18, 20, 110
Memoirs Found in a Bathtub (Lem), 49, 96, 145
Mencken, H.L., 9, 161
Menippean satire, 80, 99, 118, 182 n 15
Menippus of Gadara, 32, 93
Mérimee, Prosper, 66
Merlin, 140
Metamorphoses (Ovid), 19, 131
"Metamorphosis, The" (Kafka), 22, 84, 113
Meyerhoff, Hans, 69, 142

Miller, Henry, 152
Milton, John, 90–91, 93, 143
Miss Lonelyhearts (West), 48, 52, 95, 125, 151
modern satire: cheerless and unpleasant, vii; vigorous and creative, vii; vitally rich and prolific, 163
"Modest Proposal, A" (Swift), 133
Molloy (Beckett), 24, 114
monsters, 19, 170 n 6
Montaigne, Michel de, 21, 133
More, St. Thomas, 81
More Pricks Than Kicks (Beckett), 24
Morris, Wright, 70
motion pictures, 141
Mrozek, Slawomir, 85, 130, 134–35
muddle, 58
Mumford, Lewis, 107
Murphy (Beckett), 24, 96, 114, 151
Murphy's Law and Other Reasons Why Things Go 8uo₁Mᵢ (Bloch), 99, 102, 155, 161
Musil, Robert, 1, 15, 96, 112, 152, 156
"My Kinsman, Major Molineux" (Hawthorne), 16, 84

Nabokov, Vladimir, 13, 48, 64–66, 70, 78, 91, 96, 121
Nadja (Breton), 81
Naked Lunch (Burroughs), 150
narcissism, 187 n 10
Nausée, La (Sartre), 48
negative, the, vii, 3, 4
Nero (Nero Claudius Caesar), 18, 19
Newton, Isaac, 142
Nietzsche, Friedrich, 13, 99
1984 (Orwell), 45, 46–47, 95, 140
nonsense, 180 n 12
Notes from Underground (Dostoevsky), 4, 13, 14, 20, 48, 81, 96, 111, 153
Nova Express (Burroughs), 150
Novak, Maximillian E., 17
"NRACP, The" (Elliott), 136, 145

Oates, Joyce Carol, 70
Obermann (Sénancour), 110
Oblomov (Goncharov), 96, 111
O'Connor, Flannery, 15; and the grotesque, 168 n 22
Odyssey (Homer), 19
Oedipus (Seneca), 83, 86
Oldenberg, Claes, 2
Olympian Odes (Pindar), 131
One Flew over the Cuckoo's Nest (Kesey), 49, 96
One Hundred Years of Solitude (García Márquez), 14, 23–24, 48, 78

Index 209

O'Neill, Eugene, 9, 144
On the Beach (Shute), 48, 145
Orpheus Descending (Williams), 85
Ortega y Gasset, José, 9, 149
Orwell, George, 1, 45, 95, 140
Our Mutual Friend (Dickens), 153
Out at Sea (Mrozek), 134–35
Ovid (Publius Ovidius Naso), 19, 131

Pale Fire (Nabokov), 78
Paradise Lost (Milton), 90–91, 93
paranoia, 9, 139, 142, 180–81 n 15, 189 n 30
Parkinson, Francis, 99, 161
parody, 29, 86, 99, 180 n 18; in satire, 176 n 3
Pater, Walter, 111
Paulson, Ronald, 132
Payson de Paris, Le (Aragon), 81
"Peach in Brandy, The" (Walpole), 53–54
Peacock, Thomas Love, 98
Pearce, Richard, 88
Percy, Walker, 150
performing self, 10, 108, 166 n 5, 187 n 11
Peri Bathous (Pope), 21–22, 43, 44–45, 99–100
Perkins, Augustus Thorndike, 1
Persius (Aulus Persius Flaccus), 38
pessimism, 142
Peter, Laurence J., 99, 161
Petronius, 47, 56–57, 80–81, 84, 96, 98, 118, 133
picaresque, 30, 99, 172 n 2
Picasso, Pablo, 22, 68, 81
"Pierre Menard, Author of Don Quixote" (Borges), 78
Pindar, 131
Pinter, Harold, 2, 9, 13, 85, 144
Pirandello, Luigi, 13, 20, 75, 80
Planck, Max, 149
Player Piano (Vonnegut), 145
playfulness, 177 n 10, 179 n 2
plots in satire, 51, 67–76, 73, 77
Plumb, J.H., 161–62
Poe, Edgar Allan, 76
Pooh Perplex, The (Crews), 58
Pope, Alexander, 21, 22, 37, 39, 41, 43, 95, 99, 100, 106, 119, 155
Portnoy's Complaint (Roth), 122, 125–26
"Portrait d'une femme" (Pound), 61, 153
postmodern, the, 77, 81, 181 n 1
Pound, Ezra, 48, 61, 68, 153
power of negative thinking, 4
Praise of Folly, The (Erasmus), 81
Pricksongs and Descants (Coover), 74, 78
pride, 37, 39, 42, 43, 49–50

progress, idea of, 9, 10, 12, 17, 18, 109, 136, 142, 154, 166 n 2
Prometheus, 88, 143
Proust, Marcel, 1, 9, 13, 68, 111–12, 152
Puig, Manuel, 162–63
Purgatorio (Dante), 96
Pynchon, Thomas, 13, 54, 72, 78, 81, 113, 145, 150, 156

Queen Victoria (Strachey), 52
Quevedo Villegas, Francisco de, 43

Rabelais, François, 21, 40, 81, 98, 99, 119
Ransom, John Crowe, 14
Raphael (Raffaello Sanzio), 18
Rasselas (Johnson), 97
realism questioned, 75, 82, 182–83 n 17
recipes, 43
René (Chauteaubriand), 110
repetition, 90–102
Reynard the Fox (anon.), 21
Rhodes, Richard, 132
Rice, Elmer, 2, 144
Richardson, Samuel, 91–92
Richmond, Velma, 30
Riesman, David, 1
Rimbaud, Arthur, 65, 113
Rise and Fall of American Humor, The (Bier), 2
Rivals, The (Sheridan), 42
Robbe-Grillet, Alain, 70, 74, 78, 144
Robinson Crusoe (Defoe), 132
Roderick Random (Smollett), 119
romantic horror, 84
romanticism, 10, 12
romantic quest, 14, 86
romantic self, 11
Rosenberg, Harold, 68–69, 76
Roth, Philip, 122, 125–26
Rousseau, Jean Jacques, 110, 137
R.U.R. (Čapek), 95, 144
Ruskin, John, 110

Sacred Fount, The (James), 62–64, 70–71
Sade, Marquis de, 30
Sainte-Beuve, Charles-Augustin, 110
Salinger, J.D., 10
Sandbox, The (Albee), 70
Santayana, George, 12
Sartor Resartus (Carlyle), 81
Sartre, Jean-Paul, 48, 114, 161
satire: as anticlassical, 25; condemned by moralists, 3, 21, 157; considered unpleasant and disorderly, 4, 21; continues to be rich and fertile in our era, 157, 163; creates hosts of jargon, 59; dramatizes the triumph of folly and

vice, 51; imitates excess and imperfection, 51; as lowly writing, 21; parodies numerous literary kinds, 57–58; prevents resolution and catharsis, 51; so-called demise of, 155, 159, 191–92 n 16; provides anticlimactic, foreshortened, perplexing, defective plots, 51; as rhetoric, 176 n 4; thrives under censorship, 178 n 31; treats decline and fall, 155, 161; ultimately is creative and vigorous, 4, 6

Satire I.5 (Horace), 52
Satire I.8 (Horace), 118
satiric butts and buffoons, 59, 178 n 27
satiric grotesque: belongs to age-old tradition, 157; thrives in twentieth century, 157
satiric strategies: debases or eliminates hero, 29–35; debunks authors, 36–50; devises intrusions and disruptions, 77–82; frustrates audience expectations, 51; mocks and lampoons conventional style, diction, and language, 51–66; tampers with plot, 67–76; upsets work's climax and finale, 83–89; utilizes deliberate redundancy, 90–102; violates climax, engineering anticlimax and defeat, 95
satiric themes: cannibalism, 131–38; dystopias and triumph of machines over humanity, 139–47; ennui, 105–15; entropy and apocalypse, 148–56; scatology, 116–30
satirist: as parasite, 51; as maker of defective plots, 51–52
Saturnalia, 18
Satyricon (Petronius), 47, 56–57, 80–81, 84, 96, 99, 118, 133
savage comedy, 88
Say Cheese! (Aksyonov), 70
Scarron, Paul, 82
scatology, 2, 6, 43, 44, 116–30
Scoop (Waugh), 48, 120
Scriblerus, Martinus, 21, 43, 99, 100
"Secret Life of Walter Mitty, The" (Thurber), 144
self, 20; divided, 142, 187 n 12
self-contradiction, 188–89 n 23
semantic gravitation, 45
Sénancour, Etienne Pivert de, 110
Seneca, Lucius Annaeus, 19, 52, 80, 83, 86, 131, 155
senselessness of an ending, 83
Sentimental Education, A (Flaubert), 110
Sentimental Journey, A (Sterne), 96
"Sex Ex Machina" (Thurber), 139

Shakespeare, William, 16, 56, 66, 69, 84, 99, 108, 132, 148, 160, 163
Shaw, George Bernard, 165 n 8
Shelley, Mary, 143, 145
Sheridan, Richard Brinsley, 42
shocking the reader, 3, 5, 27, 51
Shute, Nevil, 48, 145
Sidney, Sir Philip, 20
Sillitoe, Alan, 124–25
"Simple Heart, A" (Flaubert), 97–98
Sisyphus, 5, 88, 94, 113
Six Characters in Search of an Author (Pirandello), 75
Slapstick (Vonnegut), 70
Slaughter-House Five (Vonnegut), 78–79, 134
Sloan, James Park, 70
Smollett, Tobias, 119, 122
Snow, C.P., 2, 148, 154
Snow White (Barthelme), 70, 79, 102, 153
"S.O.B." (Blake Edwards), 85
Socrates, 31, 107, 161
solipsism, 11
Somer, John, 79
Sontag, Susan, 150, 153
Sophocles, 161
Sorrows of Werther, The (Goethe), 106, 110
Sot-Weed Factor, The (Barth), 123
Sound and the Fury, The (Faulkner), 81
Southern, Terry, 2, 127–28
Spengler, Oswald, 1, 13, 30–31, 152, 160
Start in Life, A (Sillitoe), 124–25
"Star Trek" (TV program), 140
Stein, Gertrude, 81, 112
Steiner, George, 13, 109
Sterne, Laurence, 41, 81, 82, 96
Stevick, Philip, 79
Stewart, George, 121–22
Stoker, Bram, 132
Strachey, Lytton, 52
Stranger, The (Camus), 153
Stravinsky, Igor, 68, 161
Strindberg, (Johan) August, 1, 83
Studies in the History of the Renaissance (Pater), 111
Styron, William, 86–87, 88
suicide, 113
Sukenick, Ronald, 75, 79
surrealism, 12, 13, 20, 69, 76, 81
"Sweeney among the Nightingales" (Eliot), 56, 129–30
Swift, Jonathan, 9–10, 17, 21, 36, 39–40, 41, 44, 47, 49–50, 52, 58, 81, 96, 99, 106, 117, 118, 119, 133
symbolic action, 179 n 2
symbolism, 12
Sypher, Wylie, 12, 149–50

Index   211

Tacitus, 160
Tale of a Tub, A (Swift), 9–10, 39–40, 58, 81, 98, 106
Tango (Mrozek), 85
Tanner, Tony, 4, 142, 150, 151
Tantalus, 94
tedium. *See* boredom
Telling It Again and Again (Kawin), 98
Temple, Sir William, 17
Terence (Publius Terentius Afer), 5, 161
Tess of the d'Urbervilles (Hardy), 73
Thackeray, William Makepeace, 29, 117
theater of the absurd, 1, 12, 20
Thomas, D.M., 95
Thomas, Dylan, 163
Thomson, William, 148
Three Sisters, The (Chekhov), 10
"Three Versions of Judas" (Borges), 78
Thurber, James, 2, 35, 97, 139, 144, 161; and E.B. White, 48
Thyestes (Seneca), 131
Time Machine, The (Wells), 48, 95, 133, 152
Timon of Phlius, 31
Tin Drum, The (Grass), 23, 88–89, 94, 113
titter and terror, 4
Titus, 18
Titus Andronicus (Shakespeare), 132
"Tlon, Uqbar, Orbis Tertius" (Borges), 78
Toffler, Alvin, 159
Tonnies, Ferdinand, 1
traditions, breakdown of, 68–69
"Tragedy of a Character, The" (Pirandello), 75
Trajan, 18
Trial, The (Kafka), 47
Trilling, Lionel, 4, 30, 142, 160–61
Tristram Shandy (Sterne), 58, 81, 96
Trotsky, Leon, 151
"Trouble in the Works" (Pinter), 144
"Trout, Kilgore," 48
Trout Fishing in America (Brautigan), 153
Twain, Mark, 2, 14, 18, 54–55, 133, 161
"Two Bottles of Relish" (Dunsany), 133–34
two cultures, 2
"2001: A Space Odyssey" (Clarke), 145
"2001: A Space Odyssey" (Kubrick), 141

ugly, the, vii, 34
Ulysses (Joyce), 15, 120
Un-Expurgated Code, The (Donleavy), 136
Universal Baseball Association, Inc., J. Henry Waugh, Prop. (Coover), 70
universalizing of tradition, 68–69
unnatural, the, 7, 19
unpleasure, 4

Up (Sukenick), 75, 79
Updike, John, 2, 126–27, 150
Utopia (More), 81

Valéry, Paul, 111
Vanity Fair (Thackeray), 29
Velázquez, Diego, 18
Venus on the Half Shell ("Trout"), 48
Vera Historia (Lucian), 52
Verlaine, Paul, 65, 109
Vie . . . de Joseph Delorme (Saint-Beuve), 110
"Views of My Father Weeping" (Barthelme), 85
Vile Bodies (Waugh), 48, 95, 100
Villon, François, 160
violation of decorum, 84
Virgil (Publius Virgilius Maro), 19
Vision of Judgement, The (Byron), 52
Visit, The (Dürrenmatt), 14
Vitruvius Pollio, 18–19
Voltaire, 14, 43, 80, 97, 106, 128, 133
Vonnegut, Kurt, Jr., 2, 13, 45–46, 48, 69, 70, 75, 78–79, 80, 95, 102, 134, 145, 150, 156
Voyeur, Le (Robbe-Grillet), 74

Wagner, Richard, 143
Waiting for Godot (Beckett), 24, 114, 121, 151
Walker, George Lee, 70
Walpole, Horace, 53–54
Wanting Seed, The (Burgess), 48, 135
warfare, modern, 167–68 n 13
War Games (Morris), 70
War Games (Sloan), 70
War with the Newts (Čapek), 48, 135
Waste Land, The (Eliot), 50
Watt, Isa, 69
Waugh, Evelyn, 1, 2, 34, 36, 48, 53, 54, 89, 95, 97, 99, 100, 120, 134, 143–44, 155
Way of the World, The (Congreve), 42
We (Zamyatin), 95, 140, 151
Weber, Max, 1
Wells, H.G., 48, 95, 133, 152
Wertham, Frederic, 131
West, Nathanael, 1, 14, 48, 52, 84, 95, 96, 125, 151, 156
White, E.B., 48, 144
White Hotel, The (Thomas), 95
Whitman, Walt, 162
Whole Duty of Man, The (Allestree), 42
Whyte, William H., Jr., 1
Wilde, Oscar, 111
Williams, Tennessee, 20–21, 85
Williams, William Carlos, 81, 162

Willie Masters' Lonesome Wife (Gass), 79–80
Wilson, Edmund, 53, 111–12
Winner Take Nothing (Hemingway), 70
Wolfe, Tom, 33, 124
Wonderland (Oates), 70
Woolf, Virginia, 67
Wordsworth, William, 100, 108
world-city, 30

Woyzeck (Büchner), 20, 83, 96

Yeats, William Butler, 34, 111, 154

Zamyatin, Yevgeny, 2, 13, 95, 140, 151, 156
Zinsser, Hans, 131
Zoschenko, Mikhail, 60–61

www.ingramcontent.com/pod-product-compliance
Lightning Source LLC
Chambersburg PA
CBHW022059160426
43198CB00008B/287